D0253165

Peer Power

Peer Power

Preadolescent Culture and Identity

PATRICIA A. ADLER

PETER ADLER

RUTGERS UNIVERSITY PRESS
New Brunswick, New Jersey, and London

Library of Congress Cataloging-in-Publication Data

Adler, Patricia A.
    Peer power : preadolescent culture and identity / Patricia A.
Adler, Peter Adler.
        p.   cm.
    Includes bibliographical references and index.
    ISBN 0-8135-2459-8 (cloth : alk. paper). — ISBN 0-8135-2460-1
(pbk.)
    1. Peer pressure in children—United States.   2. Social
interaction in children—United States.   3. Interpersonal relations
in children—United States.   4. Cliques (Sociology)—United States.
5. Children—Social networks—United States.   I. Adler, Peter,
1951– . II. Title.
HQ784.P43A35   1998
303.3′27—dc21   97–22516
                                                                            CIP

British Cataloging-in-Publication information available

Composition by Colophon Typesetting

Manufactured in the United States of America

Contents

To Jori and Brye,
who else?

Acknowledgments

THE 1990s, when most of this book was researched and written, have witnessed profound cultural and social transformations that have left their mark particularly on children. With the burgeoning of cable television, the rise of electronic and video games, the widespread use of the Internet, the earlier introduction to peers in day care and preschool, and the movement toward increased participation in athletics for girls, along with more egalitarian roles generally, children have become more sophisticated than previous generations at the same age. Nevertheless, peers' interaction has been a constant. Friendship still remains at the heart of most children's lives. We were fortunate to have been allowed a glimpse inside their social worlds and would, therefore, like to thank all the children, teachers, administrators, and parents who unselfishly admitted us into their daily lives.

Scores of scholars, over the past ten years, have contributed their ideas to our work. While we have not heeded their every word, we have benefited greatly from their good counsel. Coincidental to the writing of this book, the sociology of children arose as a legitimate area of inquiry within the discipline. From this coterie of scholars, people such as Bill Corsaro, Donna Eder, Gary Alan Fine, Julie Gricar Beshers, Gerry Handel, Karen Hegtvedt, Donna King, David Kinney, Nancy Mandell, Michael Messner, Tim Owens, Marty Power, Geoffrey Tesson, and Fran Waksler lent their intellectual support. In the spring of 1996 we were invited to Norway and Denmark for a series of talks before a scholarly audience. The interchange of ideas with Pers-Egil Mgaatvan, Flemming Mouritsen, Jens Qvortrup, and most especially, our host, Ivar Frønes, has shaped the final stages of this book.

Many others, along the way, have been stalwart in their support of our work. They were always willing to accept a late night phone call, an e-mail, or a letter that would help us resolve a particularly puzzling question. For the better part of two decades, Mitch Allen, David Altheide, Spencer Cahill, Andy Fontana, Ruth Horowitz, John Johnson, Sherryl Kleinman, Joe Kotarba,

Donileen Loseke, Peter Manning, Pepper Schwartz, David Snow, and Carol Warren have served as role models and compatriots. Our work has also been improved by the assiduous editorial assistance of our colleagues Dale Dannefer, Norm Denzin, Rosanna Hertz, Ed Lawler, Bill Staples, and Julia Wrigley. Further, we are reminded that teaching is often a two-way street. Several of our students have been especially helpful in their willingness to listen to our ideas, serve as sounding boards, and generously give their help: Kathy Fry, Joanna Gregson, Steve Kless, Katy Irwin, Jen Lois, and Laurie Scarborough Voss. There were others, such as Paul Colomy, Dan Cress, Diane Duffy, Chuck Gallmeier, John Irwin, Dana Larsen, and Marsha Rosenbaum, who not only would talk over sociological dimensions of our research, but reminded us that life is about friendships, loyalty, trust, and love.

To conduct a study in our own community, we had to rely on the largesse of many friends and neighbors who ran interference, set up appointments, made recommendations, and were our consciences as we wound our way through the myriad activities of children. We want to especially thank Penny and Barry Barnow, Linda and Bill Jacobsen, Synneve and Charlie Jones, Betty and Joe Kelly, Koenck, Geri and Pat Lynch, Tim and Rose Petrosky, Vince and Karen Porreca, and Adair Williamson for their goodwill. To engage in such a monumental and longitudinal task, we needed the support of our respective departments. Dorene Miller and Steve Graham took care of many details while we were in the field and at our computers. We also gained a great deal of insight from the numerous print and electronic media people with whom we discussed various aspects of this research. Peter Caughey and Marianne Goodland made sure that our research was reaching the widest possible audience.

We could not imagine working with a better publishing house than Rutgers University Press. Marlie Wasserman, the director of the Press, recognized this project while it was still in its embryonic stage. It was her vision that led us to continue during the early phases of the research. We are proud to be part of a trilogy, along with Barrie Thorne's *Gender Play* and Donna Eder's *School Talk*, that will put Rutgers at the forefront of sociological studies of children. Our editor, Martha Heller, who is well on her way to becoming one of the most influential editors in the social sciences, went way beyond her duties in assisting us. Not only did she serve as an acquisitions editor, but she helped us with our prose, organization, tone, and style throughout. The credit for the title must go to Martha. Others at the Press, such as Brigitte Goldstein and Victoria Haire, lent valuable editorial assistance in seeing this manuscript to its final stages.

Our research has been informed by our own experiences as children, and we thank our parents, Ben, Pat, and Judy Heller and Bea and Jerry Adler, who provided insights into childrearing and parenting. They taught us that good parenting never ends, that it is a lifelong endeavor. We are grateful to have been parented by loving and supportive people, who created a familial atmosphere in which our relationships with our parents, as well as our siblings, could flourish. To Lois, Deedy, Woody, Rob, Nikko, and Kyra we would like to send our appreciation for furthering our understanding of the growing-up experience. Similarly, our observations of our nieces and nephews, Adam, Josh, Michael, Rebecca, Whitney, Travis, Sosie, and Alex, informed the analyses in this book. Our brother-in-law, Kevin Bacon, took time out of his hectic schedule to create the cover drawings, proving once again that his artistic talents extend in many directions. All of these people have combined to make this book truly a "family affair."

Finally, accolades go to our children, Jori and Brye, who suffered through more dinners of pizza, tuna fish, peanut butter and jelly sandwiches, and takeout Chinese food than anyone needs to endure. Now, with one of them in the twilight of her adolescence and the other just dawning in his teen years, they have spent most of their lives under the microscopic scrutiny of having every intricate detail of their lives examined. Not many children could have withstood the kind of interrogations we sometimes put them through. Even more amazingly, they seemed to thrive under the spotlight, true assistants in the ethnography of their lives. We lovingly, respectfully, and admiringly dedicate this book to them.

In the end, it has been a marvelous decade of watching, observing, and analyzing children in their natural habitats. Surely, some of our extrapolations will resonate, while others may seem outlandish. We trust that reading this book will give more insight into the vortex of the mysterious lives of preadolescent children. We tried to treat their worlds with the respect they deserve. For any oversights, misconceptions, errors, or problems we stand ready to take the blame; it is our hope, however, that the problems are few and the wisdom is that much greater.

Portions of earlier versions of chapters 1, 2, 3, 4, and 5 appear as, respectively: Patricia A. Adler and Peter Adler, "Parent-as-Researcher: The Politics of Researching in the Personal Life," *Qualitative Sociology*, Vol. 19, No. 1 (January 1996); Patricia A. Adler, Steven J. Kless, and Peter Adler, "Socialization to Gender Roles: Images of Popularity among Elementary School Boys and Girls," *Sociology of Education*, Vol. 65, No. 3 (July 1992); Patricia A. Adler and Peter Adler, "Dynamics of Inclusion and Exclusion in Preadolescent Cliques,"

Social Psychology Quarterly, Vol. 58, No. 3 (September 1995); Patricia A. Adler and Peter Adler, "Preadolescent Clique Stratification and the Hierarchy of Identity," *Sociological Inquiry*, Vol. 66, No. 2 (spring 1996), by permission of University of Texas Press; Patricia A. Adler and Peter Adler, "Social Reproduction and the Corporate Other: The Institutionalization of Afterschool Activities," *Sociological Quarterly*, Vol. 35, No. 2 (June 1994), by permission of the *The Midwest Sociological Quarterly*.

Peer Power

Introduction

MARK AND LARRY were friends; they had been ever since first grade when Larry moved into the neighborhood. Mark considered Larry his best friend; to Larry, Mark was one of his best friends. Larry was the leader of their little clique, a subgroup of the larger popular boys' group. Brad was the leader of this larger clique and dominated its decision making, trend setting, and behavior. He and Larry had been uneasy friends for years, skirmishing over power and loyalty within the group. The school had carefully avoided placing them in the same homeroom for many years. In fifth grade, however, Brad, Mark, and Larry found themselves in the same class, along with several other key players in the popular crowd. As expected, the new placement created tension within the group. During one fight, Brad ostracized Larry and forced him out of the group. Mark and Rick (Larry's other best friend) then rejected the group to support Larry. The next week brought a new shift in group dynamics, and Larry and his cohort were readmitted.

This split in the group led Brad to adopt a new strategy. Instead of combating Larry, he attempted to co-opt him, winning his submission and loyalty by acquiring his friendship. To forge this bond, he had to eliminate the competition. Brad went to Larry and talked to him about Mark, attempting to elicit negative comments. He then carried these negative remarks to Mark, asking what Mark thought of them and how he felt about Larry. Brad went back and forth between the two boys, attempting to alienate them from each other by building their mutual uncertainty and resentment. At first they would not offer bad feelings, but after hearing a steady stream of negative comments about themselves, they started to believe the tales and criticized each other. They did not approach each other, feeling awkward and not knowing what to say. While

Brad was separating the friends, he was also ingratiating himself with each party, portraying himself as the truly loyal and trustworthy friend. Eventually, tension between Mark and Larry became high.

The breaking point came on a Monday. The previous weekend, Mark and Brad had been calling each other on the phone all night. In between calls, Mark had worked up the courage to call Amanda, a girl he liked, and ask her to "go" with him. She agreed, but stipulated that if anybody found out, she would break off the relationship. Brad called Mark, heard about his success, and immediately called Larry. They decided to call girls and ask them out, although they announced their intention of only using them "to get a kiss." Monday, at school, the two boys spread the gossip about Mark throughout the class. Amanda found out, dumped Mark, and broke his heart. He attempted to retaliate by informing Larry's and Brad's girls about their manipulative scheme, but these girls did not mind. They seemed happy to be associated with the two most popular boys in the grade. Brad turned the situation to his advantage. He accused Mark of betraying him, severed Larry's friendship with Mark, and forced Mark out of the popular clique permanently by turning all the other clique members against him. Larry became Brad's new best friend.

In sixth grade, the popular girls' clique split into two subgroups, whose leaders were Tiffany and Emily. The girls from the two groups liked each other, but the leaders did not. Tiffany was jealous of the attention Emily got from her followers and from the popular boys, wanting center stage all to herself. Emily resented Tiffany's intrusions and manipulations. They polarized their groups against each other.

By spring, Tiffany could no longer control her hatred. She persuaded one of the less popular boys to steal Emily's backpack, empty it, and take it into the rest room and smear it with excrement. Emily discovered her backpack missing, searched for it, and alerted her teacher. The backpack was finally found in the boys' rest room (where it could not be traced back to Tiffany), clogging up a toilet, soaking in urine and feces. Although the school administrators interviewed numerous people to try to uncover the truth, they were never able to solve the crime.

Tiffany used Emily's anguish to ridicule her, portray her as weak, and turn the bulk of the popular people (boys and girls) against her. The following year Emily's parents sent her to boarding school.

One day Larry, Brad, and Trevor were at Rick's house. Larry had just turned twelve and had a lot of birthday money in his wallet. Brad noticed Larry's wallet lying on Rick's bed and climbed on top of it. He motioned Trevor to join him. From his perch, Brad asked Larry where his wallet was, and when Larry could not find it, Brad accused Rick of stealing it. Despite Rick's fervent denials, Brad eventually convinced Larry of Rick's guilt, whipping him into a frenzy of anger and outrage. Larry tore Rick's room apart looking for his wallet. Brad slyly showed Trevor the wallet he was sitting on, inviting him to join him in conspiratorial silence.

Brad's accusations, Larry's fear for his money and anger at Rick, and Rick's pathetic denials escalated to the point where Larry began threatening to break Rick's things if he did not turn over the wallet. Helplessly, Rick professed innocence and ignorance. Larry broke Rick's lamp. Then he smashed the telephone in Rick's room (a birthday gift) to the floor, shattering it. He stomped on video games. Rick wailed and cried. Larry ran out of the room, moving to the kitchen to find more things to destroy, his anger out of control. Rick followed him, screaming, terrified. As Larry was about to throw down a blender, Rick's mother came home and stopped him. Assessing the situation, she sent the three boys home. Searching the house, she found the wallet on the bed and called Larry's mother.

The next day in school, Brad and Trevor bragged exultantly to everybody about their caper. Rick was out of the group.

In fourth grade, Diane and Julie were best friends. Although she was new to the school, Diane rose to the position of clique leader. Together, Diane and Julie ruled over the class, gracing some girls with their attention and casting away others. They were inseparable, playing every week, and visiting each other out of town over the summer.

Returning to town one week after the start of school, Diane eagerly contacted Julie. She was disappointed to learn that they were now in different homerooms, but she tried to arrange to get together after school. Julie could not make it. Nor could she the next day or the day after that. Diane was sad and confused. Was her best friend avoiding her? Julie seemed to be hanging out with their other friends, who were in Julie's class, but not with Diane. Diane did not have any friends in her new class, a combination class of fifth and sixth graders. By Friday Diane could not stand it anymore. After another rejection, she confronted Julie outside school. "Why won't you play with me?" she asked.

Julie was wrenched. Diane had been her best friend, had done everything with her. Before school started, however, Julie's mother had told her that she did not want Julie playing with Diane anymore. After a conference with the girls' fourth-grade teacher, Julie's mother had decided that Diane was a bad person and a bad influence. Julie was banned from playing with Diane. Julie did not know how to tell this to her best friend, so she kept making excuses about

why she could not play. When Diane finally confronted her, she blurted out
the truth and ran home, distraught.

Diane was devastated. She did not know what to think; she did not understand the reasons. Her parents tried to talk with Julie's mother, but they could
neither reason with nor understand her. The girls' mutual friends, in the class
with Julie, stayed with Julie and avoided Diane too. The former clique leader,
Diane, was cast out of the clique through Julie's mother's intervention and the
class reconfiguration. Diane was eventually swept up into a new social scene.
Diane and Julie never talked again.

THIS BOOK is about the peer culture of preadolescents, children between the
ages of eight and twelve, or roughly grades three through six. It is about the
way these children live their lives when they are unencumbered by the guidance of adults. We focus on the meanings children attach to the social objects,
social behaviors, and social experiences that are important in their lives. These
meanings are found in the subculture they create that lies in and around the
culture of adults, but which exists primarily for them. Corsaro suggests that peer
culture is "a stable set of activities or routines, artifacts, values, and concerns
that children produce and share" (1992, 162), and that this culture emerges
through interaction in which children appropriate adult culture but transform
it so that it fits the situation at hand (1985, 250–254). As Fine (1987, 125)
notes, peer culture "consists of a system of knowledge, beliefs, behaviors, and
customs shared by members of an interacting group to which members can refer
and that serve as the basis of further interaction. Members recognize that they
share experiences, and these experiences can be referred to with the expecta-
tion they will be understood by other members." Children's peer culture flows
out of children's worlds, guiding and shaping children's understanding of what
happens within them. Members need not all be friends, belonging to the same
primary group, but as peers, they belong to a common secondary group (Rizzo
1989). Pence (1988) says we know almost nothing about the inside of child institutions and child groups.

We attempt to remedy this situation by portraying the world of preadolescents from their point of view. We focused our attention on those things that
children told us we should study, those things that they considered the most
important. Under their guidance we looked at friends and friendships (how children form them and what kinds of friends they have); popularity and social status (what makes children popular and what are the consequences of being
popular and unpopular); use of time (what children do with their free time and
time scheduled by adults, and the kinds of structures and experiences these activities yield); and finally, the relationships between boys and girls (what the

balance is between platonic and romantic interests, and how these evolve over the course of preadolescence).

The concept of preadolescence as an age period is a relatively new one. Children used to be thought of as going through infancy, toddlerhood, childhood, and then adolescence. Preadolescence represents the latter part of the elementary school years, a period that has been considered part of childhood. Frønes (1994, 162–163) notes that "the phases that have recently been most open to change are late childhood and early adolescence (ages eleven to fourteen, fifteen), which have merged into a new phase because of changes in the cultural configuration of childhood. This is the age period where individuation processes are at their most intense, the age period before this new puberty, loosely corresponding to the latency period, becomes critically important for social development, because certain types of competence have to be acquired during this phase." The rise of preadolescence as an age period thus corresponds to the increasing specialization of society, where members need to acquire ever more sophisticated knowledge and skills, at ever younger ages, to function successfully. Preadolescence represents an important learning period, and its peer culture contains members' distillations of society's expectations.

A Study of Children's Peer Culture

We studied the children of our city over a period of eight years. The community encompasses a population of about ninety thousand; it is predominantly white and middle- to upper-middle class. Minority groups, of which Hispanics are the largest, constitute less than 10 percent of the population. Like the large, state university located within it, the city is heavily oriented toward research and development, with some small industry. A clean, environmentally conscious town with an active recycling program and a slow-growth and liberal political environment, it is geared toward fitness, promoting outdoor athletics of many kinds, especially individual, nontraditional pursuits. The town contains a mixture of older and newer housing, fanning outward from the older, single-family dwellings in the center to the smaller bungalows, apartments, and trailer parks in the middle rings, to the larger, more modern houses near the outer areas. The community's three city recreation centers and YMCA offer subsidized athletic, social, artistic, musical, and other programs for local residents. The vast majority of young people attend the city's highly regarded public school system, consisting of two high schools, six middle (formerly junior high) schools, and ten elementary schools. The children we studied came from seven public and five private schools.

We committed ourselves to a depth, ethnographic approach for, as Deegan

(1996, 11) notes, "it allows children a more direct voice and participation in the production of sociological data than is usually possible through experimental or survey styles of research." As parents of two children, we began to study them and their community when they were young, only five and nine. (chapter 1 addresses the topic of "parent as researcher.") Having a naturally occurring membership role in the worlds that children inhabit, we sought to expand that role, making ourselves more active in the lives of children than most parents. We progressed from this early base to the friends of our children, the children of our friends, children in activities where we "hung out," and then moved into the educational and after-school organizations. We fixed our gaze, initially, on the later years of elementary school, grades three through six. After four years, however, our school board reconfigured the educational system and eliminated junior high schools and replaced them with middle schools. This moved the sixth grade out of the elementary school and into the middle school, and we focused thereafter mostly on third through fifth graders. As our children drifted out of the target population, we still followed them and their friends, but found new children entering the age group we wanted in the local neighborhoods, schools, friendship circles, and activities. Over the course of eight years, we observed, casually conversed with, and maintained an acquaintance with literally hundreds of children. We forged more intimate relationships with dozens of children, becoming close, interacting with them intensely, and conducting depth, unstructured interviews with them, sometimes repeatedly. Chapter 1 contains a more detailed discussion of the methods employed.

Perspectives on Studying Children

Unlike adults, children are a disenfranchised, powerless group in society. Where researchers situate themselves, both concretely and ideologically, in relation to children not only influences the assumptions they make, the questions they raise, and the types of answers they seek, but also has a significant effect on the outcome of their research.

CHILDREN AS INCOMPLETE ADULTS

The traditional perspective on children involves viewing them as incomplete adults. As Qvortrup (1990) insightfully points out, childhood has been studied for the purpose of understanding what it portends for future adulthood. At the same time, adulthood has been analyzed in terms of its past childhood. Both of these approaches look at childhood from the perspective of understanding adulthood, strongly embedding the value judgment that adulthood is the most important stage of the generational structure. This set of assumptions is what fueled the developmental perspective on children, for example, where children were considered to take on the qualities of adults one stage at a time. This perspective also takes a passive view of children, painting them as relatively uninvolved in their own socialization, having the characteristics of adults imparted to them or teleologically developed from within. From this position, the only authentic and worthwhile activity for children is play. Thus, childhood represents a transitional phase from which members graduate into being "real" members of society. With this in mind, Hardman (1973) raises the question, do children have an "autonomous self-regulating world that does not merely reflect the early development of adult culture?"

CHILDREN AS ACTIVE AGENTS, WORTHY OF STUDY IN THEIR OWN RIGHT

The second, more recent, perspective on children answers Hardman's question in the affirmative. Proponents of childhood as an autonomous field of study argue that childhood represents not a transitional stage in society but a permanent social category, because even though individuals grow out of it, children are always present in society, no less influenced by it and capable of being influenced by it than adults (Qvortrup 1990; 1993). Thorne (1987) endorses the "conceptual autonomy" of children, suggesting that we focus directly on the targeted group of interest. Continuing, Sutton-Smith (1982) points out that "peer interaction is not a preparation for life, it is life itself." All of these contentions build on an active view of children, whereby they are capable of independent thinking and functioning, and have social relationships and a peer culture that are unconstrained by the perspective and concern of adults. We believe strongly in this approach and therefore join with Waksler's (1986) call to study children on their own terms, to stop looking at them as incomplete adults, and to phenomenologically examine the lived experiences of childhood.

Yet the separation of these perspectives into two disparate approaches yields further problems. Having argued why children can be studied apart from adults, we ask whether they need be exclusively studied apart from adults. We feel it would be valuable to ponder the effects of childhood on adulthood and adult society, as well as the effects of adults on children. Historically, academically, and intellectually, the movement to consider children as worthy of study in their own right was critical to establishing children's studies as a legitimate field of inquiry.[1] Now that it is established, we would suggest uniting these two perspectives.

Social Psychological Frameworks

We take a social psychological approach to the study of preadolescents. We look at the daily lives of children in their social worlds, describing and analyzing their individual and patterned attitudes and behavior. Within the framework of their peer group, we look at their perceptions, interpretations, and decisions to act. This micro, interactionist approach draws on and contributes to social psychological theories about the nature of socialization and the relation between the individual and society.

DEVELOPMENTAL MODEL

Historically, the developmental model has been the dominant social psychological framework. Reviewing these perspectives, Frønes (1995) notes that most theories of social development regard childhood as a psychological process out of which the adult personality is formed. Using stage models, these theories regard childhood as progressing through phases of social development, influenced by social and cultural factors, but considerably dependent on innate, cognitive and biological foundations. The role of society lies in shaping the social and cultural surroundings of childhood (Gelman and Bailargon 1983). Major progenitors of this approach include Vygotsky (1978), who focuses on children's advances through critical periods, and the structuring of their social development by societal forces. Piaget's (1965) "genetic epistemology" links the biological facts of immaturity to the social aspects of childhood. He advances four stages of cognitive development, during which children's thinking undergoes patterned changes as they mature biologically and gain social experience. Kohlberg's (1981) theory proposes to explain the moral development of children through three stages. Finally, Erikson's (1950) developmental theory tries to combine analyses of social structure and psychoanalysis. In his view, culture is primarily an instrument for channeling psychological forces.

According to Thorne (1993), these developmental models imply that children's inner dispositions will incrementally unfold over time as they age, thereby maturing, and gain experience in their social environments. These models suffer, according to Speier (1970), from the classic adult ideological viewpoint. Heavily psycho-biological, they see social forces as influencing the social context and content of these stages by shaping the specific stages, their configurations, and the relations among them. Social change, as discussed earlier, can lead to the rise of new categories, preadolescence for example, and to the accompanying form of individual development (Frønes 1994). Among the problems associated with this model of socialization are the inadequate role it accords social content and context, its inability to satisfactorily explain class, gender, or cross-cultural divergences, its failure to explain how and why children progress through these stages in different ways and at different ages, and its general bias toward the adult model as the apex of complete development.

NORMATIVE SOCIALIZATION MODEL

Normative social psychological theories are grounded in psychological and macro sociological perspectives on socialization. The normative perspective is grounded in macro and positivist models of the individual and society, emphasizing the way children internalize society's norms and values and learn roles for future use. Practitioners conceive of individuals as born with the classic tabula rasa, where the structure and culture of society are "writ" onto them, molding them into socialized societal members (Brim 1960; Inkeles 1966; Merton 1957; Parsons and Bales 1955; Watson 1970). A second dimension of the normative socialization perspective, behaviorist theory, suggests that people learn desirable behavior in society through a system of positive and negative stimuli. Pavlov's classical conditioning model (1927) regards people as passive reactors to an impersonal environment. It leaves no room for interpretation or creativity. Skinner's system of consequences (1953) suggests that people learn and are molded to socially acceptable norms, values, and behaviors through positive and negative reinforcements. A third component, social learning theory, is a stimulus-response approach similar to behaviorism. Imitating the actions and behaviors of those around them, who serve as role models, individuals adopt their norms and values (Bandura 1969; Bandura and Walters 1963). Like the developmental model, these perspectives offer a passive view of socialization that accords children little agency, and little or no role in their own formation. In fact, socialization itself is a passive concept that moves mostly in one direction: the more powerful socialize, the less powerful get socialized; therefore adults will always be seen as socializing children (Thorne 1993).

SOCIAL CONSTRUCTIONIST PERSPECTIVE

Morss (1990) suggests that some of the flaws in development theory are tied to its lack of an empirically scientific base, since it is rooted in the assumptions of early-nineteenth-century biological and psychological theory. He notes a trend in psychology away from the search for the "universal child" toward a view of children as a social group that operates within social contexts, with childhood increasingly seen as a social construct.

These views are tied to the rise of the third, and most recently forged, social psychological framework: social constructionism. Emerging from pragmatist philosophy in the 1920s and 1930s, and tied to such key figures as James, Baldwin, Cooley, Dewey, Mead, and Blumer, social constructionism is a part of symbolic interactionist theory. Fundamental to the interactionist critique of the development and socialization models is the belief that children are active and creative agents, and that socialization is a collective process. Childhood is a socially constructed category, and not only parents, the state, and the market, but children themselves contribute to its construction (Qvortrup 1990). According to this perspective, socialization represents the development of interactional competence, as individuals become increasingly capable of taking the role of the other, developing the "looking-glass self," and competently aligning their actions with others. This competence arises as they experience society through interaction. Interactionists generally reject stage models as too neat and linear, saying that not all people advance through all stages (Musolf 1996). Corsaro and Eder (1990, 200) suggest, however, that the interpretive model does not totally reject stagelike theories, recasting them within a productive-reproductive process of "increasing density and reorganization of knowledge that changes with children's developing cognitive and language abilities and with changes in their social worlds." There is a strong emphasis on the importance of children acquiring language skills and accumulating interactive experiences, for individuals' movement from one stage to another is seen as heavily rooted in these spheres. Corsaro (1985) specifically points to the peer group as the most significant public realm for children. Denzin (1977, 2–3) is a good spokesman for the interactionist perspective when he contends that socialization is not a "structurally determined process whereby the values and goals of social systems are instilled in the child's behavior repertoires." Interactionists view social structure as circumscribing human agency, but unlike the normative socialization theorists, they do not regard structural constraints as deterministic. They emphasize the dynamic tension between structure and agency (Musolf 1996). One way that social constructionists facilitate a portrayal that simultaneously incorporates structure and agency while avoiding the adult-centric viewpoint is to start with group life rather than individuals, and to look at the social relations, the organization and meanings of social situations, and the collective practices through which children create and recreate key constructs in their daily interactions (Thorne 1993). Another is to focus on beliefs as continuing cultural constructs and to look at the role of language in constructing those beliefs (Eder 1995). In this book we begin with the construct of peer culture and examine how children are socialized within it, being shaped by its existing structures and dynamics, yet constantly creating new beliefs and behavioral patterns.

Four Dimensions of Childhood

Frønes (1994) identifies four general approaches, or perspectives, to the sociology of childhood. To gain a full understanding of childhood in its historical development and locate this work within the appropriate context, we must glance briefly at each one.

CHILDHOOD AS AN AGE GROUP

Childhood can be conceptualized as a distinct group, somewhat akin to a generation or social class. Many of the works that adopt this perspective are demographic studies, examining economic and related changes in the population of children, while others are historical studies, positing models in the development and evolution of childhood. Qvortrup (1987; 1990; 1993; 1995), a major contributor to this area, suggests that childhood is akin to a minority group, with common characteristics that distinguish members and identify relations between children and other groups. He also suggests that in the adult-centric society, children are rendered largely invisible and have lower social status and privileges. Such an analysis poses the Simmelian question of what relational features define a group if it can be analyzed in reference to adults or members of society. Qvortrup's answer is that as a group, children are distinguished by their perceived need for simultaneous protection and exclusion. They represent a precious resource yet also a costly burden. They are held in a dependent posture, given a status that ostensibly protects them but effectively excludes them from societal decision making and money earning, while mandating their compulsory school attendance. They are thus valued, revered, protected, a group we are making an investment in, while suppressed, controlled, disenfranchised, and deprived of free choice. Sgritta (1987) suggests that this attitude toward and treatment of children incorporate structural contradictions. Our society's double regime of protection and control yields the unintended consequences of greater dependence, increased passivity, and the alienation of childhood. Qvortrup (1993) agrees, adding that children have become defined as nonachievers, thereby made dependent on the achievement of their parents. This situated dependency has significant consequences for their invisibility and their entitlement to welfare provisions. In relation to adulthood, childhood is thus characterized by marginalization, protection, paternalism, individualization, institutionalization, and familialization (Qvortrup 1994).

INSTITUTIONAL ARRANGEMENTS OF CHILDHOOD

A second perspective on childhood involves focusing on the agencies and institutions concerned with children. As Frønes (1994) notes, analyses of institutional arrangements surrounding children examine their content, shape, and development. Such research includes a focus on individual institutions as well as a larger focus on the general framework of institutional development. Qvortrup (1990) points out that historically, school represents the first major institution to shape the form of childhood. Children, previously, were tied to work and family. Universal school attendance liberated children from these bonds, thrusting them instead into large-scale organization, systematization, time planning, and other features of modern society. School socializes children and "normalizes" them to society. Various features of school and their influence on children have drawn the interest of scholars. In a series of works, Hallinan (1976; 1978; 1979; 1980) examines the effects of classroom size and structure (open versus traditional) on the formation and character of children's friendships, noting that larger and more open classrooms liberate elementary school children from the bonds of the traditional popularity system and enhance their chances of finding like-minded peers. She also sociometrically charts the composition and parameters of cliques, tying the restrictiveness of their internal structures to the opportunities for friendship formation associated with the aforementioned classroom characteristics. Deegan's (1996) work takes up the issue of cultural diversity in classrooms, looking at the way elementary school children stratify primarily by gender and secondarily by race, ethnic, and socioeconomic group, but at the same time try to negotiate friendships across these lines. The diversity of their life situations proves to be the factor challenging their friendship formation, rather than strict demographic differences. In addition to the formal educational system, other significant institutional arrangements for children include child care and, especially recently, after-school activities (see chapter 5). These institutional arrangements formalize the lives of children and socialize them through their systems of qualifications, social control, supervision, formal rules, membership, timetables, and age classification (Frønes 1994).

RELATIONS AMONG GENERATIONS

A third body of works focuses on the cultural and social relations among generations, both within the family (children and parents and grandparents) as well as among historical generations (Frønes 1994). The family represents a significant institution for children, providing the anchor for their biography and sense of continuity (Kovarik 1994). Handel argues that the family group serves as the most influential socializing agency and, in Hess and Handel (1959), analyzes five families of different class levels to show variations in these patterns of family socialization. (While the family is an important influence on children, it is not a main focus for us in this book.) Postman (1994) and Holt (1974) discuss the historical emergence of childhood as a protected and controlled period in this context, as related to the defamilialization of children/hood, analyzing children's removal from the family and labor market and placement into schools. They also note the consequences of this move for the universalization of the childhood experience. Jensen (1994) analyzes the movement of children from the male to the female realm of interest and control, as childhood changed historically from an economic to an emotional asset with their removal from the workplace and placement into educational dependency. The consequences of this move, she notes, have been the rise of the single-parent family, the feminization of poverty, and the pauperization of childhood. Over the years, research has shown that many family functions have been taken over by other professionals and institutions. But parental influence has not been totally lost. Participation in some of the new institutions, such as after-school facilities, is contingent on the parental resources of time and money, thus tying children back to their families (Frønes 1994). Modern families do not have the highly autocratic authority structure that existed prior to the Industrial Revolution, however. Modern families have more democratic relations, a culture of negotiation among the generations, with work chores voluntary or paid, and parental command weaker. Children's experience within them is thus marked by greater individuation (they have greater autonomy, freedom, and individual treatment compared to siblings), defamilialization (they function outside of family bounds more), and democratization (power and decision making have been diffused among more family members).

RELATIONS AMONG CHILDREN

The final dimension concerns the relations children form among members of their own group, focusing on peer relations, child culture, and children's activities or their use of time. It includes studies rooted in child development and ethnographic works on child culture. These works emphasize the importance of play and peer relations for socialization and the development of interactional competence. They examine the way children construct meaning through play. Kovarik (1994) argues that institutional analyses have overlooked the role and importance of peers. Harris (1995) maintains that peer groups are much more critical to socialization than family groups, because intra- and intergroup processes, not dyadic relationships, are responsible for the transmission of culture and for environmental modification of children's personality characteristics. Studying children's culture, Frønes (1994) suggests that this is a construct passed down from one generation of children to the next. Opie and Opie (1959; 1969) document this transmission in their research on children's folklore, marking the recurrence of specific stories and games over generations (see also Sutton-Smith and Rosenberg 1961) and the extremely rapid and widespread diffusion of children's culture from one central location.

The ethnographic literature contains several works focusing on children's relationships, play, and culture. Conducting observations and interviews with elementary school children, Lever (1976; 1978) examines differences in boys' and girls' play and social organization. She notes that boys' play centers on competitive games, occurring outdoors in larger, more age-mixed groups, while girls play indoors in smaller, more age-homogeneous, nonhierarchical groups of intimate friends. Best (1983), who spent three years conducting participant observation in an elementary school, focuses on the dimensions of peer relations and peer culture that children learn informally within the broader confines of the educational institution. Concentrating on various aspects of the "hidden curriculum," she notes the formation of cliques and their exclusionary character, the separation of boys and girls into gendered cultures where they learn the informal peer norms of how boys and girls should behave, the evolution of sexualized attitudes and behaviors, and how these change and go "underground" after third grade, and the way boys and girls stereotype each other as so different that they cannot be friends. These developments prepare them for "intermediate" level school and its informal curriculum.

Corsaro (1985) develops his language and cultural skills with a group of Italian preschoolers as he spends time with them in their classroom and videotapes them. His struggles with communicating allow him to be taken under their wing and assisted; so he moves through the educational continuum in much the same way as the children do. His research examines friendships and peer culture within this very young group, focusing on the way children allow some children to gain access to their play groups and play spaces while protecting these against the incursions of unwanted others, and how they use exchanges to develop solidarity and mutual trust. In this, and in his work with Rizzo (Corsaro and Rizzo 1988), he examines the socialization process of preschoolers, concluding that children's creative productions of peer culture are influenced by and contribute to the reproduction of the adult world. Rizzo's (1989) own research on first graders continues this theme, focusing on the formation and character of children's peer interactions and friendships. He concentrates particularly on the kinds of things that influence children's friendships and the process through which these develop, from children's early moves to initiate relationships, to how these change over time. He concludes that children's friendships aid in their self-development and feelings of solidarity, but that the negative, conflictful, and exclusionary features of these bonds do not foster prosocial behavior with individuals beyond these primary friendships.

In Fine's (1987) study of preadolescent boys, he spends time with five pairs of Little League teams. He looks at the way these boys' friendship groups construct subcultures of masculinity that wrestle with moral development in issues like swearing, discussing girls, and talking about sex, and at how they form collective attitudes about work-related activities and appropriate expressions of violence, such as roughhousing. He notes how the norms formed by each group represent their own particular "idioculture" within the broader American culture.

Thorne's (1993) research, based on observations in one classroom in Michigan and one in California, focuses on gender. She looks at the way children are integrated by gender in their school activities, yet separated into discrete and oppositional gendered cultures in their informal relations. She then observes how children overcome these gender barriers through "crossing"; they may take the extreme action of leaving their same-gender mates to play with the other gender, or just make occasional forays into other-gender activities. The romantic overtones of the heterosexist culture impede cross-gender platonic friendships, she notes, although they facilitate the rise of romantic relationships, a means to reintroduce boys and girls to each other, toward the later elementary school years.

Eder's (1995) work examines adolescent peer culture in a middle school setting, taking these themes and following them into an older population, people in the eleven-to-fourteen age range. Informally congregating with several different friendship groups in lunchroom and recess settings, Eder and her three research assistants explore the content and dynamics of male and female friendship circles occupying high and low status levels. She follows adolescents into the social world dominated by the discourse of heterosexual romanticism and popularity, looking at how boys and girls create and align themselves within gendered cultures that dictate appropriate self-presentations. Like elementary school cultures, these images recreate traditional gender roles, fostering narrow and conservative behavioral repertoires. Whether they are teasing, insulting, gossiping, courting, or fighting, boys and girls project and protect their fragile selves within the confines of the acceptable discourse and culture. Eder shows how these traditional status and gender dimensions continue to be socially created and recreated through language, establishing power through hierarchy and differentiation.

Finally, following Eder's age group, Merten, in a series of insightful articles

(1994; 1996a; 1996b; 1996c; 1996d), analyzes ethnographic data gathered over two years on the social lives of middle schoolers, or early adolescents. He focuses on many of the same peer social issues we address here, including social hierarchy, grouping and categorization, especially as these influence identity. These issues span the continuum from the behavior and symbolic location of the high-status cheerleaders, to the social rejection, isolation, and heightened visibility of the boys on the lowest rung of the ladder, the "mels." He also looks at romantic relations, specifically the social form of "going with," documenting the awkwardness and superficiality of this early romantic link, and at the rise of adolescent aggression in its cultural context and structural framework of the transition from elementary to middle school.

Overview of This Book

Our work falls among these ethnographic studies of children's culture, developing and extending this body of work. It is unique in its scope and depth. We spent eight years observing and interviewing preadolescents in the community through our membership role as parents and researchers. This role enabled us to be with preadolescents during and out of school, on weekdays and weekends, in the daytime and at night, during periods of calm and when crises arose. We also researched a larger population, studying dozens of children closely, with intimate interaction and depth interviews, and hundreds of children less closely, with casual conversation, long-term acquaintance, and observation. This approach generated a more in-depth look at preadolescents' social worlds. We were able to consider many of the elements and characteristics identified in previous research, but to go beyond discussing *what* children do and to identify *how* and *why* their behavior unfolds. Our focus is on preadolescent peer culture, how it intermediates between individuals and groups to affect such things as status, popularity, friendships, and activities. We look at both the structure and dynamics of peer group life, at its overall blueprint, and at the progressive evolution of children's behavior over the course of several years.

In chapter 1 we provide an extensive discussion of the methods we employed in terms of what we actually did and of the implications of taking the parental research role. We present the practical and epistemological advantages of this stance, as well as some of the ethical issues that arose. This research approach, although it skirted ethically risky issues at times, offered us a powerful means of accessing children's subcultures and took us farther inside children's lives than most other approaches could have.

The first series of empirical chapters deals with issues of status, stratification, and power. Chapter 2 focuses on what makes children popular, contrasting the important dimensions for boys with those of girls. We begin to see the emergence of the variables that will separate the popular from the unpopular people, and the boys from the girls. In chapter 3 we focus on the popular people and the nature of their cliques. Our interest in this topic began as we observed the universal occurrence of this type of group formation and the power that resided in clique leaders. For many years we pondered the questions of how some individuals generated the kind of power they wielded, and how they got others to engage in the demeaning activities they demanded. Chapter 3 presents our answer to this question: clique power resides in the dynamics of inclusion and exclusion, where leaders gain and maintain their influence by determining, on a changing basis, who is accepted and who is rejected. Chapter 4 extends this discussion by looking at the stratification system pervading the entire grade, from the cliques at the top, to the wannabes surrounding them, to the middle friendship circles comprising the bulk of the population, to the social isolates occupying the bottom of the hierarchy. We describe and analyze the internal characteristics of each stratum such as leadership, decision making, loyalty and trust, and stability, and at the relations among strata. Ironically, we see that although social esteem and self-esteem are interrelated, they are only loosely coupled.

The remaining chapters focus on the activities preadolescents pursue and the peer relationships they forge within them. Chapter 5 examines after-school activities. We trace the contours of the extracurricular career, as children move from spontaneous play through a series of adult-organized stages beginning with social and recreational pursuits and moving to those featuring skill development, into various levels of competitive involvement, and finally to elite participation. Chapters 6 and 7 consider the types of friendships that preadolescents form. Critical to individuals' happiness and feelings of self-worth, friendships can be close, casual, or compartmentalized. We discuss some of the characteristics and composition of these different friendship types, the way children form them, and the patterns surrounding their prevalence. Cross-gender relationships are the subject of the last two empirical chapters, chapters 8 and 9. A main concern in the existing literature, gender segregation and integration, of both a platonic and romantic nature, is our interest here. We trace a developmental pathway, showing how peer gender norms move boys and girls through a journey that begins together, separates them, and reconnects them. Yet despite these norms, and powerful peer sanctions reinforcing them, children violate them (or desire to) on a consistent, yet cautious, basis. These two chapters deepen our understanding of the feelings children secretly harbor for individuals of the other gender as well as of the numerous similarities between the genders that lie below the surface of boys' "macho" posturing and physicality and girls' primping and restraint.

We conclude, in chapter 10, with a discussion of the implications of these findings. We weigh the role of the demographic variables salient to preadolescents' lives, particularly age and gender. We consider the encroachment of adult corporate and work values into preadolescence through the institutionalized vehicle of after-school play. Finally, we discuss the vital and often undervalued role of preadolescent peer culture in mediating between the individual and society, and in powerfully shaping preadolescents' socialization and identity.

Chapter 1   The Parent-as-Researcher

THE ETHNOGRAPHIC study of children has become a focus of growing socio-logical interest. Researchers undertaking such projects have attempted to bridge the gap between children and themselves by assuming roles in their settings that were compatible with participation in children's worlds.[1] Discussing his research with preschoolers, Corsaro (1981a, 130) argues that "becoming a participant in the children's activities was necessary for gaining insight into what *mattered most to them* in their everyday interaction" (emphasis in original). The physical and demographic differences between adults and children limit the range of participatory roles adults can take in children's settings.[2] With few exceptions, these roles are not naturally existing in children's settings, but are researcher-created, imbuing them with a certain artificiality. Moreover, they have generally been constructed within institutionalized settings, such as schools, where children are most easily found.[3] Such settings restrict the range of children's behavior available to researchers. As a result, researchers' understanding of children's culture and experiences may be lacking in both breadth and depth.

One research role that has been previously overlooked is the *parent-as-researcher* (PAR). Parents can readily gain entry to the world of children through their own children. They can then capitalize on this "complete membership role" (Adler and Adler 1987) by "opportunistically" (Riemer 1977) making the community of youth to which their children belong a focus of study. This approach offers several advantages over more conventional ethnographic roles and relationships. First, it is a naturally occurring membership role with which children are totally familiar. Second, it spans children's participation in a variety of settings, offering access into their school, home, recreational, and social lives.

Many scholars have successfully made use of their personal lives as a focus of research.[4] A smaller number have studied their own children, focusing primarily on socialization and development, including Charles H. Cooley, Jean Piaget, and Erik Erikson.[5] PARs integrate these foci, looking at their own children and those of others in the social worlds they inhabit. But rather than looking exclusively at developmental issues, PARs can follow Waksler's (1986) call to study children on their own terms, to stop looking at them as incomplete adults, and to phenomenologically examine the lived experiences of childhood.

Parental research, like the work of many who draw upon their own personal lives, encompasses a dual research-membership focus. Such role-fused postures have also been applied to the study of children through the approaches of the teacher-as-researcher[6] and the counselor-as-researcher.[7] Little reflection has been done, however, on the contours of these other dual approaches, leaving their advantages, their problems, and some of the solutions to their problems underinvestigated. The ethical implications of these role-fused approaches warrant particular reflection, as our society and its researchers forge new collective moral attitudes toward the definitions of public and private domains and the needs and rights of researchers versus those of the researched. When social scientists straddle the parental and research roles, they may find themselves in situations where the distance between the researcher and the researched diminishes and their service to these two endeavors does not always easily coincide. Some of the sensitive issues that have been raised are researchers' potential power over subjects (Corsaro 1981a) and their responsibility for the knowledge they gain during the research (Fine and Sandstrom 1988; Glassner 1976; Mandell 1988). Further issues include the moral and legal responsibilities of parental researchers and the ultimate consequences of this dual role for both the research and the researched.

In this chapter we offer an exploration of such issues. We describe the research we conducted, detailing the community we studied, our relations with community members, and the types of empirical materials we gathered. We then outline some of the conceptual features of this research role, focusing on the specifics and implications of the role advantages, role location, and role relations. We conclude by addressing the ethical issues raised by this type of research.

Research Settings and Strategies

In doing our research, we occupied several parental roles in different settings. We interacted with children, parents, teachers, and school administrators as *parents-in-the-school*, volunteering in classrooms, accompanying field trips, organizing and running school carnivals and other events, driving car pools, and serving on school committees. We interacted with children, parents, other adults, and city administrators as *parents-in-the-community*, coaching and refereeing youth sports teams, serving as team parents, being the team photographer, organizing and running the concession stand, and founding and administrating our own youth baseball league. We interacted with children, their parents, neighborhood adults and children, and adult friends and their children as *parents-in-the-home*, being a part of our neighborhood, having friends in the community, interacting with the neighborhood and friendship groups of our children, offering food and restroom facilities (our house bordered the neighborhood's playing field), nursing children through illnesses, injuries, and substance abuses, helping them with their school decisions and schoolwork (assisting with library research, editing their rough drafts, providing home computer and copying facilities), functioning as mentors and role models, serving as friends and confidantes, bailing them out of jail and other troubles, and helping them talk to their own parents. We became the "cool parents" in the group, to whom our kids and their friends could turn.[8]

These diverse roles built upon our natural parenting activities, contacts, interests, and style, taking us into locations and events populated by children. We undertook them both as they naturally presented themselves and as deliberate research strategies, sometimes combining the two as opportunities for interacting with children became available through familial obligations or work/school requirements. It helped, at times, that we were of different genders, for there were occasions where children sought us out to talk about gender-related topics, and times when our gendered experiences and insights made us more interested in and helpful about discussing different subjects.

We also took a more explicit *parent-as-researcher* role, conducting audiotaped interviews with children in our home, in their homes, and in schools. We let these interviews flow out of and build on our participant observation. We generated research topics and conceptual questions about specific and general areas through our interactions and casual conversations with people in our parental roles. When we were ready to write about a particular subject, we conducted focused, unstructured interviews. We selected theoretical samples (Glaser and Strauss 1967) of people to interview based on our knowledge of who might offer us a range of points of view and experiences with regard to the topic at hand. In choosing interviewees, we relied on our own knowledge of people in the community and got referrals from our children, their friends, parents, neighbors, and teachers we knew, and people whom we had already interviewed (Biernacki and Waldorf 1981). We contacted or were contacted by potential interviewees, arranged for parental consent, and interviewed them at the location they preferred.

We also conducted interviews with children in schools, both individually and in groups. On several occasions, we did whole-class interviews with students in the third through sixth grades, at the invitation of their teachers (some of whom had taught our children). After obtaining parental consent, we asked for their help with our research and moved through the topics on our interview schedule. This technique offered the advantage of bringing together children from a variety of social groups and asking them to resolve their different perspectives on sociological issues. In addition, we used this school base to conduct individual interviews with members of these and other classes. Instead of interviewing whole classes, we sometimes went into classes and talked about our current topic. We then solicited volunteers who wanted to be interviewed (and got recommendations from their teachers), and, after obtaining informed consent, we conducted taped interviews with individual children in unoccupied classrooms or offices. In all, we observed or casually interacted with over two hundred children, and held group or individual interviews with another hundred. We then conducted select interviews with seven teachers at three different elementary schools to get a broader overview of children's social lives and their dynamics from individuals who had worked with many different groups of children over the years.

We used this combination of personal life and school settings to generate a diverse pool of empirical materials. The informants we generated outside of schools, for both participant observation and interviewing, were influenced by our personal location in our community. We followed our daughter and son, their friends and enemies, the children of our neighbors and friends, and other children we met through our involvement in youth leisure activities through their school and extracurricular experiences. Our children inadvertently obliged us by occupying or passing through vastly different types of social groups and experiences. Our daughter moved through preadolescence in the popular group, surrounded (and occasionally overwhelmed) by a strong, although shifting, circle of friends. Her concerns included maintaining acceptance and popularity, tailoring group membership to suit her preferences, avoiding the conflicts engendered by status and power, and dealing with manipulative leaders. Our son's experiences spanned a broader spectrum of the social scale, as he grew up surrounded by a crowd that was popular but vicious, quit the group in a terrible fight that kept him hovering in and out of social isolate status for nearly a year, and finally made friends in a shifting and oscillating midlevel friendship circle. We thus used the different social locations of our children and their friends, other people we knew, and the children we gathered through our school interviews, to triangulate (Denzin 1989) our data, putting together a wide representation of people.

DIMINISHED ROLE PRETENSE

In traditional research roles, fieldworkers often enter their settings and establish identities that do not naturally exist there. They create a set of behaviors and meanings associated with studying the members, a concept that may, especially initially, be alien or forced. In creating a research role, they may feel internal and/or external pressures to reciprocally offer something back to people in the setting in exchange for their research entry and assistance. This may lead them to assume contributory roles or to act interested in or committed to the setting in ways that they really are not. Ethnographers studying children may also find their role choices restricted by the institutional nature of the settings in which children are most easily found. To study children only in school settings, for instance, limits the types of interactions ethnographers can have and observe, and they have to forge roles that somehow bypass the authority of the adult-as-stranger and construct the accessibility of the adult-as-friend (Fine 1987; Mandell 1988).[9] This may be awkward or difficult. Even in more informal leisure settings, adult-researchers must find roles, such as observer, supervisor, or friend (Fine and Sandstrom 1988), that carry with them certain limitations and artificiality.

In contrast, the PAR role is recognizable and familiar to people in the setting. In our case, we had no need to pretend to be something we were not or to create some unwieldy research persona. Our presence and role in the settings were understood and expected by participants. Children, and the adults who surrounded them, interacted with us naturally, during the course of conducting everyday business. As parents, we were expected to be in and have interest in these settings. Our parental attachments and responsibilities thus constituted our involvement in the settings, necessitating no further explanation or "contribution."

ROLE IMMERSION

Another advantage of the PAR role involved the totality of our participation in the settings. Unlike other researchers who can only interact with their informants at circumscribed times, the children we studied, particularly our own, were available to us all the time. We could observe them on the weekends as well as weekdays, in the evenings as well as daytimes, during the mundane periods of their lives as well as when crises periodically arose. In contrast to the method Eder (1995) employs in studying middle school children where she and her team of researchers observe students in the cafeteria during lunchtime, our house was "on limits" constantly. We prided ourselves on having the best snacks

in town, thereby becoming a frequent way station for children after school or
when children congregated to play sports and games. We spent many hours observing them in the backyard park from our deck or living room, often without their paying attention, to see how they negotiated and compromised with
each other. To our own children's bemused consternation, neighborhood kids
would stop by to visit with us during the summer months, when our children
were not even home. Fully cognizant of our desire to know about the shifting
social developments that commonly define the summer months, these children
would give us updates on the latest news. This immersion increased the intensity of our research, enhancing its validity as compared not only with less participatory depth interviews but with other types of field research as well.

ROLE TRIANGULATION

A third advantage of the PAR role involved our greater ability to triangulate
data in the settings. Rather than just coming upon the scene and observing or
asking subjects directly about themselves, we had many avenues by which we
could access empirical information about people. Naturally, we relied on our
own children as key informants since they were readily available, usually willing to talk (although this became more problematic as they neared adolescence), and understood the research process. However, they, like anyone else,
had their own value judgments and their own data access limitations. Supple-
menting them, we had, as noted, many widely dispersed and varied contacts in
our community. These sources were all backed up by the foundation of our own
observations. We gathered data formally, in taped interviews, or informally, as
we stood around at sporting events and chatted with other parents and their
children.

Role Location

ROLE ATTACHMENT

In cases where people assume dual research/membership roles, their involvement in and commitment to one aspect of this role may be stronger than to the
other. As in any complete-member research, our attachment was stronger to
our parental membership role. We had a greater investment in this dimension
because it was primary, deeper, longer lasting, and more central to our core identities and goals. This had the potential to affect our research and research relations. For instance, one Halloween evening, our son came home early from
trick-or-treating because some of the neighborhood bullies had been picking
on him. One, in particular, in whom we were extremely interested because of

his clique background, was extremely manipulative, denigrating our son in an effort to aggrandize himself to other boys (who eventually "ditched" him themselves). Later that evening, when his worried mother called to see if we had seen or helped her "lost" son, we could not contain our anger. We strongly expressed our feelings, described her son's behavior, and told her how unwelcome he would be in our house. She, naturally, defended her son. The next morning, when calmer heads prevailed, we called the mother to apologize, but by this time the damage had been done. We feared that we had lost any chance of having direct access to this family for research purposes.[10] In this case, our role as parental defenders superseded that of measured observers, temporarily jettisoning our research concerns. Actual conflicts with those we study are a serious problem arising from the PAR's role attachment that is less likely to occur in non-PAR research on children.

ROLE OBLIGATIONS

At times, our membership role in the settings created obligations and responsibilities for us. Although we were often able to align our membership efforts with our research interests, this was not always the case. Membership role obligations occasionally ran independently of and in opposition to the values and philosophies we developed and espoused in our research role. For instance, during the course of this research we founded, along with two other couples, our own competitive youth baseball organization. We had written about some of the detrimental effects associated with the adult control of youth recreation and the pressure this brought upon young people, fostering highly competitive and goal-oriented attitudes toward sport at ever younger ages (Adler and Adler 1994). Still, we tried to develop a program that incorporated the positive aspects while restraining the negative ones. Not surprisingly, however, we began to see some of the same disappointing aspects in our league as in other youth sports leagues. While we were frustrated and disappointed with the league, having already obligated ourselves to the other members of the board of directors, we could not pull out; we were committed to operating the new organization.

These membership role obligations worked the same way in our own household. We often heard children denigrate the importance of school, making fun of kids who did well, or distancing themselves from educational investment. While we could nonjudgmentally accept the decisions and attitudes of these people, and could talk about their lives and options within the parameters they had set, we could not take that same approach with our own children. Our responsibilities as parents necessitated that we uphold our family values and goals. There were also times when we were called upon by other parents to assume the parental mandate and join with them in enforcing membership obligations. For example, we were awakened in the middle of the night to hear that our daughter and her friend had sneaked out of someone's house, and were enjoined to track them down; we were alerted that a carload of our girls was seen filling up the trunk with beer and heading out of town, and were recruited to find and stop them at the city limits.[11] In these kinds of cases we held relationships with other parents, shared things from a parental perspective, and collectively enforced parental norms. Our membership role carried with it a set of responsibilities and requirements that could not be avoided.

Though these role obligations precluded some data from coming our way, we had fewer obligations from artificially structured research bargains that we had to pay off. Often in field research, ethnographers must ingratiate themselves with their subjects to equalize the moral exchange. Since our role was a naturally occurring one, we did not have to "pay back" people in this way. Our favors to others were done in socially expected venues, and when we did not reciprocate, it was because it was not expected. All meaningful field research relations carry within them the necessity for reciprocal exchange. The difference between ours, as a membership role, was that the nature of our obligations was clearly articulated and part of our daily responsibilities, while for nonmember researchers they are negotiated or stipulated.

ROLE IDENTIFICATION

In contrast to other research roles, PARs have a greater relational identification by themselves and others with their children-as-subjects. This anchors their location in the settings and gives them a reflected identity.

Being affiliated with our children-as-subjects enhanced our ties to some people in the settings. For instance, our close ties to our children's friends led them to say things to us that they might never have revealed to other parents or researchers. We were fearful, for example, in studying clique dynamics (see chapter 3), that we would never learn how powerful clique leaders actually felt about the way they acted toward others, or whether they were consciously aware of their manipulations. Yet our daughter and her friends poured forth about these matters freely, speaking to us as they would only have to extreme insiders. Similarly, we had easy access to teachers in the local schools. Having made contacts with them when they taught our children, we were able to return to their classrooms for years following. They contacted parents for us, vouched to kids for us, and proudly hung up articles from the local newspaper about our work in their classrooms. We received help from other parents, too, who shared their inner feelings and frustrations about their kids with us, knowing that as parents we could understand and relate to their troubles and turmoils. Whole networks of people were also opened up to us through our role identification, particularly the after-school activities in which our children participated. For years, when we needed more data, when we needed answers to particularly puzzling questions or when we needed to triangulate data on people or events about which we were dubious, we had merely to walk down to the Little League fields on a Saturday and drift from group to group. By the end of several hours, we had harvested all the latest tidbits, scheduled a dozen interviews, and rounded up assistants who would search for the types of others we still needed.

Being parents of children in the community even enhanced our ties to people who did not know our kids. For instance, Patti was interviewing a third-grade girl outside school one day about the stratification hierarchy of kids in her grade. The girl mentioned a particularly mean clique leader by first name, and later in the conversation pointed him out as he passed by. Patti recognized him as the younger brother of a mean bully who had given our son a black eye and acknowledged, to the girl, the acquaintance. Her eyes grew wide as she exclaimed, "Oh, you know him?" She subsequently turned toward Patti, confidentially, and revealed a whole array of secret, negative information that she had previously withheld.

On the other hand, our close identification with our children and their friends diminished our access to other people in the settings. People who disliked our children tended to avoid us as well. This included children who were our children's enemies, parents of children whom they had treated badly, and those parents, noted earlier, with whom we had fought defensively on their behalf. Other times we had difficulty gaining direct information from people who thought ill of our children. In interviews with one of our son's former teachers and one of his former friends, these people had to delicately step around descriptions of behavior that they thought damaging because they found it embarrassing to say negative things that they believed applied to our son. Further, despite our promises of confidentiality, there were people who probably did not want to say things to us that they feared would get back to our kids or to others, through our kids. Finally, there were others who tried to hide their marginal behavior, such as smoking cigarettes or having sex, because they thought it might affect the way we felt about them. These types of diminished access are less likely to occur in non-PAR research on children.

Role Relations

ROLE EFFECTS

Casting a research dimension onto a previously existing membership role may have numerous effects on the incumbent role and its associated relationships.

This may, in some respects, be damaging. Studying their children and community may impinge upon researchers' relationships with their children or other community members. In pursuing depth information and feelings, researchers may intrude into people's personal lives and invade their private areas. There were times when our children resisted our interest in and curiosity about them. They were particularly sensitive about anything concerning their relationships with members of the other gender. Adding the research role into the relationship also brought with it added responsibilities for our children. While at times they relished our interest in their friends, they also tired of facilitating our search for information and insight. Finally, the research relationship is characterized by an informational exchange. To some, this may be seen as having manipulative overtones that could negatively impinge on the relationships it touches.[12]

In other respects, the added role may enhance researchers' relationships with their children and others by deepening their intimacy, involvement, and understanding. Our children grew up with the security that their parents were interested and actively involved in their lives. We knew intimately about their inner feelings and the vicissitudes of their social worlds. We took their questions and problems as our own. When they needed help, our suggestions reflected our depth immersion in their experiences. Our commitment to studying our children thus afforded us the opportunity to invest time in their worlds that we might otherwise have had to divert to other research settings. We also developed an enhanced intimacy with our children's friends. Several of them told us that they lacked the closeness with their parents that our children had with us. They never tried to explain their feelings and behavior to their parents, they said, because their parents were so unfamiliar with their lives that they would never understand them. Not only our own children, then, but these others told us about their personal lives or came to us for guidance. The addition of the research role deepened and enhanced our involvement in the lives of our children and their friends.

ROLE CONFUSION

Using the dual roles of parent and researcher was occasionally a source of confusion. Some people, usually acquaintances or distant others, did not understand our roles and questioned our behavior. Children who came into contact with us or our children were sometimes surprised to find us so interested in their lives. One time Peter and our son were out shopping one evening when they ran into some acquaintances from our son's class. They stopped to say hello, and Peter ended up engaging them in a long conversation, during which he chatted with them about other kids at school and about themselves. When they saw our son at school the next day, they asked him why his father was so curious about their friends and their lives. They were not used to talking to parents who knew so much about or were so interested in them. There were adults, too, who misunderstood our relationship with their children when they glimpsed it superficially. For instance, after our daughter and her friends got into trouble one evening, when they were supposed to be at our house, one mother accused us of being too permissive. She claimed that the girls congregated at our house because we allowed them to do things that others prohibited. This was not true, in fact, for we maintained the same curfew and behavioral standards as others. We knew, though, what the girls were generally doing, how and to whom they were lying, and when and where to balance liberty with control, rather than imposing strict unilateral rules. In contrast to this mother, who had to rely on rigid regulations that made her daughter hide everything from her and flee, we used our knowledge and our judgment to work within their culture, moderating its excesses. In these cases, people misunderstood the relationship between, and the way we integrated, our research and parental roles.

Other instances of role confusion were brought about by people, usually close others, who did not understand our seeming behavioral inconsistencies. These arose from conflicts we had between our values as parents and our desire to watch children as they naturally behaved. We occasionally seemed to flip in our attitudes, as we struggled between the nonjudgmental value stance of the research role and the moral imperative of the parental role. For instance, our interest in popularity led us to discern that, for some, academic achievement was not a trait critical to the hierarchy of popularity (see chapter 2). When we would force our children to read challenging books, to edit and rewrite their papers, or to stay home to study, this confused some of their friends. While we seemed to understand (better than their parents) their needs for faddish clothes, their desire to see an R-rated movie, their obsession with a weekly television show, or the necessity of acquiring their own phone line, we also had strong moral judgments about time that robbed them of their academic focus.

ROLE INTEGRATION

Most of the time we were able to integrate the research and the membership roles, engaging in them simultaneously. The commitment to time, place, and behavior, which would have been split between our personal lives and our research lives, was fused in the PAR approach. The parental role served as the base, and the research role flowed out of it. This is generally the case with opportunistic member-research, for the membership role precedes and is unlikely to be meaningfully transformed by the research addition. The character of our research posture was influenced by our natural membership inclinations in several ways. We have always tried to follow a laissez-fairist parental posture (Adler and Adler 1984), avoiding intervention in children's disputes and letting them learn (wherever possible) from the "natural consequences" of their own experiences.

The integration of the research and membership roles offered several advantages for us. First, we could be simultaneously engaged in gathering data while living our daily lives. Second, as noted, instead of having to ferret it out, data would come to us immediately and regularly as important events occurred. We were thus able to see people's initial, instead of reconstructed, emotional reactions and the way they individually and collectively forged their responses. Third, research questions arose for us in the pursuit of everyday life, questions which could then be addressed and answered in this same realm. Other people in the settings, both children and adults, were particularly helpful in this regard, since they found our questions fascinating and enjoyed discussing them with us. Fourth, when we entered settings (such as schools) exclusively for the purpose of gathering data, we were able to apply our membership knowledge to facilitate rapport, as when we brought our own "Pogs" (playing pieces for a popular children's game) to elementary schools and used them to play with kids on the playground in between interviewing them in their classes.

The PAR role thus represents an integration of self, enabling researchers, in large part, to synthesize their work and play, their personal and professional dimensions. PARs can then focus their research lens on topics that have meaningful interest to their lives, at the same time as they use their research skills to pursue the understanding and analysis of personal interests.

ROLE BIFURCATION

While these roles meshed comfortably most of the time, there were occasions when they were better separated or distinguished. The prompt to bifurcate these roles could come from either ourselves or others.

We initiated this distinction when we wanted to clarify our research interests or goals to people with whom we primarily shared a membership relationship. For example, our daughter and several of her friends had been invited to the "homecoming" dance of the rival high school by several boys with whom they were not "going," something that rarely occurred in their circle. Our queries about who these boys were and why they would invite our daughter's friends were met with a series of rebuffs and denials of knowledge. The morning of the dance, in unsuccessfully raising the question once again, Patti finally said to her, "Okay, I'm not asking as your mother anymore. I want to know as a sociologist." Suddenly a different expression crossed her face, and she explained that these boys were the stars of the football team, the boys with the highest status in the school. She and her friends represented the cream of the popular girls' group at her school. Since her school held higher local status than its rival, these boys bypassed the popular girls at their own school to seek the highest-status girls in town, even if it meant inviting girls with whom they were not romantically involved. It was as if this role as informant was separate from her role as our daughter.

Similarly, one day at school we saw our son, who had trouble making friends, hanging out with a "nice" boy. When we asked him why he did not invite this boy over to play, he informed us that this was a "school friend," not someone with whom he played at home. Intrigued, we asked him to explain this concept further, but he walked away annoyed. Exhortations that this relationship could prove of research interest were only met with further rebuffs. This shift in posture from parent to researcher, although not always successful in evoking data, was articulated to clarify a shift in goals that carried with it a rise in the confidentiality, impersonality, and generic interest of the communication.

At other times, the prompt to bifurcation came as the result of role conflict. Sometimes others tried to invoke our allegiance to one role over the other. This created dilemmas for us that we had to resolve individually, balancing our needs as parents, our children's needs, the needs of their friends, and our research needs. In some instances we allied with parents and the parental perspective. We responded to a call to join with other parents, for example, in holding a meeting with our son's basketball team to tell the boys that their collective behavior was inappropriately mean and hurtful. This was difficult because we had been pursuing noninterventionism as we gathered rich data, observing, interacting with, and carpooling the boys as they talked about each other and enacted their intricate clique manipulations. On another occasion, we responded to the direct query of a mother by informing her that her daughter had not arrived at our house by her curfew. This caused a breach in our trust relationship with the child, one that we were eventually able to recoup, but not without some difficulty. Nonparental researchers might not have had the same moral obligations to the surrounding adult community.

Occasionally, we sensed the role conflict ourselves and had to take a stance between research and membership pulls. We established standards to guide our conduct with children. In most cases we leaned toward the membership role, particularly in behavior involving our own children. We abandoned detachment and value neutrality when we felt that their welfare or moral development was in jeopardy. Yet with other children, we followed a policy of passive acceptance (but not active facilitation) of problematic behavior. We made it perfectly clear to our informants, for example, that while we would not seek out their parents to volunteer our knowledge, neither would we lie for them. When asked directly, as noted above, we would tell. We also drew the line between knowing about deviant behavior and enabling it. While we recognized that some people used alcohol and drugs, we neither permitted the use of illicit substances in our house nor assisted people in obtaining them. Finally, we refrained from engaging in any deviant behavior or consuming any illicit substances (including alcohol) with our informants. This culminated in our having to take the strongest membership stance of our research career: excluding a topic from study.

While conducting interviews about clique dynamics, we were told by several people that we should interview them about drugs, that drugs were coming in and tearing their cliques apart, that drugs were salient to the hierarchy of status and the confines of group membership. We pursued the topic, obtaining a Certificate of Confidentiality from the federal Department of Health and Human Services, which would have protected the data we gathered from the curiosity of parents or the subpoena of law enforcement. After thinking about the project for a long time, however, we finally decided to abandon it because of the potential role conflict and ethical issues it might engender. We did not want to put ourselves in situations where we would feel torn between the research loyalty of protecting informants' confidences and the membership loyalty of protecting them and their families from dangerous behavior.

Role bifurcation occurred, then, when we deliberately detached one role from the other, drawing the distinction between the researcher and membership position. We stepped out of research/membership role fusion when we thought it would clarify our purpose, when we needed to assert authority and distance, or when we took an ethical stance with regard to a particular behavior.

ROLE BETRAYALS

As Lofland and Lofland (1995) and Punch (1994) state, any foray into the field may yield the sense of betrayal. When researchers gain intimate knowledge of people's lives and write about it, the subjects may feel as if they have been betrayed (Rochford 1985; Vidich and Bensman 1964). Subjects may also feel betrayed when researchers leave the field, especially if they have taken a membership role. In contrast to these "active" membership roles (Adler and Adler 1987) that researchers may quit, the parental research role is one that endures. Once the research is terminated, participants remain within the setting. Nevertheless, role betrayals (by researchers to others and vice versa) can still arise during complete membership research. When any party interacts through one role, he or she may betray the commitment of self and others to the alternate role.

The issue of role betrayal came up repeatedly in our interaction with our own children. We often expected them to treat their lives toward us as research, while we acted toward them as parents. They, in turn, wanted us to accord them the acceptance and value neutrality of the research stance (which we gave their friends), while they treated their lives toward us as personal. We were thus caught with them between the relationships of parent-child and researcher-friend. While this often worked, making us friends with our children, it also occasionally created feelings of role betrayal toward each other. During the instances, then, when we applied our parental standards to them, as opposed to our research standards, they felt betrayed. On the other hand, when we felt obligated to apply our research standards rather than our parental standards, we felt impinged upon. This double standard was a confusing aspect of our dual roles.

Manipulation was another potential betrayal factor. We had to ask ourselves if our behavior was sometimes imbued with too great of an instrumental purpose. We reflected, at times, about whether we were treating the children instrumentally because of the "side-bets" (Becker 1960) we had with them, and wondered if they occasionally thought the same. We questioned our acceptance of friends and acquaintances our children brought home who were not to our liking, but whom we found empirically interesting. At the same time, we questioned their offerings to and requests from us.

Ethical Issues

POWER

A common charge leveled against ethnography is that researchers have more social power than their subjects. This imbalance can be especially pronounced when researchers are studying children (Corsaro 1981a). In our case, power differentials existed in the areas of age, status, education, financial resources, potential influence (over them through their parents), and occasionally direct authority (over our own children). Common to much of ethnography, power differentials, or "studying down" (Nader 1972), are oft-discussed forms of relations between researchers and their subjects.[13] However, in no other research relationship, with the possible exceptions of the teacher-researcher or counselor-researcher, does the question of direct authority over the researched stand out as critically as it does with the parent-researcher role.

In our role, power issues are primarily germane to problems associated with pressuring children to reveal data (the power of authority) or using data gathered through research to harm children in their personal life (the power of knowledge). Fine and Sandstrom (1988) note that preadolescence is the first age period where children develop the power to control or contain research over them, leaving researchers at their mercy. When researchers ask for entrée or inquire about specific topics, their requests carry a certain weight merely by having been made, but preadolescents have a keen sense of their privacy and deflect unwanted prying. The role of adult, parental-friend, or friend's parent was not a sufficiently formal authority role to enable us to compel data from others' children. We had no more ability to compel these participants to divulge data or to harm them through the knowledge we gathered than researchers do about any subjects they study.

The power of PARs more centrally involves their relationships with their own children. This is a role conflict issue, arising when PARs tip the balance between research and membership excessively toward the former. In an imperfect world, it is possible to imagine researchers abusing, exploiting, or in some other way harming their own children. However, we feel that the likelihood of this happening is remote. The emotional and familial primacy of the parental role dictates that the issues of protection, safety, and affection will take precedence over instrumental or career gains for the vast majority of researchers, as they did for us.[14]

GUILTY KNOWLEDGE/BEHAVIOR

A second potential ethical issue arises when PARs possess guilty knowledge about the behavior of others' children. Such guilty knowledge may also be viewed as guilty behavior when it involves withholding information about, or nonreporting, potentially problematic incidents. Ethnographic researchers studying children frequently encounter this problem, because youth is a period during which people learn by experimenting and testing boundaries. Scholars of children's behavior must weigh the moral obligation associated with knowing secrets about children's norm and rule violations, with the damage to trust that results when researchers inform on their subjects. In most cases, researchers studying children have located the ethical imperative in maintaining the confidence of their subjects (Fine and Sandstrom 1988; Glassner 1976; Mandell 1988). Fine and Sandstrom (1988, 55) argue that "children must be permitted to engage in certain behavior and speak certain words that the adult researcher finds distressing. Further, in some instances, the researcher must act in ways that are at least supportive of these distressing behaviors." Polsky (1967), in discussing research on the crime and deviance of adults, takes this one step far-

ther. He suggests that researchers studying such groups must be willing to engage in violations themselves, if only by not reporting these to the authorities,
and must prove to their informants that these actions are consistent with their
beliefs. This ethical issue is compounded when researchers' subjects are children, however, because behavioral standards for juveniles are different from
those for adults, with morals issues added to legal issues. Although the morality of children is partly legislated by society, children also fall under the moral
guidance of their parents. Each family's standards are sui generis in a category
of their own, and they may differ from the standards of researchers. This leads
to questions, discussed earlier, about how researchers should treat children
whose parents have different standards and expectations for their behavior.

For researchers to turn to parental or other authorities whenever they wit-
ness a mean-spirited, deviant, or delinquent activity not only would be im-
practical but would bring the research process to a screeching halt. Such action,
moreover, would violate the membership norms of parental behavior, since parents deem it inappropriate to report to each other everything they know. Yet
researchers may find occasions where either reporting or intervention is appropriate. Here, the guideline of endangerment can serve as a rule of thumb.
When researchers observe children engaging in behavior that could be harmful to either themselves or others, or when they encounter behavior committed by others that could be harmful to children, they should step out of the
neutral posture and attempt to help. This can take the form of reporting such
behavior to the appropriate person(s) and/or directly intervening themselves.

The responsibility for making this judgment can only lie with researchers
themselves. No structure of bureaucratic regulations can substitute for the interpretive judgment of participating individuals, because children's behaviors
are understood and given meaning within the context of their situations. If researchers deem that these behaviors fall within the parameters of children's
"normal" deviance, then they can give them some latitude. Thus, we acquiesced
to remaining silent about children's bullying, exclusion, and lying, just as Mandell (1988) permits children to urinate in the corner without telling the teachers and Fine (1987) witnesses stealing without reporting it. When the younger
boys we studied engaged in such antisocial behavior, we did not necessarily stop
them or break up their fights, believing that such dominance plays were a common feature of male preadolescent culture. Yet in other cases, we intervened
directly with our informants about their behavior, especially their alcohol con-
sumption, sexual exploits, and binge eating, acting on the basis of our concern
for their welfare. We advised them about safer techniques, health issues, and
problematic behavioral patterns, but neither told on them to their parents nor
severely chastised them. It was our belief that they would experiment with these

acts anyway, and we felt that if we could gain their confidence, we could impart information that would, in effect, be more beneficial than stringent admonitions for abstinence. We never encountered behavior that warranted, in
our opinion, reporting to either parents or authorities, such as Weiss (1994)
finds in her study of deformed children, when she observes these youngsters
being maltreated by their families and has to report this to the social welfare
service.

RESPONSIBILITY

A third issue concerns the moral and legal responsibilities of the PAR and how
these differ, if at all, from those of the parent as nonresearcher and the researcher
as nonparent. Whether or how the responsibilities and liabilities of parents
change upon the addition of the research dimension has never been specifically addressed. Guidelines to these concerns can only be deduced through in-
ference, if at all.

In reviewing our planned research, our institutional review boards suggested that following our customary parental behavior was appropriate as long
as we restricted ourselves to interacting naturalistically within the confines of
the "parental role." Only when we moved outside of this role to conduct taped
interviews did we need to obtain formal review and parental consent. In so
doing, we were carefully instructed in how to handle issues of disclosure, consent, and anonymity, and screened for areas involving sensitive topics, participants' law violations, and the ethical treatment of our subjects. We were told
to refrain from addressing sensitive topics, either to avoid asking about sex,
crime, and drugs or to inform subjects that we could not protect data they gave
us about their law violations, and that we would have to inform the authorities if we witnessed any instances of abuse or maltreatment, even if it meant
violating subjects' trust. Once we stepped out of the parental role, then, we were
to act as agents of the state.[15]

Over the years, we have seen the increasing expansion and bureaucratization of official behavior, encumbering greater numbers of people with formalized regulations and obligations. At the same time, we have witnessed the rise
in public intervention into people's private lives through the vehicle of
government-mandated reporting. A host of people in different roles have been
required to assume the responsibility of coming forward to reveal information
where they might previously have avoided involvement, particularly in areas
involving the potential physical or sexual abuse of women and children. This
no longer applies only to medical and educational personnel, but now to social
researchers as well. Parents, then, are asked to assume a different social and legal

responsibility, even if their moral responsibility feels the same, when they bring the research enterprise into their lives.

Moral standards and concerns in the academy have shifted dramatically over the last decade. Heightened attention has been brought to bear on areas that might previously have been considered unproblematic, the concept of vulnerable populations has been brought to the fore, and a host of heretofore common practices have been questioned on moral grounds. This rise in the ethical imperative and movement toward interventionism reflect a general shift in the broader societal ethic away from an emphasis on the good and the rights of the individual, toward the benefit and needs of the collective. We are increasingly being asked to give less weight to the interests of individual freedom and liberty against those of the collective welfare.

In deriving conclusions about the ethical responsibilities of the PAR, we get no assistance from those who have developed the corresponding roles of teacher-as-researcher and counselor-as-researcher. These practitioners have been less reflective about their behaviors than traditional academics.[16] Parent-researchers work in a research area where two sets of standards operate concurrently: the public arena of the research role, and the private arena of the parental role. We are asked to find a balance between two, often conflicting, sets of guidelines: those of a social moral order that is changing, and that of a personal moral order that holds constant; those of a social moral order that seeks elaborated rules and guidelines to protect the vulnerable from the potentially capricious judgment of the individual, and the personal moral order that seeks flexibility and discretion to uphold the traditional goals of family, reciprocal loyalty, and trust. Until such time as we develop clearly integrated norms that obviate the need for such tightrope balancing, we can only advise PARs to seek the good in both sides, to equilibrate, as best they can, the benefits intended by the moral collectivists with the loyalty and judgment that come from the heart of the moral individualists.

Chapter 2   Popularity

Oɴᴇ ᴏꜰ ᴛʜᴇ strongest dimensions of life that preadolescents wrestle with is popularity. They are forever talking about who is popular, who is unpopular, and why they are popular. Children strive, much to parents' chagrin, to enhance their own popularity, often at considerable expense. In this effort, there are some things that they can influence, and others that fall beyond their control. Factors affecting children's popularity and unpopularity are different for boys and girls. These are rooted in the strong gendered peer cultures that arise during youth, as children attempt to discern the contours of adult gender dimensions and adapt them, as relevant, to their own age cultures. Segregated sexual cultures have been observed as early as preschool (Berentzen 1984; Cahill 1994; Corsaro 1985; Gunnarsson 1978; Joffe 1971), as boys and girls separate and begin to evolve their own interests and activities. Studies of preadolescent and adolescent gendered peer cultures have examined the influence of play (Lever 1976), exclusiveness of friendships (Eder and Hallinan 1978), conversation rules (Maltz and Borker 1983), extracurricular activities (Eder and Parker 1987), and cross-gender relations (Eisenhart and Holland 1983) on the construction of gender roles.

In educational institutions, children develop a stratified social order determined by their interactions with peers, parents, and other social elements (Passuth 1987). According to Corsaro (1979), children's knowledge of social position is influenced by their conception of status, which may be defined as popularity, prestige, or "social honor" (Weber 1946). In the school environment, boys and girls have divergent attitudes and behavioral patterns in their gender role expectations and the methods they use to attain status, or popularity among peers.

In this chapter, we examine differences in the factors affecting girls' and boys' popularity in their gendered peer cultures.

Boys' Popularity Factors

Boys' popularity, or rank in the status hierarchy, was influenced by several factors. Although the boys' popularity ordering was not as clearly defined as the girls', there was a rationale underlying the stratification in their daily interactions and group relationships.

ATHLETIC ABILITY

The major factor affecting boys' popularity was athletic ability.[1] This was so critical that individuals who were proficient in sport attained both peer recognition and upward social mobility. In several schools we observed, the best athlete was also the most popular boy in the grade.

Two third- and fourth-grade boys considered the question of what makes kids popular:

> NICK: Craig is sort of mean, but he's really good at sports so he's popular.
>
> BRIAN: Everybody wants to be friends with Gabe, even though he makes fun of most of them all the time. But they still all want to pick him on their team and have him be friends with them because he's a good athlete, even though he brags a lot about it. He's popular.

In the upper grades, the most popular boys all had a keen interest in sports even if their athletic skills were not very adept. Those with moderate ability and interest in athletic endeavors fell primarily into lower-status groups. Those least proficient athletically were potential pariahs.

Because of their physicality, contact sports occasionally degenerated into conflicts between participants. Fighting, whether formal fights or informal pushing, shoving, or roughhousing, was a means to establish a social order for the boys. More popular boys often dispensed these physical actions of superiority, while the less popular boys were often the recipients. The victors, although negatively sanctioned by the adults in the school, attained more status than the defeated, who lost considerable status. Less popular boys were the ones most frequently hurt and least frequently assisted during games on the playground. For example, Mikey, an unpopular boy with asthma who was fairly uncoordinated and weak, was often the victim of rough playground tackles in football or checks in soccer. Boys knew they could take the ball away from him at will. When he was hurt and fell down crying, he was blamed for the incident and mocked.

COOLNESS

For boys, being "cool" generated a great deal of peer status. As Lyman and Scott (1989, 93) note, "a display of coolness is often a prerequisite to entrance into or maintenance of membership in certain social circles." Cool was a social construction whose definition was in constant flux. Being cool involved individuals' self-presentational skills, their accessibility to expressive equipment, such as clothes, and their impression management techniques (Fine 1981).

Various social forces were involved in the continual negotiation of cool and how the students came to agree upon its meaning. As Mrs. Slade, a sixth-grade teacher, commented: "The popular group is what society might term 'cool.' You know, they're skaters, they skateboard, they wear more cool clothes—you know, the 'in' things you'd see in ads right now in magazines. If you look at our media and advertising right now on TV, like the Levi commercials, they're kinda loose, they skate, and they're doing those things. The identity they created for themselves, I think, has a lot to do with the messages the kids are getting from the media and advertising as to what's cool and what's not cool."

There was a consensus among the students on what type of expressive equipment was socially defined as cool. Although this type of apparel was exhibited mostly by the popular boys, boys in the other groups also tried to emulate this style. Aspects of this style included: (1) high-top tennis shoes, such as Nike Air Jordans or Reeboks, that were often unlaced at the top eyelets or untied completely; (2) baggy designer jeans that were rolled up at the cuff; (3) loose-fitting button-down shirts, that were not tucked into their pants (or only tucked in in front) so that the shirt tails hung out, or T-shirts with surfing, skateboarding, or designer logos on them, such as Hilfiger, Mossimo, Calvin Klein, Polo, and Bad Boy; (4) hairstyles such as the "buzz," the "bow," or moussed to give the hair a "wet look" or make it stand up straight; (5) denim jackets; (6) Sony Walkmans or other brands of portable stereo receivers/cassette players; and (7) skateboards.

TOUGHNESS

In most of the schools we studied, the popular boys, especially in the upper grade levels, were defiant of adult authority, challenged existing rules, and received more disciplinary actions than boys in the other groups. They attained a great deal of peer status from this type of acting out. This defiance is related to what Miller (1958) calls the "focal concerns" of lower-class culture, specifically "trouble" and "toughness." Trouble involves rule-breaking behavior and, as Miller (1958, 176) notes, "in certain situations, 'getting into trouble' is overtly recognized as prestige conferring." Boys who exhibited an air of nonchalance in the face of teacher authority or disciplinary measures enhanced their status among their peers, as witnessed by Fine (1987) in his study of Little League boys.

Two fourth-grade boys described how members of the popular group in their grade acted:

> ANDY: They're always getting into trouble by talking back to the teacher.
>
> TOM: Yeah, they always have to show off to each other that they aren't afraid to say anything they want to the teacher, that they aren't teachers' pets. Whatever they're doing, they make it look like it's better than what the teacher is doing, 'cause they think what she's doing is stupid.
>
> ANDY: And one day Josh and Allen got in trouble in music 'cause they told the teacher the Disney movie she wanted to show sucked. They got pink [disciplinary] slips.
>
> TOM: Yeah, and that's the third pink slip Josh's got already this year, and it's only Thanksgiving.

Toughness involved displays of physical prowess, athletic skill, and belligerency, especially in repartee with peers and adults. In the status hierarchy, boys who exhibited "macho" behavioral patterns gained recognition from their peers for being tough. Often, boys in the high-status crowd were the "class clowns" or "troublemakers" in the school, thereby becoming the center of attention.

In contrast, boys who demonstrated "effeminate" behavior were referred to by pejorative terms such as "fag," "sissy," and "homo," and consequently lost status (cf. Thorne and Luria 1986). One boy was constantly derided behind his back because he got flustered easily, had a "spaz" (lost his temper, slammed things down on his desk, stomped around the classroom), and then would start to cry.

Two fifth-grade boys described a classmate they considered the prototypical fag:

> TRAVIS: Wren is such a nerd. He's short and his ears stick out.
>
> NIKKO: And when he sits in his chair, he crosses one leg over the other and curls the toe around under his calf, so it's double-crossed, like this [shows]. It looks so faggy with his "girly" shoes. And he always sits up erect with perfect posture, like this [shows].
>
> TRAVIS: And he's always raising his hand to get the teacher to call on him.
>
> NIKKO: Yeah, Wren is the kind of kid, when the teacher has to go out for a minute, she says, "I'm leaving Wren in charge while I'm gone."

SAVOIR FAIRE

Savoir faire refers to students' sophistication in social and interpersonal skills. These included interpersonal communication skills such as being able to initiate sequences of play and other joint lines of action, affirmation of friendships, role-taking and role-playing abilities, social knowledge and cognition, providing constructive criticism and support to one's peers, and expressing feelings in a positive manner. Boys used their social skills to establish friendships with peers and adults both within and outside the school environment, thereby enhancing their popularity.

Many of the behaviors composing savoir faire depended on students' maturity, adroitness, and awareness of what was going on in the social world around them. Boys who had a higher degree of social awareness knew how to use their social skills more effectively. This manifested itself in a greater degree of sophistication in communicating with peers and adults.

Miss Hoffman, a fourth-grade teacher, commented on some of the characteristics she noted in the group leaders: "Interpersonal skills, there's a big difference there. It seems like I get a more steady gaze, more eye contact, and more of an adult response with some of the kids in the popular group, one-on-one with them. The ones who aren't [in the popular group] kind of avert their gaze or are kind of more fidgety; they fidget a little more and are a little more uneasy one-on-one."

A parent also remarked on this difference between popular leaders and less popular followers in discussing a burglary attempt that had been inadvertently foiled by a group of third-grade boys who returned home early one day and surprised some thieves in the house: "They all got a good look at the pair, but when the police came, only Kyle and Devin were able to tell the police what went on. The rest of the boys were all standing around, pretty excited and nervous, and they couldn't really explain what had happened or understand what had happened. . . . And when the police took them down to the station to give a description and to look through the mug books, Kyle and Devin did all of the talking. I know my kid could not have done what they did. He's a little more in outer space somewhere. Kyle, especially, has always been more mature than the rest."

Many boys further used their savoir faire to their social advantage. In their desire to be popular, they were often manipulative, domineering, and controlling. They set potential friends against each other, vying for their favors. They goaded others into acting out in class and getting into trouble. They set the attitudes for all to follow and then changed the rules by not following them themselves. One mother sighed about her son Trevor's friendship with Brad (see the introduction), the leader of the popular group: "I'm glad they're not in the same class together this year. Every year he [her son] has chased after Brad, trying to be his best friend. He has gotten into a lot of trouble and put himself into a lot of competition with other kids over Brad. And then he's been left high and dry when Brad decided he wanted to be best friends with someone else."

Group leaders with savoir faire often defined and enforced the boundaries of an exclusive social group. While nearly everyone liked them and wanted to be in their group, they only included the kids they wanted (see chapter 3). They communicated to other peers, especially unpopular boys, that friendships did not exist or that play sessions were temporary. This maintained social boundaries by keeping others on the periphery and at a marginal status. These kinds of social skills did not seem to emerge along a developmental continuum, with some children farther along than the rest. Rather, certain individuals seemed to possess a more proficient social and interactional acumen, and to sustain it from year to year, grade to grade.

In contrast, those with extremely poor savoir faire had problematic social lives and low popularity (cf. Asher and Renshaw 1981). Their interpersonal skills were awkward or poor, and they rarely engaged in highly valued interaction with their peers. Some of them were either withdrawn or aggressively antisocial. Others exhibited dysfunctional behavior and were referred to as "bossy" or mean. These individuals did not receive a great deal of peer recognition yet often wanted acceptance into the more prestigious groups.

A group of second-grade boys discussed these behaviors in regard to their classmate Bud:

> STEVE: Bud, he's the worst bugger in the whole school. He always bugs
> people a lot.
> TIMMY: And he always pushes all of us around, and he calls us all names.
> Q: *Is Bud popular?*
> ALL: NO.
> SAM: Because he calls everybody names and kicks everybody and
> pushes us.
> STEVE: You know what he's best at? [*"No, what?"*] Annoying people.

Many of the students who lacked savoir faire to an extreme were disagreeable in conversations with their peers. Not only did they lack the social skills necessary to making it in the popular group, they could not maintain relationships with other less popular individuals.

CROSS-GENDER RELATIONS

Although cross-gender friendships were common in the preschool years, play and games became mostly gender-segregated in elementary school and there was a general lack of cross-gender interaction in the classroom (cf. Hallinan 1979). After kindergarten and first grade, boys and girls became reluctant to engage in intergender activities. Social control mechanisms, such as "rituals of pollution" and "borderwork" (Thorne 1986), reinforced intragender activities as the socially acceptable norm.[2] Also, peers often viewed intergender activities as romances, which made them highly stigmatized and therefore difficult to maintain. Elementary school boys sometimes picked out one girl that they secretly "liked," but they were reluctant to spend much time talking with her or to reveal their feelings to anyone for fear of being teased. When these secrets did get out, children were made the butt of friends' jokes. Most boys, whatever their popularity, were only interested in the select girls from the popular group.

Sometime during the fourth or fifth grade, both male and female students began to renegotiate the social definition of intergender interactions due to pubertal changes and the emulation of older children's behavior (cf. Thorne 1986).[3] Eder and Parker (1987, 201) note that preadolescence is the stage where "cross sex interactions become more salient." As we show in chapter 9, during the later elementary years it generally became more socially acceptable for the members of male and female groups to engage in intergender interactions. This took the form of boys talking with girls in the protected enclave of their social group. They would tease girls or ask them silly or awkward questions. They sometimes wrote anonymous prank letters with their friends to girls they secretly liked, asking or challenging these girls about "mysterious" features of puberty.

By the sixth grade, boys began to display a stronger interest in girls, and several—usually the most popular boys—initiated cross-gender relations. As Mr. Clark, a fifth-grade teacher, remarked: "The big thing I think is that they are with the girls. They've got some relationships going with the girls in the class, whereas the less popular group does not have that at all."

As Fine (1987) notes, sexual interest is a sign of maturity in preadolescent boys, yet it is problematic for inexperienced boys who are not fully cognizant of the norms involved. For safety, boys often went through intermediaries (cf. Eder and Sanford 1986) in approaching girls to find out if their interests were reciprocated. Rarely were such dangerous forays made face-to-face. Boys gathered with a friend after school on the phone to call girls for each other, or passed notes or messages from friends to the girl in question. When mutual interest was confirmed, they then asked the girl to "go" with them.

One sixth-grade boy described the Saturday he spent with a friend: "We were over at Bob's house, and we started calling girls we liked on the phone, one at a time. We'd each call the girl the other one liked and ask if she wanted to go with the other one. Then we'd hang up. If she didn't say yes, we'd call her back and ask why. Usually they wouldn't say too much. So sometimes we'd call her best friend to see if she could tell us anything. Then they would call each other and call us back. If we got the feeling after a few calls that she really was serious about no, then we might go on to our next choice, if we had one."

Getting a confirmation from a girl that she accepted the commitment only affected the interaction between them in school to a certain degree. Boy-girl relations posed considerable risks by representing "innovative situations" (Lyman and Scott 1989) that called for displays of coolness. Yet when a boy went with a girl, he was free to call her on the phone at home and to invite her to a boy-girl party, to a movie, or to the mall with another couple or two.

Once the connection was established, boys pressured each other to "score" with girls. Boys who were successful in "making out" with girls (or who claimed that they were) received higher status from their friends. This put considerable pressure on the boy-girl relationship, as Matt, a sixth-grade boy, explained: "I liked Amy, and we had been going together for a few months, nothing much, mostly going to the mall or bowling on weekends with some other kids, but some of the other guys were going with girls who made out [kissed]. One couple would even make out right at school, right in front of everybody. So the guys put a lot of pressure on me to get to first base with Amy. I knew she didn't want to because she had told me, but at one party it just got so intense, and the guys were on me so much, that I told her she had to. So she got all mad and started to cry, and then her friends came over and got all 'round her, and then they all left the party, and so I guess we're sort of broken up."

Boys who were successful in getting girls to go with them developed the reputation of being a ladies' man and gained status among their peers.

ACADEMIC PERFORMANCE

The impact of academic performance on boys' popularity was negative for cases of extreme deviation from the norm, but changed over the course of their elementary years for the majority of boys from a positive influence to a potentially degrading stigma.

At all ages, boys who were skewed toward either end of the academic continuum suffered socially. Thus, boys who struggled scholastically, who had low self-confidence in accomplishing educational tasks, or who had to be placed in remedial classrooms lost peer recognition. One third-grade boy, for example, who went to an after-school tutoring institute shielded this information from his peers, for fear of ridicule. Boys with serious academic problems were liable to be called "dummies." At the other end of the continuum, boys who were exceedingly smart but lacking in other status-enhancing traits such as coolness, toughness, or athletic ability were often stigmatized as "brainy" or "nerdy."

The following discussion, by two fifth-grade boys, highlighted the negative status that could accrue to boys with excessive academic inclinations and
performance:

> GLEN: One of the reasons they're so mean to Seth is because he's got
> glasses and he's really smart. They think he's a brainy-brain and a
> nerd.
> SETH: You're smart too, Glen.
> GLEN: Yeah, but I don't wear glasses, and I play football.
> SETH: So you're not a nerd.
> Q: *What makes Seth a nerd?*
> GLEN: Glasses, and he's a brainy-brain. He's really not a nerd, but
> everybody always makes fun of him 'cause he wears glasses.

In the early elementary years, academic performance in between these extremes was positively correlated with social status. Younger boys took pride in
their work, loved school, and loved their teachers. Many teachers routinely
hugged their students at day's end as they sent them out the door. Yet sometime during the middle elementary years, by around third grade, boys began to
change their collective attitudes about academics. This coincided with a change
in their orientation, away from surrounding adults and toward the peer group.
Their shift involved the introduction of a potential stigma associated with
doing too well in school. The macho attitudes embodied in the coolness and
toughness orientations led them to lean more toward group identities as rene-
gades or rowdies. This stance affected their exertion in academics, creating a
ceiling level of effort beyond which it was potentially dangerous to reach. Boys
who persisted in their pursuit of academics while lacking other social skills were
subject to ridicule as "cultural dopes" (Garfinkel 1967). Individuals who had
high scholastic aptitudes, even with other culturally redeeming traits, became
reluctant to work up to their full potential for fear of exhibiting low-valued behavior. By diminishing their effort in academics, they avoided the disdain of
other boys. One fifth-grade boy explained why he put little more than the minimum work into his assignments: "I can't do more than this. If I do, then they'll
[his friends] make fun of me and call me a nerd. Jack is always late with his
homework, and Chuck usually doesn't even do it at all [two popular boys]. I
can't be the only one."

Not only did this diminished academic effort preclude boys' ostracism from
popular groups, it also demonstrated support and solidarity for others less able
than themselves. This functioned as a technique of collective face-saving. The
group identity was managed so that "low achievers" were able to occupy positions of high status. Discussing the dynamics of boys' groups, Miss Moran, a

fourth-grade teacher, stated: "It was like they all had that identity and they all hung together like none of us do it, none of us are gonna do it. If we do it, it's gonna be half, and if we do any better than half the job, then we're gonna give it to you on the slide."

Some boys who were scholastically adept tried to hide their academic efforts or to manage good performance in school with other status-enhancing factors so as to avoid becoming stigmatized. They gave their friends answers when friends were called on by the teacher, and were disruptive and off-task during instructional periods, socializing with their friends and occasionally playing the class clown. These behaviors nullified the label of "goody-goody" or "teacher's pet" by demonstrating a rebellious attitude to adult authority. Thus, by the second half of elementary school, the environment provided more of a social than an educational function for them, and this had a negative effect on their desire for academic success (cf. Coleman 1961).

Girls' Popularity Factors

The major distinction between the boys' and girls' status hierarchies lay in the factors that conferred popularity. Although some factors were similar, girls used them in a different manner to organize their social environment. Consequently, they had different effects on their status hierarchies.

FAMILY BACKGROUND

As with the middle school girls studied by Eder (1985), elementary school girls' family background was one of the most powerful forces affecting their attainment of popularity. Their parents' socioeconomic status and degree of permissiveness were two of the most influential factors.

Socioeconomic Status (SES). Maccoby (1980) suggests that among the most powerful and least understood influences on a child are the parents' income, education, and occupation. In general, many popular girls came from upper- and upper-middle-class families. These students were able to afford expensive clothing, which was socially defined as stylish and fashionable. These "rich" girls had a broader range of material possessions, such as expensive computers or games, a television in their room, and/or designer phones in their room with their own separate line (some girls even had a custom acronym for the number). They also participated in select extracurricular activities, such as horseback riding, skiing, and vacation travel to elite locations. Some girls' families owned second homes in resort areas to which they could invite their friends for the weekend. Their socioeconomic status gave these girls greater access to highly regarded symbols of prestige. While less privileged girls often referred to them as "spoiled," they secretly envied their lifestyle and possessions.

Two fourth-grade girls in the unpopular group discussed the issue of popularity versus unpopularity:

> ALISSA: If your mom has a good job you're popular, but if your mom has a bad job then you're unpopular.
>
> BETTY: And if, like, you're on welfare, then you're unpopular because it shows that you don't have a lot of money.
>
> ALISSA: They think money means that you're great, you can go to Sophia's [a neighborhood "little store" where popular people "hang out"] and get whatever you want and stuff like that. You can buy things for people.
>
> BETTY: I have a TV, but if you don't have cable [TV] then you're unpopular, because everybody that's popular has cable.

Family background also influenced girls' popularity indirectly, through the factor of residential location. Neighborhoods varied within school districts, and girls from similar economic strata usually lived near each other. Not only did this increase the likelihood of their playing together, and not with girls from other class backgrounds, but the social activities in which they engaged after school were more likely to be similar, and their parents more apt to be friends. In addition, the differences in their houses could be considerable, intimidating some and embarrassing others. One girl, who lived in one of the poorer areas in the district, referred to the houses of her classmates as "mansions." When she invited these girls over to her house, she had difficulty bringing them into her room, since her clothes were kept in cardboard Pampers boxes, out of which her mother had fashioned a dresser. As her mother remarked: "I think sometimes it's a lot easier for Angela to just play with the neighborhood girls here than to try to make friends with some of the other girls in her class. They're popular, and they do all the fun things that Angela wants to get involved with, but it's hard for her when they come over here and stare. . . . And she knows she can't afford to do all the things they do, too."

Thus, although there were some popular girls who were not affluent, for the most part they came from families with high socioeconomic status. Girls believed that having money influenced their location in the social hierarchy.

Laissez-faire. Laissez-faire refers to the degree to which parents closely supervised their children or were permissive, allowing them to engage in a wide range of activities. Girls whose parents let them stay up late on sleepover dates, go out with their friends to all kinds of social activities, and who gave them a lot of freedom while playing in the house were more likely to be popular. Girls who had to stay home (especially on weekend nights) and "get their sleep," who were not allowed to go to mixed-gender parties, who had strict curfews, or whose parents called ahead to parties to ensure that they would be adult "supervised" were more likely to be left out of the wildest capers and the most exclusive social crowd.

Whether for business, social, or simply personal reasons, permissive or absentee parents oversaw the daily nuances of their children's lives less closely. They had a less tightly integrated family life and were less aware of their children's responsibilities, activities, and place in the social order. These girls had a valuable resource, freedom, that they could both use and offer others. They were also the most likely to spend time socializing away from the house or to organize activities with their friends that others perceived as fun and appealing. Their freedom and parental permissiveness often tempted them to try out taboo activities, which was a source of popularity among peers. Their activities sometimes served to make the group a wild or fast crowd, further enhancing their status.

In some instances, girls who received less support or supervision in their home lives developed an "external locus of control" (Good and Brophy 1987) and became major figureheads in the popular crowd. Using the peer group as a support mechanism, they manipulated others in the group to establish their central position and to dominate the definition of the group's boundaries. These ringleaders could make life difficult for members of their own clique, as Diane, one member of the fifth-grade popular group (see the introduction), lamented:

"I've really been trying to break away from Tiffany this year because she can be so mean, and I don't know when I go in to school everyday if she's been calling up other girls talking about me behind my back and getting everybody against me or not. Like, if I don't call everyone in my clique every night, I might find myself dropped from it the next day. Or she might decide at school that I've done something she doesn't like and turn everyone against me. That's why I'd like to break away from her, but I'm afraid, because she controls everybody and I wouldn't have any friends."

PHYSICAL APPEARANCE

Another powerful determinant of girls' location in the stratification system was their physical attractiveness.[4] Others have noted that appearance and grooming behavior are not only a major topic of girls' conversation but also a source of popularity.[5] The norms of popular appearance included designer clothing, such as Calvin Klein, Gap, Banana Republic, and J. Crew. In the upper grades, makeup was used as a status symbol, but as Eder and Sanford (1986) note, wearing too much makeup could inhibit a girl's social mobility since other members of the group were highly critical of this practice. Finally, girls who were deemed pretty by society's socially constructed standards were attractive to boys and had a much greater probability of being popular.

Girls were socialized into these norms of appearance at very early ages. A group of five second-grade girls had bad feelings about another girl in their class because they felt that she was popular and they were not:

> JEN: It's just that she has a lot of money but we don't, so it's like that's why she has the prettiest clothes and, you know, the prettiest makeup.
>
> LIZ: And she thinks, like, she's the prettiest girl in the whole school. Just because she's blond and all the boys like her.
>
> ANITA: And she thinks only she can have Erin [a well-liked girl] as her friend and not even us, she doesn't even play with us, and that's not very nice.

The perception that popularity was determined by physical traits was fully evidenced by these second graders. These aspects of appearance, such as clothing, hairstyles, and attractiveness to boys, were even more salient with the girls in the upper grades. As an excerpt from one of our field notes indicated: "I walked into the fifth-grade coat closet and saw Debby applying hairspray and mousse to Paula's and Mary's hair. Someone passed by and said, 'Oh, Mary I like your hair,' and she responded, 'I didn't do it, Diane did it.' It seemed that Diane, who was the most popular girl in the class, was socializing them to use the proper beauty supplies which were socially accepted by the popular clique. I asked what made girls unpopular, and Diane said, 'They're not rich and not pretty enough. Some people don't use the same kind of mousse or wear the same style of clothing.'"

As girls learn these norms of appearance and associate them with social status, they form the values that will guide their future attitudes and behavior, especially in cross-gender relationships (cf. Eder and Sanford 1986, 290). This correlates with other research suggesting that physical appearance is closely related to attaining a mate, that people who perceive themselves as being unattractive have difficulties in establishing relationships with others, and that there is a correlation between opportunities for occupational success and physical attractiveness (see Berscheid et al. 1971).

SOCIAL DEVELOPMENT

As with the boys, the most precocious girls achieved dominant social positions, but they were also more sensitive to issues of inclusion and exclusion. Precocity and exclusivity were crucial variables in influencing girls' formation of friendships and their location on the popularity hierarchy.

Precocity. Precocity refers to girls' early attainment of adult social characteristics, such as the ability to express themselves verbally, an understanding of the dynamics of intra- and intergroup relationships, skills at convincing others to see things their way and manipulating them into doing what they want, and an interest in more mature social concerns (such as makeup and boys). As with the boys, these social skills are only partly developmental; some girls just seem more precocious from their first arrival in kindergarten.

Mrs. Appleyard, a teacher, discussed differences in girls' social development and its effects on their interactions: "Communication skills, I can see a definite difference. There is not that kind of sophistication in the social skills of the girls in the unpopular group. The popular kids are taking on junior high school characteristics pretty fast just in terms of the kinds of rivalries they have. They are very active after school, gymnastics especially. Their conflicts aren't over play as much as jealousy. Like who asked who over to their house and who is friends. There is some kind of a deep-running, oh, nastiness as opposed to what I said before. The popular group, they seem to be maturing; I wouldn't call them mature, but their behavior is sophisticated. The unpopular girls seem to be pretty simple in their way of communicating and their interests."

The most precocious girls showed an interest in boys from the earliest elementary years.[6] They talked about boys and tried to get boys to pay attention to them.[7] This group of girls was usually the popular crowd, with the clothes and appearance that boys (if they were interested in girls) would like. These girls told secrets and giggled about boys, and in class and in the halls they passed them notes that embarrassed but excited the boys. They also called boys on the phone, giggling at them, asking them mundane or silly questions, pretending they were the teacher, singing radio jingles to them, or blurting out "sexy" remarks.

When Larry (see the introduction) was in third grade, he described the kinds of things a group of popular girls said to him when they called him on the phone: "Well, usually they just call up and say like, 'This is radio station KNUB, and we're here to call you,' but sometimes they say things like, 'Babe, will you go out with me tonight,' or one time Jim [his brother] answered the phone and they said, 'Get your sexy brother on the phone right now.' And one time last year when we were out to dinner, they called and filled up our whole phone machine with messages, around twenty of them, and my mom had to call their moms and tell them to stop it."

Girls who did not participate in these kinds of interactions often looked down on these girls as boy-crazy, but the interactions sharpened the interest of the boys. While boys could not let their peers know they liked this, they appreciated the attention. The notice they repaid to the girls then enhanced these girls' popularity (cf. Schofield 1981).

By around fourth to sixth grade, it became more socially acceptable for girls to engage in cross-gender interactions without being rebuked by peers. The more precocious girls began to experiment further with flirting with boys, calling them on the telephone, "going" with them, going to parties, and, ultimately, dating. Although some were adventurous enough to ask a boy out, most girls followed traditional patterns and waited for boys to commit themselves first. Kara, a popular fourth grader, described what it meant to "go" with a boy: "You talk. You hold hands at school. You pass notes in class. You go out with them, and go to movies, and go swimming. . . . We usually double-date."

In the upper grades, if a girl went with a popular boy, she was able to achieve a share of his prestige and social status. Several girls dreamed of this possibility and even spoke with longing or anticipation to their friends about it.[8] When popular girls went with popular boys, this reinforced and strengthened both parties' status. This was the most common practice, as one fifth-grade girl noted, "It seems that most of the popular girls go out with the popular boys; I don't know why." One fourth-grade girl referred to such a union as a "Wowee" (a highly prestigious couple), because people would be saying "Wow!" at the magnitude of their stardom.

Yet to go out with a lower-status boy would diminish a girl's prestige. Three fourth-grade girls responded to the question "What if a popular girl went with an unpopular boy?"

> ALISSA: DOWN! The girl would move down, way down.
> BETTY: They would not do it. No girl would go out with an unpopular boy.
> LISA: If it did happen, the girl would move down and no one would play with her either.

A high-status girl would be performing a form of social suicide if she interacted with a low-status boy in any type of relationship whatsoever. While girls acknowledged themselves as very sensitive to this issue, they doubted that a popular boy's rank in the social hierarchy would be affected by going with a girl from a lower stratum. They thought that boys would not place as much weight on such matters.

Exclusivity. Exclusivity refers to individuals' desire, need, and ability to form elite social groups using negative tactics such as gossiping, rumormongering, bossiness, and meanness. There were one or two elite groups of girls in each of the grade levels who jointly participated in exclusionary playground games and extracurricular activities. This formed clearly defined social boundaries because these girls granted limited access to their friendship circles.

In one fourth-grade class, a clique of girls had such a strong group identity that they gave themselves a name—the Swisters—and a secret language. Three of the members talked about their group:

> ANNE: We do fun things together, the Swisters here, um, we go roller skating a lot, we walk home together and have birthday parties together.
>
> CARRIE: We've got a secret alphabet.
>
> ANNE: Like an "A" is a different letter.
>
> DEBBIE: We have a symbol and stuff.
>
> ANNE: But we don't sit there and go like mad and walk around and go, "We're the Swisters and you're not, and you can't be in and anything."
>
> CARRIE: We don't try to act cool; we just stick together, and we don't sit there and brag about it.

This group of girls restricted entrée to their play and friendship activities, although they did not want to be perceived as pretentious or condescending. Many girls in the less popular groups did not like the girls in the highest-status crowd, even though they acknowledged their popularity (cf. Eder 1985). One sixth-grade girl, Melody, who was in an unpopular group remarked that "with a few exceptions, most of the girls in the fifth grade are snobby, and with the sixth grade most of them are snobby too, especially Carol, but they're popular. That might be what makes them popular."

Two lower-status fourth-grade girls commented further on the girls' social hierarchy:

> BETTY: The popular girls don't like the unpopular girls.
>
> Q: *Why not?*
>
> LAUREN: Because they don't think they look good and don't dress well, and Anne, Carrie, Debbie, and all those guys have an attitude problem.

Q: *What do you mean?*

ALISSA: An attitude problem is just coming in to impress people and
    like beating people up constantly or being really mean.

BETTY: If you're not popular, you mostly get treated like you're really
    stupid. They stare at you and go, "Uhhh." Like if someone does
    something bad, then the popular girl will tell all the other popular
    girls, and they'll go, "Oh, I hate you, you're so immature." Then
    they'd tell their whole gang, and then their whole gang won't like
    you one bit.

Thus, one of the most common forms of boundary maintenance among
friendship groups, both intra- and interclique, involved the use of rumors and
gossip (Parker and Gottman 1989). Shared secrets were passed among friends,
cementing their relational bonds (Simmel 1950), while derisive rumors were
told about outsiders. During class, many of the girls were preoccupied with passing notes to one another. These behaviors primarily involved the girls in the
popular cliques, who often derided the girls in the unpopular groups. Such tactics served not only to separate the groups but also to maintain the popular
crowd's position at the top of the social hierarchy. As Simmel (1950, 314) notes,
"The lie which maintains itself, which is not seen through, is undoubtedly a
means of asserting intellectual superiority and of using it to control and sup-
press the less intelligent (if intelligence is measured as knowledge of the social
situation)."

ACADEMIC PERFORMANCE

In contrast to the boys, elementary school girls never seemed to develop the
machismo culture that forced them to disdain and disengage from academics.
While not all popular girls were smart or academic achievers, they suffered little stigma from performing well scholastically. Throughout elementary school,
most girls continued to try to attain the favor of their teachers and to do well
on their assignments. They gained status from their classmates for getting good
grades and performing difficult assignments. The extent to which a school's policies favored clumping students of like abilities in homogeneous learning groups
or classes affected the influence of academic stratification on girls' cliques. Homogeneous academic groupings were less common during the early elementary
years but increased in frequency as students approached sixth grade and their
performance curve spread out wider. By fifth or sixth grade, then, girls were more
likely to become friends with others of similar scholastic levels. Depending on
the size of the school, within each grade there might be both a clique of acad-

emically inclined popular girls and a popular one composed of girls who did not perform as well and who bestowed lower salience on schoolwork.

THESE FINDINGS on gendered peer cultures accord well with other research. Studies of elementary school children have pointed out that girls value social and nurturant roles (Best 1983; Borman and Frankel 1984) while beginning to focus on appearance and romantic issues (Eisenhart and Holland 1983). Boys have been found to gain status from competitive and aggressive achievement-oriented activities, with an emerging interest in the later grades in romance (Best 1983; Eisenhart and Holland 1983; Goodwin 1980a,1980b; Lever 1976). Yet our research suggests that many of these peer focal concerns arise and become differentiated earlier than has been previously shown—in elementary school rather than adolescent gendered cultures. Thus, girls we observed were already deriving status from their success at grooming, wearing the "right" clothes, and other appearance-related variables; social sophistication and friendship ties; romantic success as measured through popularity and going with boys; affluence and its correlates of material possessions and leisure pursuits, and academic performance. Boys, even in the predominantly white, middle-class schools that we studied, were accorded popularity and respect for distancing themselves from the deference to authority and investment in academic effort, and for displaying traits such as toughness, troublemaking, domination, coolness, and interpersonal bragging and sparring skills.

Chapter 3

Clique Dynamics

A DOMINANT FEATURE of children's lives is the clique structure that organizes their social world. The fabric of their relationships with others, their levels and types of activity, their participation in friendships, and their feelings about themselves are tied to their involvement in, around, or outside the cliques organizing their social landscape. Cliques are, at their base, friendship circles, whose members tend to identify each other as mutually connected.[1] Yet they are more than that; cliques have a hierarchical structure, being dominated by leaders, and are exclusive in nature, so that not all individuals who desire membership are accepted. They function as bodies of power within grades, incorporating the most popular individuals, offering the most exciting social lives, and commanding the most interest and attention from classmates (Eder and Parker 1987). As such, they represent a vibrant component of the preadolescent experience, mobilizing powerful forces that produce important effects on individuals.[2]

The research on cliques is cast within the broader literature on elementary school children's friendship groups. A first group of such works examines independent variables that can have an influence on the character of children's friendship groups.[3] A second group looks at the features of children's inter- and intragroup relations.[4] A third group concentrates on the behavioral dynamics specifically associated with cliques.[5] Although these studies are diverse in their focus, they identify several features as central to clique functioning without thoroughly investigating their role and interrelation: boundary maintenance and definitions of membership (exclusivity); a hierarchy of popularity (status stratification and differential power), and relations between in-groups and out-groups (cohesion and integration).

In this chapter we look at these dynamics and their association, at the way clique leaders generate and maintain their power and authority (leadership, power/dominance), and at what it is that influences followers to comply so readily with clique leaders' demands (submission). These interactional dynamics are not intended to apply to all children's friendship groups, only those (populated by one-quarter to one-half of the children) that embody the exclusive and stratified character of cliques.

Techniques of Inclusion

The critical way that cliques maintained exclusivity was through careful membership screening. Not static entities, cliques irregularly shifted and evolved their membership, as individuals moved away or were ejected from the group and others took their place. In addition, cliques were characterized by frequent group activities designed to foster some individuals' inclusion (while excluding others). Cliques had embedded, although often unarticulated, modes for considering and accepting (or rejecting) potential new members. These modes were linked to the critical power of leaders in making vital group decisions. Leaders derived power through their popularity and then used it to influence membership and social stratification within the group. This stratification manifested itself in tiers and subgroups within cliques composed of people who were hierarchically ranked into levels of leaders, followers, and wannabes (see chapter 4). Cliques embodied systems of dominance, whereby individuals with more status and power exerted control over others' lives.

RECRUITMENT

Initial entry into cliques often occurred at the invitation or solicitation of clique members. (Cf. Blau, 1964, on small groups and organizations.) Those at the center of clique leadership were the most influential over this process, casting their votes for which individuals would be acceptable or unacceptable as members and then having other members of the group go along with them. If clique leaders decided they liked someone, the mere act of their friendship with that person would accord them group status and membership. (Cf. Eder,1985, on popular middle school girls.)

Potential members could also be brought to the group by established members who had met and liked them. The leaders then decided whether these individuals would be granted a probationary period of acceptance during which they could be informally evaluated. If the members liked them, the newcomers would be allowed to remain in the friendship circle, but if they rejected them, they would be forced to leave.

Tiffany, a popular, dominant girl, reflected on the boundary maintenance she and her best friend Diane, two clique leaders, had exercised in fifth grade:

Q: *Who defines the boundaries of who's in or who's out?*
TIFFANY: Probably the leader. If one person might like them, they might introduce them, but if one or two people didn't like them, then they'd start to get everyone up. Like in fifth grade, there was Dawn Bolton and she was new. And the girls in her class that were in our clique liked her, but Diane and I didn't like her, so we kicked her out. So then she went to the other clique, the Emily clique.

Timing was critical to recruitment. The beginning of the year, when classes were being reconstructed and people formed new social configurations, was the major time when cliques considered additions. Once these alliances were set, cliques tended to close their boundaries once again and stick to socializing primarily within the group. Kara, a fifth-grade girl, offered her view: "In the fall, right after school starts, when everyone's lining up and checking each other out, is when people move up, but not during the school year. You can move down during the school year, if people decide they don't like you, but not up."

Although people could play with friends who were in different classes, getting together at lunch, recess, and before and after school, individuals in elementary school were more tightly bound to their classrooms than they would be once they got to middle or junior high school (Hallinan 1979; Hansell 1984). At the beginning of the year, individuals separated from their key clique allies (as often happened through conscious school planning), assessed the new pool of eligibles in their classes, and tried to recruit them into the clique (through what Rizzo, 1989, calls "friendship bids").[6]

Most individuals felt that invitation to membership in the popular clique represented an irresistible offer. They repeatedly asserted that the popular group could get anybody they wanted to join them. One of the strategies used was to try to select new desirables and go after them. This usually meant separating the people from their established friends.

Melody, an unpopular fourth-grade girl, described her efforts to hold on to her best friend who was being targeted for recruitment by the popular clique: "She was saying that they were really nice and stuff. I was really worried. If she joined their group, she would have to leave me. She was over there, and she told me that they were making fun of me, and she kind of sat there and went along with it. So I kind of got mad at her for doing that. 'Why didn't you stick up for me?' She said, 'Because they wouldn't like me anymore.'" Melody subsequently lost her friend to the clique.

When clique members wooed someone to join them, they usually showed only the better side of their behavior. It was not until they had the new person firmly committed to the group that the shifts in behavior associated with leaders' dominance and status stratification activities began.

Diane recalled her inclusion into the popular clique and its aftermath: "In fifth grade I came into a new class and I knew nobody. None of my friends from the year before were in my class. So I get to school, a week late, and Tiffany comes up to me and she was like, 'Hi Diane, how are you? Where were you? You look so pretty.' And I was like, wow, she's so nice. And she was being so nice for like two weeks, kiss-ass major. And then she started pulling her bitch moves. Maybe it was for a month that she was nice. And so then she had clawed me into her clique and her group, and so she won me over that way, but then she was a bitch to me once I was inside it, and I couldn't get out because I had no other friends. 'Cause I'd gone in there and already been accepted into the popular clique, so everyone else in the class didn't like me, so I had nowhere else to go."

Eder (1985) also notes that popular girls are often disliked by unpopular people because of their exclusive and elitist manner (as befits their status).

APPLICATION

A second way for individuals to gain initial membership into a clique occurred through their actively seeking entry (Blau 1964). Several factors influenced the likelihood that a person would be accepted as a candidate for inclusion, as Darla, a popular fourth-grade girl described: "Coming in, it's really hard coming in, it's like really hard, even if you are the coolest person, they're still like, 'What is *she* doing [exasperated]?' You can't be too pushy, and like I don't know, it's really hard to get in, even if you can. You just got to be there at the right time, when they're nice, in a nice mood."

According to Rick, a fifth-grade boy who was in the popular clique but not a central member (see the introduction), application for clique entry was more easily accomplished by individuals than groups. He described the way individuals found routes into cliques: "It can happen any way. Just you get respected by someone, you do something nice, they start to like you, you start doing stuff with them. It's like you just kind of follow another person who is in the clique back to the clique, and he says, 'Could this person play?' So you kind of go out with the clique for a while and you start doing stuff with them, and then they almost like invite you in. And then soon after, like a week or so, you're actually in. It all depends. . . . But you can't bring your whole group with you, if you have one. You have to leave them behind and just go in on your own."

Successful membership applicants often experienced a flurry of immediate popularity. Because their entry required clique leaders' approval, they gained associational status.

Status and power in a clique were related to stratification, and people who remained more closely tied to the leaders were more popular. Individuals who wanted to be included in the clique's inner echelons often had to work regularly to maintain or improve their position.

Like initial entry, this was sometimes accomplished by people striving on their own for upward mobility. In fourth grade, Danny was brought into the clique by Mark, a longtime member (see the introduction), who went out of his way to befriend him. After joining the clique, however, Danny soon abandoned Mark when Brad, the clique leader, took an interest in him. Mark discussed the feelings of hurt and abandonment this experience left him with: "I felt really bad, because I made friends with him when nobody knew him and nobody liked him, and I put all my friends to the side for him, and I brought him into the group, and then he dumped me. He was my friend first, but then Brad wanted him. . . . He moved up and left me behind, like I wasn't good enough anymore."

The hierarchical structure of cliques, and the shifts in position and relationships within them, caused friendship loyalties within these groups to be less reliable than they might have been in other groups. People looked toward those above them and were more susceptible to being wooed into friendship with individuals more popular than they. When courted by a higher-up, they could easily drop their less popular friends.

Cliques' stratification hierarchies might motivate lower-echelon members to seek greater inclusion by propelling themselves toward the elite inner circles, but membership in these circles was dynamic, requiring active effort to sustain. More popular individuals had to put repeated effort into their friendship alignments as well, to maintain their central positions relative to people just below them, who might rise up and gain in group esteem. Efforts to protect themselves from the potential incursions of others took several forms, among them co-optation, position maintenance, follower realignment, and membership challenge, only some of which draw upon inclusionary dynamics.[7]

Follower realignment involved the perception that other clique members were gaining in popularity and status and might challenge leaders' position. But instead of trying to hold them in place (position maintenance) or exclude them from the group (membership challenge), leaders shifted their base of support; they incorporated lesser but still loyal members into their activities, thereby replacing problematic supporters with new ones. This happened when Joe, a fifth-grade clique leader, began to get the feeling that Davey was becoming very popular in his clique, developing followers who were loyal to him exclusively and not to Joe. He stopped inviting Davey over to his house after school and to sporting events with his family, and began to play with other clique members, who were outside of Davey's circle. This realignment pushed Davey and his group out of the center of the clique, elevating Joe's new best friends to the fore.

Co-optation involved leaders diminishing others' threats to their position by drawing them into their orbit, increasing their loyalty, and diminishing their independence. Clique members gaining in popularity were sometimes given special attention. At the same time, leaders might try to cut out their rivals' independent base of support from other friends.

Darla, a fourth grader, had occupied a second-tier leadership position with Kristy, her best friend. She explained what happened when Denise, the clique leader, came in and tore their formerly long-standing friendship apart: Me and Kristy used to be best friends, but she [Denise] hated that. 'Cause even though she was the leader, we were popular and we got all the boys. She didn't want us to be friends at all. But me and Kristy were, like, getting to be a threat to her, so Denise came in the picture and tore me and Kristy apart, so we weren't even friends. She made Kristy make totally fun of me and stuff. And they were so mean to me." Such tactics by Denise and other clique leaders illustrate Simmel's (1950) concept of the *tertius gaudens*, the one who draws advantage from the quarrels of others by dividing and conquering.

Diane's experiences illustrated what it felt like to be the one being realigned into the higher circle of popularity. She elaborated further on how she, in fifth grade, had been induced by Tiffany, the dominant clique leader, to drop her former best friend: "Yeah, Tiffany tore me and Julie apart. 'Cause I still wanted to be Julie's friend and Tiffany was like, 'She's a bitch, we don't want to be friends with her. She's ugly, she's mean.' And I was like, 'Yeah, you're right.'" Hence, friendship realignment involved clique members' abandoning previous friendships or plowing through existing ones in order to assert themselves into relationships with those in central positions. These actions were all geared toward improving instigators' position and thus their inclusion. Their outcome, whether anticipated or not, was often the separation of people and the destruction of their relationships.

INGRATIATION

Currying favor with people in the group, like previous inclusionary endeavors, can be directed either upward (supplication) or downward (manipulation).

Addressing the former, Dodge et al. (1983) note that children often begin their attempts at entry into groups with low-risk tactics; they first try to become accepted by more peripheral members, and only later do they direct their gaze and inclusion attempts toward those with higher status. The children we observed did this as well, making friendly overtures toward clique followers and hoping to be drawn by them into the center.

The more predominant behavior among group members, however, involved currying favor with the leader to enhance their popularity and attain greater respect from other group members. One way they did this was by imitating the style and interests of the group leader. Marcus and Adam, two fifth-grade boys, described the way borderline people would fawn on their clique and its leader to try to gain inclusion:

> MARCUS: Some people would just follow us around and say, "Oh yeah, whatever he says, yeah, whatever his favorite kind of music is, is my favorite kind of music."
>
> ADAM: They're probably in a position where they want to be more *in* because if they like what we like, then they think more people will probably respect them. Because if some people in the clique think this person likes their favorite group, say it's REM, or whatever, so it's say Bud's [the clique leader's], this person must know what we like in music and what's good and what's not, so let's tell him that he can come up and join us after school and do something.

Fawning on more popular people not only was done by outsiders and peripherals but was common practice among regular clique members, even those with high standing. Darla, the second-tier fourth-grade girl mentioned earlier, described how, in fear, she used to follow the clique leader and parrot her opinions: "I was never mean to the people in my grade because I thought Denise might like them and then I'd be screwed. Because there were some people that I hated that she liked and I acted like I loved them, and so I would just be mean to the younger kids, and if she would even say, 'Oh she's nice,' I'd say, 'Oh yeah, she's really nice!'" Clique members, then, had to stay abreast of the leader's shifting tastes and whims if they were to maintain status and position in the group. Part of their membership work involved a regular awareness of the leader's fads and fashions, so that they could accurately align their actions and opinions with the current trends in a timely manner. (See also Eder and Sanford 1986.)

Besides outsiders supplicating to insiders and insiders supplicating to those of higher standing, individuals at the top had to think about the effects of their actions on their standing with those below them. While leaders did not have to explicitly imitate the style and taste of their followers, they did have to act in a way that held their adulation and loyalty. This began with people at the top making sure that those directly below them remained firmly placed where they could count on them. Any defection, especially by the more popular people in a clique, could seriously threaten their standing.

Leaders often employed manipulation to hold the attention and loyalty of clique members.[8] Another manipulative technique involved acting different ways toward different people. Rick recalled how Brad, the clique leader in fifth grade, used this strategy to maintain his position of centrality: "Brad would always say that Trevor is so annoying. 'He is such an idiot, a stupid baby,' and everyone would say, 'Yeah, he is so annoying. We don't like him.' So they would all be mean to him. And then later in the day, Brad would go over and play with Trevor and say that everyone else didn't like him, but that he did. That's how Brad maintained control over Trevor." Brad employed similar techniques of manipulation to ensure that all the members of his clique were similarly tied to him. Like many leaders, he would shift his primary attention among the different clique members, so that everyone experienced the power and status associated with his favor. Then, when they were out of favor, his followers felt relatively deprived and strove to regain their privileged status. This ensured their loyalty and compliance.

To a lesser degree, clique members curried friendship with outsiders. Although they did not accept them into the group, they sometimes included them in activities and tried to influence their opinions. While the leaders had their in-group followers, lower-status clique members, if they cultivated them well, could look to outsiders for respect, admiration, and imitation. This attitude and behavior were not universal, however; some popular cliques were so disdainful and mean to outsiders that nonmembers hated them.

Diane, Tiffany, and Darla, three popular girls who had gone to two different elementary schools, reflected on how the grade school cliques to which they had belonged displayed opposing relationships with individuals of lesser status:

> DARLA: We hated it if the dorks didn't like us and want us to be with them. 'Cause then we weren't the populerest ones 'cause we always had to have them look up to us, and when they wouldn't look up to us we would be nice to them.
>
> DIANE: The medium people always hated us.
>
> TIFFANY: They hated us royally, and we hated them back whenever they started.
>
> DARLA: Sometimes we acted like we didn't care, but it bothered me.
>
> TIFFANY: We always won, so it didn't matter.

Thus, while there were notable exceptions (see Eder 1985), many popular clique members strove to ingratiate themselves with people less popular than they, from time to time, to ensure that their dominance and adulation extended beyond their own boundaries, throughout the grade.

Techniques of Exclusion

Although inclusionary techniques reinforced individuals' popularity and prestige while maintaining the group's exclusivity and stratification, they failed to contribute to other, essential, clique features such as cohesion and integration, the management of in-group and out-group relationships, and submission to clique leadership. These features are rooted, along with further sources of domination and power, in cliques' exclusionary dynamics.

OUT-GROUP SUBJUGATION

When they were not being nice to try to keep outsiders from straying too far from their realm of influence, clique members predominantly subjected outsiders to exclusion and rejection.[9] They found sport in picking on these lower-status individuals. As one clique follower remarked, "One of the main things is to keep picking on unpopular kids because it's just fun to do." Eder (1991) notes that this kind of ridicule, where the targets are excluded and not enjoined to participate in the laughter, contrasts with teasing, where friends make fun of each other in a more lighthearted manner but permit the targets to remain included in the group by also jokingly making fun of themselves. Diane, a clique leader in fourth grade, described the way she acted toward outsiders: "Me and my friends would be mean to the people outside of our clique. Like, Eleanor Dawson, she would always try to be friends with us, and we would be like, 'Get away, ugly.' "

Interactionally sophisticated clique members not only treated outsiders badly but managed to turn others in the clique against them. Parker and Gottman (1989) observe that one of the ways people do this is through gossip. Diane recalled the way she turned all the members of her class, boys as well as girls, against an outsider: "I was always mean to people outside my group like Crystal, and Sally Jones; they both moved schools. . . . I had this gummy bear necklace, with pearls around it and gummy bears. She [Crystal] came up to me one day and pulled my necklace off. I'm like, 'It was my favorite necklace,' and I got all of my friends, and all the guys even in the class, to revolt against her. No one liked her. That's why she moved schools, because she tore my gummy bear necklace off and everyone hated her. They were like, 'That was mean. She didn't deserve that. We hate you.' "

Turning people against an outsider served to solidify the group and to assert the power of the strong over the vulnerability of the weak. Other classmates tended to side with the dominant people over the subordinates, not only because they admired their prestige but also because they respected and feared the power of the strong.

Insiders' ultimate manipulation in leading the group to pick on outsiders involved instigating the bullying and causing others to take the blame. Davey, the fifth-grade clique follower mentioned earlier, described, with some mystery and awe, the skilled maneuvering of Joe, his clique leader: "He'd start a fight and then he would get everyone in it, cause everyone followed him, and then he would get out of it so he wouldn't get in trouble."

Q: *How'd he do that?*

DAVEY: One time he went up to this kid Morgan, who nobody liked, and said, "Come on Morgan, you want to talk about it?" and started kicking him, and then everyone else started doing it. Joe stopped and started watching, and then some parapro[fessional] came over and said, "What's going on here?" And then everyone got in trouble except for him.

Q: *Why did he pick on Morgan?*

DAVEY: 'Cause he couldn't do anything about it, 'cause he was a nerd.

Getting picked on instilled outsiders with fear, grinding them down to accept their inferior status and discouraging them from rallying together to challenge the power hierarchy.[10] In a confrontation between a clique member and an outsider, most people sided with the clique member. They knew that clique members banded together against outsiders, and that they could easily become the next target of attack if they challenged them. Clique members picked on outsiders with little worry about confrontation or repercussion. They also knew that their victims would never carry the tale to teachers or administrators (as they might against other targets; see Sluckin 1981) for fear of reprisal. As Mike, a fifth-grade clique follower, observed, "They know if they tell on you, then you'll 'beat them up,' and so they won't tell on you, they just kind of take it in, walk away."

IN-GROUP SUBJUGATION

Picking on people within the clique's confines was another way to exert dominance. More central clique members commonly harassed and were mean to those with weaker standing.[11] Many of the same factors prompting the ill treatment of outsiders motivated high-level insiders to pick on less powerful insiders.

Rick, a fifth-grade clique follower, articulated the systematic organization of downward harassment: "Basically the people who are the most popular, their life outside in the playground is picking on other people who aren't as popular, but are in the group. But the people just want to be more popular so they stay in the group, they just kind of stick with it, get made fun of, take it. . . . They come back everyday, you do more ridicule, more ridicule, more ridicule, and they just keep taking it because they want to be more popular, and they actually like you but you don't like them. That goes on a lot, that's the main thing in the group. You make fun of someone, you get more popular, because insults is what they like, they like insults."

The finger of ridicule could be pointed at any individual but the leader. It might be a person who did something worthy of insult, it might be someone who the clique leader felt had become an interpersonal threat, or it might be someone singled out for no apparent reason (see Eder 1991). Darla, the second-tier fourth grader discussed earlier, described the ridicule she encountered and her feelings of mortification when the clique leader derided her hair: "Like I remember, she embarrassed me so bad one day. Oh my God, I wanted to kill her! We were in music class and we were standing there and she goes, 'Ew! what's all that shit in your hair?' in front of the whole class. I was so embarrassed, 'cause, I guess I had dandruff or something."[12]

Often, derision against insiders followed a pattern, where leaders started a trend and everyone followed it. This intensified the sting of the mockery by compounding it with multiple force. Rick analogized the way people in cliques behaved to the links on a chain: "Like it's a chain reaction, you get in a fight with the main person, then the person right under him will not like you, and the person under him won't like you, and et cetera, and the whole group will take turns against you. A few people will still like you because they will do their own thing, but most people will do what the person in front of them says to do, so it would be like a chain reaction. It's like a chain; one chain turns, and the other chain has to turn with them or else it will tangle."

COMPLIANCE

Going along with the derisive behavior of leaders or other high-status clique members could entail either active or passive participation. Active participation occurred when instigators enticed other clique members to pick on their friends. For example, leaders would often come up with the idea of placing phony phone calls to others and would persuade their followers to do the dirty work. They might start the phone call and then place followers on the line to finish it, or they might pressure others to make the entire call, thus keeping one step distant from becoming implicated, should the victim's parents complain.

Passive participation involved going along when leaders were mean and manipulative, as when Trevor submissively acquiesced in Brad's scheme to convince Larry that Rick had stolen his money (see the introduction). Trevor knew that Brad was hiding the money the whole time, but he watched while Brad whipped Larry into a frenzy, pressing him to deride Rick, destroy Rick's room and possessions, and threaten to expose Rick's alleged theft to others. It was only when Rick's mother came home, interrupting the bedlam, that she uncovered the money and stopped Larry's onslaught. The following day at school, Brad and Trevor could scarcely contain their glee. As noted earlier, Rick was demolished by the incident and cast out by the clique; Trevor was elevated to the status of Brad's best friend by his coconspiracy in the scheme.

Many clique members relished the opportunity to go along with such exclusive activities, welcoming the feelings of privilege, power, and inclusion. Others were just thankful that they weren't the targets. This was especially true of new members, who, as Sanford and Eder (1984) describe, often feel unsure about their standing in a group. Marcus and Adam, two fifth-grade clique followers introduced earlier, expressed their different feelings about such participation:

> Q: *What was it like when someone in your group got picked on?*
>
> MARCUS: If it was someone I didn't like or who had picked on me before, then I liked it. It made me feel good.
>
> ADAM: I didn't really enjoy it. It made me feel better if they weren't picking on me. But you can't do too much about it, so you sort of get used to it.

Like outsiders, clique members knew that complaining to persons in authority did them no good. Quite the reverse, such resistance tactics made their situation worse, as did showing their vulnerabilities to the aggressors.[13] Kara, a popular fifth-grade girl, explained why such declarations had the opposite effect from that intended: "Because we knew what bugged them, so we could use it against them. And we just did it to pester 'em, aggravate 'em, make us feel better about ourselves. Just to be shitty."

When people saw their friends in tenuous situations, they often reacted in a passive manner. Popular people who got in fights with other popular people might be able to count on some of their followers for support, but most people could not command such loyalty. Jeff, a fifth-grade boy, explained why people went along with hurtful behavior: "It's a real risk if you want to try to stick up for someone because you could get rejected from the group or whatever. Some people do, and nothing happens because they're so high up that other people listen to them. But most people would just find themselves in the same boat. And we've all been there before, so we know what that's like."

Clique members thus went along with picking on their friends, even though they knew it hurt, because they were afraid (see also Best 1983). They became accustomed to living within a social world where the power dynamics could be hurtful, and accepted it.

STIGMATIZATION

Beyond individual incidents of derision, clique insiders were often made the focus of stigmatization for longer periods of time. Unlike outsiders who commanded less enduring interest, clique members were much more involved in picking on their friends, whose discomfort more readily held their attention. Rick noted that the duration of this negative attention was highly variable: "Usually at certain times, it's just a certain person you will pick on all the time, if they do something wrong. I've been picked on for a month at a time, or a week, or a day, or just a couple of minutes, and then they will just come to respect you again." When people became the focus of stigmatization, as happened to Rick, they were rejected by all their friends. The entire clique rejoiced in celebrating their disempowerment. They would be made to feel alone whenever possible. Their former friends might join hands and walk past them through the play yard at recess, physically demonstrating their union and the discarded individual's aloneness

Worse than being ignored was being taunted. Taunts ranged from verbal insults to put-downs to singsong chants. Anyone who could create a taunt was favored with attention and imitated by everyone (see Fine 1981). Even outsiders, who would not normally be privileged to pick on a clique member, were able to elevate themselves by joining in on such taunting (see Sanford and Eder 1984).

The ultimate degradation was physical. Although girls generally held themselves to verbal humiliation of their members, the culture of masculinity gave credence to boys' injuring each other (Eder and Parker 1987; Oswald et al. 1987; Thorne 1993). Fights would occasionally break out in which boys were punched in the ribs or stomach, kicked, or given black eyes. When this happened at school, adults were quick to intervene. But after hours or on the school bus, boys could be hurt. Physical abuse was also heaped on people's homes or possessions. People spit on each other or others' books or toys, threw eggs at their family's cars, and smashed pumpkins in front of their house.

EXPULSION

While most people returned to a state of acceptance following a period of severe derision (see Sluckin, 1981, for strategies children use to help attain this end), this was not always the case. Some people became permanently excommunicated from the clique. Others could be cast out directly, without undergoing a transitional phase of relative exclusion. Clique members from any stratum of the group could suffer such a fate, although it was more common among people with lower status.

When Davey, mentioned earlier, was in sixth grade, he described how expulsion could occur as a natural result of the hierarchical ranking, where a person at the bottom rung of the system of popularity was pushed off. He described the ordinary dynamics of clique behavior:

> Q: *How do clique members decide who they are going to insult that day?*
> DAVEY: It's just basically everyone making fun of everyone. The small
> people making fun of smaller people, the big people making fun of
> the small people. Nobody is really making fun of people bigger than
> them because they can get rejected, because then they can say, "Oh
> yes, he did this and that, this and that, and we shouldn't like him
> anymore." And everybody else says, "Yeah, yeah, yeah," 'cause all
> the lower people like him, but all the higher people don't. So the
> lowercase people just follow the highercase people. If one person is
> doing something wrong, then they will say, "Oh yeah, get out,
> good-bye."

Being cast out could result either from a severely irritating infraction or from individuals standing up for their rights against the dominant leaders.

Sometimes expulsion occurred as a result of breakups between friends or friendship realignments leading to membership challenges (mentioned earlier), where higher-status people carried the group with them and turned their former friends into outcasts. Brad was able to undercut Larry's rising popularity and co-opt his friendship by cutting off the support of Larry's longtime friend Mark (see the introduction). By pretending to be best friends with both Larry and Mark but secretly encouraging them both to say bad things about each other, he finally wounded Mark severely enough that he retaliated against Brad in a way that Brad used to turn both Larry and the whole clique against Mark, expelling him from the group.

On much rarer occasions, high-status clique members or even leaders could be cast out of the group (see Best 1983). One sixth-grade clique leader, Tiffany, was deposed by her former lieutenants for a continued pattern of petulance and self-indulgent manipulations:

Q: *Who kicked you out?*

TIFFANY: Robin and Tanya. They accepted Heidi into their clique, and they got rid of me. They were friends with her. I remember it happened in one blowup in the cafeteria. I asked for pizza and I thought I wasn't getting enough attention anymore, so I was pissed and in a bitchy mood all the time and stuff, and so I asked them for some, so she [Robin] said like, "Wait, hold on, Heidi is taking a bite," or something, and I got so mad I said, "Give the whole fuckin' thing to Heidi," and something like that, and they got so sick of me right then, and they said like, "Fuck you."

When clique members get kicked out of the group, they leave an established circle of friends and often seek to make new ones. Some people have a relatively easy time making what Davies (1982) calls "contingency friends" (temporary replacements for their more popular friends), and, according to one fifth-grade teacher, they are "hot items" for the unpopular crowd. James, a sixth-grade clique follower, explained why popular clique expulsions might be in demand with nonclique members: "Because they want more people, who are bigger, who have more connections, because if you get kicked out of the group, usually you still have a friend who is still going to be in the group, so then they can say, 'Oh yeah, we'll be more popular even though this person isn't respected anymore, at least there is one person who still respects them in the group, so he'll get a little higher up or more popular, or we just should give him a chance.'"

Many cast-outs found new friendships harder to establish, however. They went through a period where they kept to themselves, feeling rejected, stigmatized, and cut off from their former social circle and status. Because of their previous behavior and their relations with other classmates, they had trouble being accepted by unpopular kids. Others had developed minimum acceptability thresholds for friends when they were in the popular crowd, and had difficulty stooping to befriend unpopular kids. When Mark was ejected from his clique in fifth grade, he explained why he was unsuccessful in making friends with the unpopular people: "Because there was nobody out there I liked. I just didn't like anybody. And I think they didn't like me because when I was in the popular group we'd make fun of everyone, I guess, so they didn't want to be around me, because I had been too mean to them in the past."

Occasionally, rejects from the popular clique had trouble making friends among the remainder of the class due to the interference of their former friends.

If clique members got angry at one of their friends and cast him or her out, they might want to make sure that nobody else befriended that individual. By soliciting friendship with people outside the clique, they could influence outsiders' behavior, causing their outcast to fall beyond the middle crowd to the status of pariah, or loner. Darla explained why and how people carried out such manipulations:

Q: *Have you ever seen anyone cast out?*

DARLA: Sure, like, you just make fun of them. If they don't get accepted to the medium group, if they see you like, "Fuck, she's such a dork," and like you really don't want them to have any friends, so you go to the medium group, and you're like, "Why are you hanging out with THAT loser, she's SUCH a dork, we HATE her," and then you be nice to them so they'll get rid of her so she'll be such a dork. I've done that just so she'll be such a nerd that no one will like her. You're just getting back at them. And then they will get rid of her just 'cause you said to, so then, you've done your way with them. If you want something, you'll get it.

People who were cast out of their group often kept to themselves, staying in from the playground at recess and coming home after school alone. They took the bus to school, went to class, did what they had to do, but didn't have friends. Their feelings about themselves changed, and this was often reflected in the way they dressed and carried themselves. Being ejected from the clique thus represented the ultimate form of exclusion, carrying with it severe consequences for individuals' social lives, appearance, and identity.

THE TECHNIQUES of inclusion and exclusion represent the means by which the behavioral dynamics of cliques are forged. As such, they offer the basis for a generic model of clique functioning that interweaves these processes with the essential clique features of exclusivity, power and dominance, status stratification, cohesion and integration, popularity, submission, and in-group and out-group relations.

Lemert (1972) outlines some of the features of the exclusionary dynamic, focusing on how paranoid persons become ostracized from informal groups and organizations. He notes the secret nature of decision making within groups, the isolation of individuals who oppose the policies of leaders, and the removal of these individuals from access to information and power as critical features of the exclusion process. Yet he fails to elaborate them thoroughly or to explicitly tie them to the corresponding dynamic of inclusion.

These two dynamics work hand in hand. The inclusionary dynamic is central to cliques' foundation of attraction. Cliques' boundary maintenance makes them exclusive. They can recruit the individuals they want, wooing them from competing friendships, and reject the supplications of others they evaluate as unworthy. The popularity of their membership (with leaders to lend status and followers to lend power) strengthens their position at the center of activity. Upheavals and friendship realignments within cliques keep the hierarchical alignment of prestige and influence fluid, giving those successful at maneuvering toward and staying near the top the greatest esteem among their peers. The systematic upward ingratiation of individuals toward the leading members, and leading members' ability to easily ingratiate themselves downward with others, thereby securing the favors they desire, enhance the attractiveness of inclusion in the clique.

The exclusionary dynamic is central to cliques' bases of cohesion. Clique members solidify together in disparaging outsiders, learning that those in the in-group can freely demean out-group members, only to have their targets return for renewed chances at acceptance. They learn sensitivity toward changes in group boundaries, acting one way toward insiders and another way toward outsiders. This lesson manifests itself not only at the group's outer edges but within the clique, as individuals move in and out of relative favor and have to position themselves carefully to avoid the stigma of association with the disfavored. They learn the hierarchy of group positions and the perquisites of respect and influence that go with those roles, submitting to the dominance of clique leaders in order to earn a share of their reflected status and position. The periodic minicyclings of exclusion serve to manipulate followers into dependence and subservience, at the same time enhancing leaders' centrality and authority. The ultimate sanction of expulsion represents a dramatic example of the effects of exclusion, weakening or bringing down potential rivals from positions of power while herding other group members into cohesion. The dynamic of inclusion lures members into cliques, while the dynamic of exclusion keeps them there.[14]

These dynamics have a further cyclical effect, affecting individuals' roles in the clique and sense of self. Both Eder (1985) and Blau (1964) posit cyclical models in their portrayals of clique, small group, and organizational dynamics. Eder follows girls' progression into cliques as, once inside, they lose their recently gained popularity, since the old friends they abandoned rise up to devastate them. Blau suggests that individuals first inflate their worth in order to be accepted into groups, then deflate it to promote integration and stability. In both of these models individuals peak in popularity and acceptance shortly after joining groups, falling thereafter due to either outsiders' evaluations or their own self-diminution. The cycle of inclusion and exclusion presented here adheres to this general form, in that individuals experience their greatest feelings of acceptance and self-worth shortly after they are included in the clique. If they are recruited by clique leaders, they are showered with attention, as followers maintain themselves by keeping abreast of leaders' current favorites. If they are accepted as applicants, their approval by clique leaders similarly casts them into a world filled with welcoming new friends. This honeymoon period does not endure, however; the positive treatment diminishes as clique leaders and members shift their focus elsewhere. Higher-status members then subjugate the new participants to ensure that their own positions are not challenged, and followers are freed to vie more openly with the newcomers for status and popularity. Individuals go through a cycle of being drawn into the group, cut off from outside friends, put down into positions of subservience, and kept there by the concerted status striving of others. This cycle of inclusion and exclusion then repeats itself as members are redrawn toward the center by the renewed interest of leaders, only to be pushed toward the periphery again and again as new people rise in favor.

While this model partially resembles those of Eder and Blau, it differs from theirs in two respects. First, it is recurrent. Second, the process of being brought in and being put down is handled by clique insiders, not by outsiders (as Eder suggests) or voluntarily, by the individuals involved (as Blau suggests). Outsiders lack the power to effect such a diminution, and the individuals involved lack the motivation. Leaders maintain their positions, then, not through the attractive qualities and important contributions they can offer the group, as Blau maintains, but through their inherent grasp of the subtleties of these dynamics and their ability to successfully manipulate them.

Chapter 4   Clique Stratification

WHILE THE MEMBERS of these popular cliques were under considerable duress to identify and keep abreast of the constantly unfolding new developments in their circles, individuals in other friendship groups had very different social experiences. A range of social group formations existed beyond the popular clique, lodged primarily within social worlds defined by children's school attendance. Preadolescents' group affiliation affected them profoundly, as having a circle of close and loyal friends could signify the difference between an active, exciting, and secure social life, and one filled with uncertainty, insecurity, and degradation. Groups also differed in their character and composition. While research on adolescents has shown that their friendship groups form the most salient element of their school experience and provide the basis for their forming and connecting to the peer culture, not much has been much written about preadolescent friendship groups.[1] Yet preadolescent friendship groups are not only organized but highly stratified.

Studies of adolescent friendship groups, from middle and junior high school to high school, have found that teenagers cluster along a multidimensional scale into groups composed according to individuals' social types and interests.[2] This diverse differentiation has not been noted at the elementary level, where there is little variety in the types and rankings of groups available; instead, a unidimensional scale exists, with the popular clique located atop a hierarchy of friendship groups that descends in prestige and power.[3] Research on the friendship groupings of elementary school–aged children has focused either on gender clusterings (Thorne 1993), on divisions within the group (Best 1983), or only tangentially on social stratification (Kless 1992). These treatments overlook the sophistication with which preadolescent children typologize each other both within and between groups according to their recognition and respect, elements of which status is composed.

Social psychologists have identified people's self-concept or identity as the location of their feelings about themselves, that image they hold as experiencing beings interacting with the world.[4] Scholars have explored numerous sources that contribute to the foundation of identity, among them appearance (Stone 1962), occupation (Hughes 1971; Snow and Anderson 1987), linguistic structures (Goodwin 1990), and interaction partners (Robinson and Smith-Lovin 1992).

In this chapter we highlight the stratification of preadolescents' friendship groups, the complex interrelations and movements between groups, and the role of these groups in affecting their conceptions of self. Children learn, in interacting both within and between friendship groups, what kind of social competence, currency, and charisma they possess. Their efforts locate them in clearly identifiable positions along the peer status hierarchy.

The Status Hierarchy

Children from all the schools we studied described the arrangement of members of their grade into a hierarchy based on peer status. Variations in the nature and composition of these strata might be influenced by the size of the school, the demographics of its population, the grade level, and the organization of classrooms (open versus closed) (Hallinan 1979). For every age level, within each gender group, and in every school with a population of over eighty students per grade, the social system was composed of four main strata: the high, wannabe, middle, and low ranks.[5] At the high end was the popular clique, comprising the exclusive crowd. Below them were the wannabes, the group of people who hung around the popular clique hoping for inclusion. Next was the middle group, composed of smaller, independent friendship circles. At the bottom were the social isolates, who found playmates only occasionally, spending most of their time by themselves.[6]

THE POPULAR CLIQUE

Composition and Character. The popular clique formed the largest friendship circle in the grade. In some grades it was an integrated whole; in others it was composed of interrelated and overlapping subgroups. The size of this clique grew as children advanced through the elementary grades, starting out small and incorporating new members each year.[7] By the fourth and fifth grades it usually encompassed around one-third of the population.

Taylor, a fifth-grade boy, outlined the relative size of the four social groups he saw in his grade: "The cool group is at the top, say 35 percent of the kids. Then you've got the cool followers [wannabes], the ones that follow the cool kids around, they're around 10 percent. The medium group is the biggest, around 45 percent. They're all divided up into little groups, but there's a lot of them. Then the rest are in the outcast group, maybe 10 percent there too."

Members of the popular clique had the most active social lives, both during school and outside of it, had the largest number of friends, appeared to have the most fun, and, as Eder (1995) notes, commanded the most attention in the grade. They spent their time talking and whispering, running from one activity to the other, busying themselves with friends, and having dates and parties after school and on weekends. The greatest amount of cross-gender interaction occurred within this group, as boys and girls talked on the phone after school, socialized at parties and movies together, and "went" (steady) with each other, as Best (1983) and Merten (1996d) also describe. Their activities, social liaisons, and breakups were known about not only within their own circle but by the rest of the grade as well.

This group of people set the tone for, and in many ways influenced, the behavior of the entire grade. Miss Moran, a fourth-grade teacher, offered her observations on the popular clique's dominance: "I see the popular clique as controlling the rest of the class, so the middle group, although they're not part of it, depending on the agenda of the powerful clique, they will respond in a certain way or they will act in a certain way. They're not totally separate. The popular clique controls everything, classroom climate, as far as who feels comfortable blurting out an answer to a question. They just have a lot of power. So that even the people who are not popular but relatively comfortable will always keep an eye on the popular clique." Although nonmembers did not directly engage with the popular people in their activities, jokes, or games, they were aware of them and set their attitudes and behavior in relation to them.

Another feature that differentiated the popular crowd from the others in the grade was its exclusivity. Cliques are closed friendship groups, guarding their borders from undesirable interlopers.[8] Located at the top of the status hierarchy, popular clique members accepted as friends only those judged worthy. They might dangle membership in front of others, as the members of Best's (1983) exclusive Tent Club did, but this did not mean that they would let them into the clique.

Rick offered his view on the exclusionary behavior of clique leaders: "I've noticed a lot of things called clubs, and they usually have enrollment tests, and I've seen these be very demanding, and I've seen these be kind of trivial and stupid, but always it's something for the leader to laugh at the other one, and, for instance, give the leader control of the other person. But I still think that by doing that, and the other people doing that, they're kind of telling the leader, 'Okay, I'll do whatever you want.' And so then that goes into a cycle, so the leaders ask for more, they do it, they ask for more, they do it, and on and on and on."

The more individuals could be manipulated into self-debasing actions, the slimmer their chances of being accepted into the group, the more they were taunted with futile opportunities for membership just to amuse the leaders and reinforce their influence. Most cliques admitted new members only when an existing member sponsored them and the leader approved, when people who moved into the school system or neighborhood looked highly desirable, or when power plays or fights broke out, motivating conflicting members to include and elevate newcomers who would support them.

Role Stratification. Although the movement of people within a clique might be fluid and shifting, people moved among a cluster of positions that were characterized by certain regular features.[9] Differences in popularity, power, and control separated members in positions more central to the group from those at the periphery.

The most powerful and pivotal role in the clique was the leader's. Cliques usually took the single-leader mode, with one person serving as the most forceful of the group, dominating over all the others. The leader had the power to set the clique boundaries, include or exclude potential members, raise or lower people in favor, and set the collective trends and opinions. Single-leader cliques coalesced around this central person and had an undisputed pyramid structure with different layers of subordinate strata arranged below.

A second form cliques less commonly took involved two leaders. Two leaders could operate in tandem, as friends, or more independently, often with an element of competition. When two friends ran a clique together, they tended to be best friends, to operate in a unified manner on issues, and to use their combined power to dominate over others, such as Denise did with Emily in fourth grade. In other cases, two powerful leaders might belong to a clique and not align themselves so completely. Mark, in fourth grade, explained how his broader clique was divided into a large group with one subgroup, led by Brad and Larry: "Larry had people who liked him more than Brad, but still liked Brad. Brad had others who liked him more than Larry, but still liked Larry. They formed together into one group and played together. But Brad had more followers than Larry, and so he was the most powerful. Larry's group was really a part of his. But he couldn't always get Larry and his friends to follow him all the time."

Just below the leaders were the second-tier clique members. This notch was usually occupied by one or two people at a time. Individuals in this position were close to the top, with the next tier falling a significant step below them. Darla, who had occupied the second tier with a friend, described the structure of her fourth-grade clique: "We had three levels, kind of. There was Denise in the center, and then me and Kristy kind of just close to the center, and then there was another level beyond us, way beyond us. But we were pretty much scared of Denise."

Individuals could attain second-tier status in one of two ways. Some came to this highly placed position because they were best friends with the leader. This type of relational status was dependent, however, on the favor of the clique leader. If friendships and alliances shifted, as they were apt to do, the person(s) in the second-tier position could be replaced with a new status occupant. Darla discussed how she was ejected from the role she had occupied in her fourth-grade clique when her best friend, the leader, abandoned her: "Yeah. Denise liked me best for awhile, and she and I were real close. So, even though she was the leader, I was up there too. But then the boys started liking Kristy because she was a blond. And my boyfriend dumped me and went off with Kristy. And then Denise was best friends with Kristy and was just a bitch to me. I went way down, way."

The other way people attained a position close to the top was through their own power. They might have followers who liked and supported them, they might have had high ranking before the current leader assumed prominence, or they might have contributed to unseating a previous leader.

The third clique role was occupied by the followers, who formed the bulk of the people in the group. Although less visible than the leaders, followers formed an indispensable part of the clique, for their unhesitant acceptance of leaders' actions and authority legitimated the leaders' role. They were connected to the group by their relation to one or more central members and occupied positions that varied in status.

Blake, a fifth grader, described the hierarchy of members in his clique, carefully noting the gap between the two higher tiers and the followers: "Bob was at the top, number one, and Max was number two. They were pretty much the most popular people. Then there was a jump between them and the rest of the group. Nobody was at three, but Marcus was a three and a half, and so were three other guys. A few people were at three and three-quarters, then Josh was a four, and John was a four. Everyone else moved between three and a half and four, including me. It could shift a lot."

The composition of the followers, while marked by subtle shadings, was fluid, with members moving up or down as they were targeted for favor or ridicule by more leading members. Some people were secure followers, while others held a more precarious position. Yet while different followers had their own clump of immediate friends, all of the clumps sought to associate with the leaders.

Relationships. Popular clique members were sensitive to their social position, both within the grade and within the clique. Maintaining their membership in the popular crowd and at the highest rank within it took a concerted effort.[10] Friendships were strongly influenced by underlying status concerns. Less popular people tried to curry favor with more popular people to improve their standing in the group. They imitated leaders' behavior and supported leaders' opinions to enhance their acceptance and approval. In turn, leaders acted to maintain their own popularity and control by seeking the continuing endorsement of other group members. Actions and friendships, then, were always subtly influenced by the consequences they might have on power and position, making them more self-consciously manipulative.

Several factors undercut the strength of the loyalty bonds that might have developed among members of the popular clique, giving their relationships a fragile quality. First, the underlying preoccupation with rank and status created an atmosphere of competition, setting members against each other in their quest to remain accepted and well-regarded. (Cf. Best 1983, on the Tent Club.) Second, the dynamics through which leaders carved out and maintained their power undercut loyalty. One of the primary ways leaders held dominance was by alternately gracing followers with their favor and then swinging the other clique members against them. Over time, everyone had the opportunity to experience the vicissitudes of this treatment, with its thrill of popularity and its pain of derogation. This shifting treatment prevented potential rival leaders from gaining a toehold of influence at the same time as it reinforced leaders' control over clique followers. Clique members liked and admired, but also feared, their leaders and these people's power to make their lives miserable. Few had the courage to defy the leaders and stand up against them when they or their friends became the butt of teasing and exclusion.[11] They knew that alliance with stigmatized clique members would cast them into the painful position these others occupied. As a result, they learned that the price of loyalty was severe, and that it was safer not to stick up for their friends but to look out for themselves instead. They thus joined with leaders in ridiculing other group members. A third factor weakening the loyalty bond within popular clique relations lay in the means by which clique members were chosen. Group leaders, rather than the general membership, selected new members, and followers often embraced the newcomers because they were popular with the leaders rather than because they, themselves, liked them. As a result, when these individuals were cast into disfavor, others did not jump to their defense. (See Eder 1995.)

Tracy, a fourth-grade girl from the middle level, offered her view of the fickleness of the relationships that characterized the popular people: "Some of the popular group, they just hang out with those people to be popular and they are not their friends, and if someone is being teased, they will just say in some instances, 'Like I don't really care since she was only in there to be popular, not really to be my friend.' And for the popular group, some of the people who are really mean, they don't have that many people to help them out when other people are doing the same thing to them since they have been so mean to others."

Members of the popular clique might thus find themselves in a group with people that they liked only slightly or not at all.

Some members of the popular clique did, however, have long-lasting relationships. Constancy among best friend pairs existed, and connections within smaller subgroups often endured. But like status and position, individuals' relationships and membership within the popular clique were frequently in a state of flux. Popular people changed their friends from time to time, getting sick of hanging out with some people and moving on to others within the group.[12] As one popular fifth grader noted in reflecting on the fluidity of people's friendship patterns, "They move around a lot. Some of them are friends with most of the same people, but most of them are friends with different people." In addition, people moved into and out of the group. Of those exiting, some left to join with new friends while others were expelled.

Any clique member could be thrown out of the group, and this awareness was widespread, although some were more vulnerable than others. Followers were the most easily dislodged, since they had the weakest base of support and least power. They could be cast out if the leaders turned against them and turned everybody else against them.

But leaders, too, could be dumped if they acted bad enough, as Best (1983) notes in describing Billy's fall from leadership in the Tent Club. Todd, a popular fifth grader, recalled the expulsion of one clique leader: "Preston used to be the most popular kid in school, but he got too lazy and he took advantage of kids. So kids dumped him."

> Q: *That's not so easy to dump the most popular kid, is it?*
> TODD: Yeah. When everybody doesn't like him, it's like, "See ya."
> Q: *And what makes everyone turn against someone?*
> TODD: If they take advantage of you. Like, say, Preston used to always say, like, "Go get me that piece of paper," and if you didn't get that piece of paper you were *uncool* [inflects with overdramatic flair]. People didn't like being *uncool* for not serving somebody. So he got kicked out.

Preston's expulsion was consequential and enduring. Even after six months, none of his former friends had taken him back. He had fallen hard, tumbling down past the followers and wannabes into a threesome in the middle ranks.

More common than these permanent actions, however, were temporary expulsions. Individuals could be kicked out by their friends and readmitted shortly thereafter. Ryan, a fourth-grade boy, talked about the vicissitudes of people's exits from and reentries into relationships with the popular clique: "It's happened to me before. I've been kicked out, and some other people. You have to watch what you wear, what you say. It's hard, but you get over it. Like just some days people are in bad moods. Other days, they let you in. So it kind of depends on mood."

Membership in the popular clique, because of its exclusive character, was thus fragile and uncertain.

THE WANNABES

Composition and Character. Wannabes were the people referred to by Taylor, earlier, when he fairly accurately noted that the "cool followers" comprised around 10 percent of the grade. Clique members occasionally invited individuals from outside their strict borders to join them in their games or activities. These individuals had a peripheral, or borderline, status, since they were not explicitly members of the clique but liked to hang around the group. They fell below the clique followers, even those who had some friends outside the group, on the stratification hierarchy because the followers were fully accepted group members. Wannabes usually had most of their friends outside of the group but were partly accepted by some people on the inside.

Mr. Clark, a fifth-grade teacher, described the configuration of the wannabes: "I think a lot of those kids want to be liked by the popular kids, so therefore they are willing to hang out until they are accepted. And then when the group accepts them and lets them in, even if it's for just a while, then they feel good because all of a sudden these popular kids are now their friends. They feel good because they are getting acknowledged by somebody from that top group. If they are going to widen the group, these are the people they will turn to. They're not really in, but they're not altogether out."

Wannabes held the lowest status of any near-clique members.

Attempts at Inclusion. In most instances when clique members deigned to play with outsiders, these marginals were readily available. Stacy, a fourth-grade popular girl, described why the pool of borderline people waited to be included: "The wannabes try to hang around, and try to be in, and try to do stuff that is cool, but they aren't really cool. But they think they are, and if we play with them, they think they'll get cooler, so they're always ready if we want them."

In making efforts to be included, wannabes copied the behavior of the popular people. They imitated their clothing and hair styles, bought the same kind of music, and tried to use the same vocabulary.[13] According to fifth graders, they would use remarks like, "Hey man, what's up?" instead of "Hello," or they'd say they were "hanging out" instead of "playing." The thrust of these linguistic efforts was to assert their coolness through a pseudomaturity, to act like teenagers. Several middle-rank third-grade girls secretly mocked the cool wannabe girls because they all adopted the leader's habit of running her fingers through her hair and shaking her head in a distinctive manner. Every time one of them did this, these other girls would look at each other and try not to laugh, often unsuccessfully. Wannabes also tried to lure popular people into friendship with what Rizzo (1989) calls "friendship bids": overnight or party invitations, material possessions such as sport cards to trade or clothes to borrow, and trips with their family to movies or other entertainment events. For these offerings they received some attention, but it was often short-lived.

Their efforts to be included also resulted in their exhibiting some extreme behavior. They would run and fetch things for popular people, carry their messages to others, and threaten to beat people up who were out of favor with the crowd. Even when they were not being belittled, they acted out and made fools of themselves. In the children's peer culture, such vulnerability was quickly noticed and regarded as a sign of insecurity and weakness.[14] Rather than helping them become accepted, it was taken as a sign of desperation, thrusting them further outside the group.

Temporary Inclusion. People around the periphery might join the popular clique's activities for a variety of reasons. Boys' play, which usually involved sports, commonly occurred within moderately large groups (Lever 1976; Thorne 1993). If their clique was too small to accommodate a particular sport, boys often invited outsiders to participate. Ryan, the fourth-grade boy quoted earlier, explained who participated in his clique's activities: "The more people that you have playing football or basketball or something the better, because then you have more people to pass to, and more people to block, or whatever, so . . . if we are playing sports, they like to include more people. But if we're just kind of hanging out, just kind of sitting around and talking, it's just the main people and no borderline ones."

In addition to simply having larger and more differentiated teams, boys often invited marginals to play with them because it was easier to play aggressively against people who were less close friends. In fact, poor treatment of the people who occupied borderline status seemed fairly common. This involved a complex combination of acceptance and rejection: on the one hand they were more accepted than the total rejects, yet they experienced the bulk of the rejection behavior, since they were the ones who tried to be included, and were alternately welcomed and shunned.

Darla, looking back at fifth grade, tried to explain her clique's relationship with and treatment of the borderline tier: "We would pretty much treat them like shit, but they were our friends. We would treat them like shit, but we would be nice to them, and they would always just come back."

> Q: *They were in the crowd, but they were on the margins?*
> DARLA: Yeah. It kind of just depended on what we wanted. We kind of used them in a way. But we were friends with them, but sometimes we were just like "Pffft" [gestures condescendingly, like she is blowing them off]. . . . Just to have somebody to be mean to, that's who we'd be mean to.

Individuals who stood outside the main circle of the group's membership thus filled the important function of defining clique boundaries, as shifting as they were, and of making all fully accepted clique members, no matter what their ranking, appreciate the benefits of their insider status. Clique members usually recognized the positive role these people filled, and although they derided wannabes, they worked to retain their attention.

Buffering the Popular Clique. When they were not playing with the cool kids, the wannabes formed smaller friendship groups of their own. They hung out alone or congregated with each other in circles of two, three, or four people. These were not strong friendship groups, however, for each person thought he or she was better than the rest and belonged with the popular clique. Wannabes also served as a buffer zone, accepting rejects from the top group.

Miss Moran, the fourth-grade teacher mentioned earlier, offered her observations on the status differentials between the popular clique and the wannabes, and the way the wannabes buffered the popular clique:

> Q: *When kids fall out of the popular group, what usually happens to them?*
> *Do the lower groups embrace them?*
> MISS MORAN: It depends why they fall out. If they fall out because they're popular and having a tiff with somebody else in the popular group, then boy, they're a hot product in the wannabe and middle groups, like wow. But if they fell out because they're a wannabe, one

of the ones trying to fit in, then sometimes they'll fall all the way
down and no one will grab them except at the very bottom.

Wannabes accepted the popular rejects to improve their own status, since
most popular rejects maintained at least a few ties to people who were still popular. But popular people saw right through this transparent strategy. In scoffing
at the wannabes, Lauren, a popular fourth grader, noted, "People that we dump
go into the middle, and the wannabes down there all think they are cool because they used to be cool and they are talking to them, but what really happened is they got booted." Accepting rejects diminished wannabes' status
further with the people whose acceptance they sought. Yet even though the
popular people scoffed at the wannabes from their high perch, when they became the object of exclusion, they valued wannabes' intermediate status. Holding some ties to the popular clique, wannabes were not as far removed from the
upper echelons as were members of the middle circles.

Ryan, the popular fourth-grade boy, discussed the role of the wannabes in
his fall from and return to popularity:

Q: *When you got kicked out of the cool group, who did you hang out with?*
RYAN: I hung out with, like, the wannabes of the cool kids. For, like, a
couple of weeks. And then my old friends said, "This guy's okay,"
and they let me back in. And then I was back in the cool group.
Q: *So you didn't go down to the medium kids?*
RYAN: No. I knew that if I hung out with the medium kids for too long I
was never going to get back into the cool group.
Q: *So the wannabes of the cool kids are higher up than the medium kids?*
RYAN: Yeah. Because they're like risking it, they're just enough trying to
be cool that they are noticed. And sometimes the cool kids let them
in. So they're kind of on the map, the edges.

MIDDLE FRIENDSHIP CIRCLES

Composition and Character. The middle rank comprised people who were considered nonpopular, who didn't try to be cool or to be accepted by the cool
people. Constituting approximately half of each grade, this group was large and
fairly amorphous, made up of many different subgroups and subtypes. Mrs.
Perkins, a fifth-grade teacher, offered her observations on the composition of
the middle group: "They're not all one group, they're very diverse. On the
strong end, they're very well-adjusted kids, who may be above the popular
games, who may not want to get into the teasing, they may not want to get
into the power struggles, and sometimes are very stable kids. Then I've got

some kids who are just not as socially astute, who don't wear the right clothes, but still well-rounded kids, healthy. And then I'd say you have some computer nerd types who seem to be very socially inept, but not in a bad sense. Just in a kind of dorky sense."

People in the middle rank clustered into small groups of friendship circles, anywhere from pairs of best friends or threesomes, to slightly larger groups. Middle friendship circles rarely got too large, or they tended to develop cliquish tendencies. Nicole, a fourth-grade girl from the middle stratum, described the social clusters surrounding her: "They're the people that mind their own business, sort of people that get in a group, maybe three to five people. They just stick to that group, don't even attempt to make other friends, and nobody attempts to penetrate into the group, except for just a few exceptions." Others corroborated this assessment, referring to the middle friendship circles as "just a slop of two- or three-person groups" or as "a couple of people in a parking lot, just all standing together, talking in little groups of three, couple of them are friends."

In contrast to the popular clique's strongly tiered ranking, middle friendship circles had only a weak hierarchical system, operating between the different friendship circles rather than within them. The higher-status clumps might accept and be considered acceptable by the popular group's rejects, such as by Preston, the formerly popular clique leader who tumbled down into the middle range. The intermediate circles minded their own business and played among themselves. The lower middle circles might be just one step above the social isolates. Todd, the popular fifth grader, characterized these latter groups by saying, "These are the kids who have the guts not to just hang out in the sandbox, but are still pretty far down."

Most nonpopular people recognized their middle-level status and accepted it. They shared the realization that they were not the type to be included in the elite circles, offering various accounts to explain this. Some described themselves as too quiet or too shy to be the "popular type," while others described themselves as "the type that other people don't like." If they were ever unsure about this, the popular people made sure to reinforce these perceptions by picking on them and deriding them, both individually and in groups.

One of the strongest features differentiating middle friendship circles from the cliques found at the upper end of the status hierarchy, apart from their size, was their willingness to accept people. Whereas popular groups were exclusive, maintaining tight control over their boundaries and keeping important members in and undesirables out, middle friendship groups more readily welcomed people who wanted to join in or play with them. Timmy, a third-grade boy from a middle circle, described how his group accepted outsiders to play: "Sometimes, a lot of people who really aren't in will get together and form a big game of basketball, and they will let anyone come in because they are a lot nicer. So if someone gets ejected from a group, they usually come over. We've had a lot of people from the popular group come over to the unpopular people because they want to play a game and the popular people usually cheat or don't treat them fairly."

Another characteristic differentiating middle friendship circles from cliques was their democratic leadership structure. While cliques had clearly defined leaders and a strongly articulated hierarchy of internal stratification, friendship circles were much more egalitarian. They were not identified by a single core person, no one person led the decisions about what they should do or think, and no leader dominated the delineations of the borders. Mary, a fifth-grade nonpopular girl, talked about the democratic nature of the leadership structure in the middle circles: "Usually, someone would just suggest something, and usually we either like it or we, if we don't like it, then somebody else would suggest something else. We don't usually have a person that chooses what we're gonna do. We just all of a sudden choose something, and we see if everybody else likes that idea."

Relationships. Relationships in the middle circles were often more intimate and intense than those in the popular or wannabe groups. This was partly due to the small size of these friendship circles and the frequency of members' interactions. Popular people had many more people with whom they regularly socialized, and they tended to regard all members of the clique as their friends. Wannabes had a weak and diffused group that never coalesced, being focused instead around the popular clique. In contrast, members of middle circles had many fewer individuals with whom they interacted. Nikko, a fifth-grade nonpopular boy, offered his observations about the difference in friendship relationships between the middle and popular levels: "I would probably say that if you were a member of the smaller groups that you would have more one-on-one experience, and you would probably get even closer and closer. And if you're in the more popular groups, you probably wouldn't stay with one person for very long, and you'd keep on moving from subgroup to subgroup, because the whole group is larger. They're like groups of twenty or thirty kids."

The lack of competition for status stratification within the nonpopular circles also affected the character of their relationships. People did not have to be as conscious about who was in better favor, about losing favor, or about getting picked on by their own friends as they did in the popular clique. Consequently, they had a greater degree of loyalty and trust among their friends and felt freer to discuss sensitive issues. Ariana, a nonpopular fourth grader, talked about the nature of the relationships in her circle: "I have lots of friends that are not in the popular group, that are in the middle, so I always knew that there was someone to turn to. With my friends you can always express your feelings and say that this person is really hurting my feelings, and then maybe we will all talk it over. There's no one who is mean in our group, who thinks she's better than the rest of us, or who lords it over all of us. So we know we can really count on each other, like if anyone makes fun of us, we know that our friends will always stick up for us."[15]

Like the popular cliques, middle friendship circles exhibited both turnover and constancy in their relationships and membership. Some people remained in their groups or friendships over long periods. They bonded tightly with friends, spent considerable time at school, home, and recreational activities together, and developed close relational ties. Others developed an orbit surrounding a certain group that they moved into and out of over a period of time.

Jarrad, a fifth-grade boy, described the ebb and flow of his relationship with his core middle friendship group:

Q: *So would you say that these groups are fairly stable, or that this kind of breaking off and reforming is more common?*

JARRAD: I would say it's in between. I have gone from together for two years, broken up for a week, together for two days, broken up for three weeks, over and over.

Q: *And when you get back together, do you go back to the same people or do you go into another group?*

JARRAD: Same people.

Miss Moran, the fourth-grade teacher, summed up the pattern of stability and flux among the people in the middle circles: "There's a lot of going back and forth among the group, like for instance, one week two people do something and the next week another two people will do something out of the same group. But it doesn't seem to be a big deal, like who's with who this week. People shift around more comfortably in the middle range, but also you've got your lasting friendships too. You've got some friends who are just good friends. They spend the weekend together, hang out together."

Individuals had a greater degree of social security, however, because they did not have to contend with capricious, demanding leaders ready to expel them from the group. People left middle circles because they got in fights with other people in the group, or because they did not want to do what others wanted to do. Sometimes two people would gang up on one, leaving that person isolated and alone. Other times a larger group would get fed up with someone.

Nick, a fifth-grade boy from a middle circle, described the collective group dynamics associated with people's exit from such groups:

Q: *So one could get kicked out of a group like that?*

NICK: Right, but only if most of the people got agreement from each other. They could use persuasion, they could use insults, they could use reasons why the other people would want that person kicked out. They could make up stories, which I've seen a lot, about the other person, they could spread rumors, etcetera. But what they can't do, which the popular people do, is to have one person decide that you're uncool and just kick you out on his own.

SOCIAL ISOLATES

Composition and Character. These individuals had no real friends. As loners, drifters, dweebs, and nerds, they occupied the bottom stratum of the grade and stuck out to everyone. Kless (1992) labels these people pariahs, while Eder (1995) refers to them as isolates, Best (1983) calls them losers, Rubin, LeMare, and Lollis (1990) identify them as withdrawn, and Merten's (1996b) subjects call them "mels."

Other kids noticed the social isolates and clearly differentiated them from the middle people at the low end of the acceptable realm. These were the people who wandered around the playground at recess, making up a game by themselves, talking to an adult playground aide, or just hanging around the sidelines. At lunch they ate by themselves, since nobody wanted to sit with them. When it came time to form into groups, they were chronically left out. When asked to reflect on the reasons for people's isolation, Tracy, a middle-rank fourth-grade girl, replied, "There are some kids who just go outside and try to hang around people, but they don't really fit in with them, so they just stay there but not talk." Jarrad, a middle-rank fifth-grade boy, responded to the same question as follows: "They're different. It's a lot like segregation. If you're different, you go off and sit alone." Tracy and Jarrad's remarks indicate that people perceived these individuals as apart from the rest of the grade, mostly due to something inherent in their own nature.[16] They were different; they did not fit in with the others. Something about the way they looked or the way they acted deviated from the norm.

While the composition of the social isolates might vary, the number of people in this category held relatively constant. Mr. Goodwin, a fourth-grade teacher, reflected on the size of this group:

Q: *In thinking of the group of people at the bottom, how many would there be of these?*

MR. GOODWIN: Thinking in terms of every year, I would say, total, in the last five years, there's probably twelve or thirteen of those kids. So out of the 125 or so students I have had, that's about 10 percent. I don't know. There's regular nerds and then there's kids who are real behavioral problems, who frighten the other kids. They're the ones who're really way out there, just socially not fitting in.[17]

The Spiral of Rejection. Although they spent considerable time alone, social isolates longed to be included in the interaction and play of their classmates. From time to time, as Merten (1996b) poignantly describes, they would make attempts to join in various conversations and games.

These efforts occasionally yielded some success, with their being taken into activities, tolerated or somewhat included in the lunchroom. Ryan, the popular fourth-grade boy discussed earlier, explained the way people without friends could get included in the activities of the popular group: "There are some people who have no friends, or maybe sometimes one or two, and sometimes they just sit down and read in the classroom or sit outside and kind of don't do much. But sometimes even if we don't like the person, sometimes the really unpopular kids get included just because they're needed in a game, and say six people are needed and maybe we have five people. They want one more people [sic] to make teams even, then they can ask someone who is just sitting around if they want to do something." In a case like this, the added people would feel included for the duration of the game.

Timmy, the middle-rank third grader, talked about a friend of his who was very isolated. He discussed his friend's attempts to be included in interactions with others:

Q: *Does he try to be included in groups?*
TIMMY: Yeah, he does that a lot, and he usually gets included, except he's not really part of it, like if someone's having a conversation with someone, he tries to be a part of it, but he doesn't really know anything about it, so he's not part of the whole thing. I think that's what makes him feel lonely because he's not . . . with anyone, he's not part of, like, the group of kids, really.

More often, however, isolates' attempts at inclusion were unsuccessful.[18] When they summoned the nerve to ask other people if they could join them in play, they would be laughed at and treated poorly. People made sport out of teasing them and picking on them.[19] While popular leaders degraded their followers, followers degraded the wannabes, and wannabes degraded the middle people, everyone could safely offset their own humiliation by passing it on to individuals at the lowest stratum. No one came to these individuals' defense, and everyone could unite in feeling superior to them. People called them names, started fights with them, made fun of their clothing and appearance, and talked about them as having "cooties" (Thorne 1993). People rebuffed those labeled as losers from play with hardly a care for their feelings.

Sean, a fourth-grade middle-level boy, discussed the way loners were rejected cruelly by groups of people, particularly those at the popular rank: "At recess they [isolates] maybe just go out and talk or something to other people, but they don't really play games or anything. They try to, but some people don't let 'em. Sometimes people say, just to be mean, that the game is full, when there's only five people or ten people, but then they let other people in after."

After a series of such encounters, the potential benefit of social interaction tended to no longer seem worth the risk of degradation and humiliation. Mary, the middle-level fifth-grade girl discussed earlier, offered her observation of what frequently happened when social isolates made repeated unsuccessful attempts to be included with others: "People shatter their self-confidence so they don't try again."

Such encounters often led loners to retire further into seclusion and cease interacting with people.[20] They ate lunch by themselves every day, often stayed inside at recess, and went home right after school. People who experienced prolonged or severe isolation sometimes invoked the ultimate recourse: they transferred to another school.

Relationships. While isolates spent much of their time alone, they drifted in and out of some relationships and sought out people in lesser positions whom they could more safely befriend.[21] Social isolates could be found drifting by themselves in the playground or being taunted and teased by more socially successful people. When people assembled into groups for play, these loners were left hanging around the edges.

In many cases, however, rather than forming their own groups, isolates' reaction to others in similar situations to themselves was mutual rejection. They were no more eager to befriend these outcasts than were others in the class. Meredith, a third-grade social isolate, expressed her lack of interest in her social peers:

Q: *So what might you do then at recess?*
MEREDITH: Well, sometimes I look at how people are playing, it makes me feel good. Sometimes I just play a simple game by myself. Just games by myself that I make up.
Q: *Are there other kids who are also playing by themselves?*
MEREDITH: Well I have to say there're sure to be, but very little. A very little group of them.

Q: *So do you ever play with any of them?*
MEREDITH: No, not really.
Q: *How come? You don't like them?*
MEREDITH: Sort of that. There's different reasons.

Miss Moran, the fourth-grade teacher, explained why she thought social outcasts shunned each other:

Q: *Is it a stigma to be friends with another person down there?*
MISS MORAN: Yeah. Well, for instance, if I were to say, 'Okay, make groups,' and there's two or three of them standing around, and they have to be in a group with each other, it's obvious to everyone that those are the leftovers. And some of them are knowledgeable enough to not want to be in that situation, although a few seem so out of it that they are oblivious.

Despite the potential stigma, there came a time when social isolates got desperate and made friends. They could no longer stand the loneliness and boredom, and overcame their feelings of distaste for other pariahs. They managed to put up with annoying behavior and overlook the teasing of high-status people, even if it increased when they joined with other isolates.[22]

Tracy, the fourth-grade middle-level girl, described how some loners joined together: "Eventually some of them will meet someone else that they kind of like, and then they will start hanging out with them, and then after about half the year it will become a little group of two or three people."

Q: *So people don't always stay by themselves forever?*
TRACY: Right, eventually some of them find someone, or they just get so lonely they force themselves to be with someone.

Mrs. Perkins, the fifth-grade teacher, gave her view of how social isolates overcame their aversion to being friendly and came to form relationships: "Their friendships are based on availability, not on any commonality. I mean the commonality, I guess, is that they're social outcasts. Some kids don't want to accept that. They eventually do accept it, and I think they're happier when they finally do accept that and say, 'Okay, I've got a friend here, even though I know what everyone thinks of this friend.'"

Despite their stigma on the peer social hierarchy, most individuals were able to turn somewhere, even if it was not in their school or in their grade, to find companionship. Having some friend, even if that person was of lower status, was critical. Otherwise isolates spent all their time after school and on weekends watching television, playing video games, reading books, participating in organized after-school activities, and hanging around with their parents.

Forming friendships with younger people was easier for social isolates because they were often able to leave the stigma of their outcast status behind and adopt a high status in the new school or neighborhood crowd based on their advanced age and grade.

Roger, a severe third-grade pariah, described his most steady companion: "Mostly I play with my next-door neighbor, Eric, he's two years old. I really help out with him, 'cause his dad's usually at work, and his mom has arthritis. So when I come over, it's a big help for them. They go run errands. Mostly Eric wants me to come along. They say it's okay because they could get more done when they're doing errands when I'm around. Like I take care of Eric, tell him not to take the things off the shelf, it helps them a lot. 'Cause if he sees something when they're not looking, then they have to go there and put it back, and then they have to find the area again, and he does it again, a lot of junk. So I help out a lot."

Roger was able to find a regular playmate by going outside of both his school's status system and his age system. When pariahs made inroads into new crowds, their acceptance was sometimes short-lived, however. As news traveled, their outside friends discovered their pariah status and often dropped them as a result.

The Identity Hierarchy

People's location at the various levels of the social stratification hierarchy led them to vastly dissimilar interactional experiences. The size of their group, the type and intensity of its activities, the nature of the relationships within it, and its relative super/subordination to other groups were all colored by this ranking system. These features led people to develop feelings about themselves, or self-concepts, that were anchored in their social-relational placement. This resulted in a second form of stratification: the identity hierarchy.

THE POPULAR CLIQUE

Individuals in the elite, leader stratum of the popular clique sat atop the identity hierarchy. They compared other people unfavorably with themselves, regarded their own activities as the most exciting and fun, and believed that everybody was jealous of them. They basked in the attention they received from the rest of the grade and were proud to think that they could persuade anyone they wanted to follow them or to join their group. They thought their interest in those lower than them should be looked on as a prize, to be received with eagerness. Some children believed that cool leaders had the most positive self-identity merely by virtue of their position, although Eder (1995) notes that they were also frequently disliked. Mary, the fifth-grade middle-level girl, expressed this viewpoint: "Well, I think that with the leaders of the big group, they usually have the most self-esteem because there's no one else to make fun of them, there's no one else for them to be competing with unless there's another person that's a leader, and they can really do anything that they want, so I think they have the most self-esteem."

Yet other members of the group did not share this positive identity. Followers suffered through their subordination to the leaders, by being bossed around, derided, and stigmatized, and by frequently worrying about losing their position in the group. Despite how they presented themselves to outsiders, Blake, the popular fifth-grade boy, noted that "the people in the top group are insecure also, especially the followers, because you get made fun of, then your self-esteem goes." Mr. Clark, the fifth-grade teacher, explained why this came back to affect the self-concepts of all members of the popular group: "Your self-esteem, the day-to-day worries about self-esteem, are going to be much more pronounced with the popular group, even if you're on the top. You're going to have setbacks, and your popularity's such a big issue that you're always feeling either attacked or you're feeling on top of things."

MIDDLE FRIENDSHIP CIRCLES

After those in the popular clique, members of the middle friendship circles had the most positive self-identities, lacking both the social pretensions and the status insecurities plaguing the popular clique members. Individuals in the middle group generally felt good about themselves. While they had to endure status derogation from popular clique members, they derived significant security from the loyalty of their friends. They did not have to worry about coming in to school and finding that all their friends had been on the phone the night before and had decided that they were out of favor. They could trust their friends to stick up for them and not betray them. They knew that fights might occur, but that they would be over, and that their friends would still be faithful to them.

Mary, the fifth-grade middle-level girl, talked about the feelings of confidence she derived from the relationships within her group: "I would rather be in my own circle of friends and be, everyone's nice and everything, instead of having to deal with what the leader says and being bossed around, having to do what they say and do to be in that group. It makes me feel like I am worth something, instead of always having to sell myself to be popular."

People in the middle level held many shared views about members of the other strata. There was some degree of envy toward the popular clique, both for the abundance of their friends and the excitement of their activities, yet their feelings toward them were predominantly negative. They often noted the way cool people acted as though they were superior, and referred to them as having "swelled heads" and "big egos," as being "full of themselves." As Eder (1995) also observed, they rejected the popular people's attitude of superiority toward them.

Sean, the fourth-grade middle-rank boy mentioned earlier, offered his views of the popular crowd:

Q: *What do you think of the kids that think they're cool?*
SEAN: Mostly they're just jerks.
Q: *Why is that?*
SEAN: 'Cause they treat other kids a lot more mean, they pick on kids, pick on little kids, they screw up loads. They spray paint on the walls and stuff. They like to get in trouble.

Middle people reserved their harsher criticism for the wannabes, however. Like the popular people, they regarded the wannabes as weak and insecure. They watched as the wannabes unsuccessfully imitated the popular people. Ariana, the fourth-grade girl noted earlier, offered a commonly held negative view of the wannabes: "[We] laugh at how they are being dragged around by other people."

Q: *They are making fools of themselves for people?*
ARIANA: Right. How they will go to any extent to be with those people.
What makes them happy? All they want is to be with those people.
But they never get the job, 'cause they always get shoved out.
There's no sense of, there's nobody being themselves.

Thus, while members of middle friendship circles suffered from being ridiculed by the popular people, they enjoyed an autonomy that the status-seeking wannabes lacked. Individuals at the middle rank derived a great deal of security and self-esteem from the loyalty of their friends. They might not have the status and excitement of the large popular group membership and the most privileged activities, but their relationships flourished because they were internally focused and supportive, and their identities were strong.

WANNABES

Although the wannabes ranked higher on the status hierarchy than the people from the middle rank, they paid a high price for it in self-esteem. The wannabes' position in the social status system was unique. They were defined not by their own social group but by their relation to a group to which they only marginally belonged. They were not members of the popular clique, yet neither were they independent of it. They forged their behavior, attitudes, and relationships by fervently looking up to the clique above them, hoping for a trickle down of attention that would draw them into greater favor. They desperately aspired to be accepted by people who toyed with them, using them for their own benefit. They suffered by always desiring something that they never really attained, enduring the frustration of experiencing it temporarily only to lose it again. They knew that the people they wanted as friends did not want them, and mocked, teased, and derided them.

Scott, a fourth-grade wannabe, explained the contradictory treatment he received from the popular people: "With the popular group you get to do more stuff, you get to have more play, you get to have more fun at recess, you get to play with all the people that are kind of up on theirselves, have big egos, and really think they're great. You play with them, but they don't, in football they never pass to you, and in basketball they never really pass to you. So there're advantages to being in the popular group, but there's a lot of disadvantages to being in the popular group."

The wannabes did not have secure membership in their own friendship circles to use as a safety net. If they let go of their grip on the popular crowd, they knew that they might tumble into the isolate rank. They therefore clung to the liminality of the in-between, striving for acceptance but never fitting in. Mr. Goodwin, the fourth-grade teacher, analyzed the way this made them feel: "The ones who are really feeling the pain are the ones who're hanging onto this popular group, but I think they're the ones who are really low in self-esteem. They don't seem to enjoy anything for the sake of it; they're just kind of analyzing things from the outside. And therefore, if they're not part of the group, they're trying to figure out what's wrong with them. . . . I guess the point I'm really trying to make is that there's that small group of kids who don't fit in either group; they're not happy. They're not happy with themselves, they're not happy with where they are, and they try so hard. . . . I would say they have some social problems, identification problems. They don't know who they are really yet, or where they want to be."

Wannabes' intense status aspirations yielded them intense status insecurity. They suffered the continual anguish of domination and exclusion at the hands of the popular clique. They lacked the loyalty and trust of the true friendships found in the middle circles. Their identities were stronger than the isolates only by virtue of the companionship and social activities in which they were able to engage, which gave them some feeling of self-worth.

SOCIAL ISOLATES

At the bottom of the status hierarchy, isolates were also at the bottom of the identity hierarchy. Most isolates recognized the effects of their low social status on their ability to form relationships and be included in social activities. Although they tried not to think that there was something wrong with them, their doubts about themselves sometimes surfaced.[23] Mr. Clark, the fifth-grade teacher, expressed his concerns about the feelings and identities of the social isolates: "I think some who are down there, who are kind of nice kids, are feeling quite a bit of pain. They probably sit there now and then and say, 'What's wrong with me? Why does no one . . . ? I know where I am, I'm way down here with these weird kids,' and I think there's some pain there. I've asked myself this question, 'Why are these kids down there?' and I'm sure that they probably do too."

Unlike people in the other three strata who all had some group that they disdained, whether higher or lower, the pariahs held contempt for no group. Their feelings about the people in the other groups fell into one of two categories: envy and dislike. Many isolates envied the social standing and relationships accompanying location in the higher strata. They looked longingly at the activities of the popular crowd and wished they could join in.

According to Rudy, a third-grade isolate, "[The cool kids] do a lot of cool things at recess. They dig in the sandbox, they always get in a long group of, like a lot of bunch of kids, like in different grade classes, but then they break up to another group of kids."

> Q: *So you think that would be better, to be in a bigger group of kids?*
> RUDY: Well, it would be more comfortable, for me anyways.

Social isolates' exclusion from nearly all social activities coupled with the extreme degradation they suffered at the hands of the popular and wannabe crowds left them with the lowest sense of self-worth. Social isolates' exclusion, rejection, ostracism, and limited scope of activities carried a heavy toll on their feelings about themselves. They tried to deceive themselves into thinking they had friends or that they were accepted, but they could only sustain this image for so long. They occasionally tried to manage their stigma by ignoring it, but they ultimately had a hard time disguising their pariah status and had to accept their disvalued identity.

ELEMENTARY SCHOOL children's social experiences are strongly affected by the location of their friendship group along the continuum of status and popularity. Those who attain membership in the elite popular clique enjoy the benefits of a more expansive social life and a superior position relative to other crowds, but pay for this with a greater anxiety about their place within the group. Wannabes, forming the periphery around the popular crowd, have the opportunity to participate in some popular group activities and derive a measure of reflected status, but they never attain membership in the group that they fervently seek. Most people fall into the largest category, composed of smaller midlevel friendship circles that garner low prestige and suffer degradation from the popular people, but whose members care less about their social ranking and enjoy secure relationships with friends. At the bottom of the ladder are the social isolates, combining pariah social status with a virtual lack of viable peer friendships.

The identity stratification of the groups is somewhat different from their hierarchical arrangement based on status, in that the top and bottom strata remain constant but the positions of the middle rank and wannabes are reversed. Owing to the loyalty and support the middle circles receive from their peers, they hold more positive self-concepts than the higher-status wannabes, despite the latter's circulation within the broader confines of the popular clique.

Chapter 5   After-School Activities

S‍INCE THE EARLY 1970s, we have witnessed the broad expansion and institutionalization of the adult-controlled "after-school" period.[1] While the time period immediately following the conclusion of formal school instruction has been in existence ever since the massification and democratization of public education, only recently has it assumed distinct organizational features and character.[2] Myriad adult-organized activities for children are available, from which youngsters and their parents can make their selections. Instead of merely coming home and playing in the house, neighborhood, or schoolyard, elementary, middle school, and junior high youths are likely to be registered in some extracurricular activity organized through a local YMCA, recreation center, community center, or private association founded for this purpose. Classes, sports, and activities are offered on specific schedules, and each season parents engage in a mad frenzy to ensure that children are enrolled in the most desirable activity, with their preferred circle of friends. As a result, after-school activities have become one of the most salient features of many families' child-rearing experience and are instrumental in defining the developing identities of participating youth.

The rise of the institutionalized after-school phenomenon may be rooted in two cultural conditions that have occurred over the last generation: the greater influx of women into the labor force, and the fear of children occupying public space.[3] The consequent demand for supervised after-school activities has led to a boom industry of offerings and associated sponsoring organizations. With programs packaged in a way that is appetizing to both youngsters and adults, the success of these organizations has been reinforced and fueled by their appeal to families regardless of whether they are in direct need of child-care services.[4] When we couple this with the declining budgets that prohibit many public schools from offering extracurricular activities, it is easy to see why these programs have burgeoned. Although the after-school phenomenon is anchored in the middle class, it has become a significant social experience among a broad diversity of social classes (Larreau 1991).[5]

Previous research on children's after-school activities has focused primarily on organized youth sports. Scholars have differed dramatically over the socializing influences of such adult-dominated activities, with some emphasizing the positive dimensions and others fearing its outcomes.[6] In chapter 10 we will analyze some of the implications for individuals and society that result from the rise of the after-school phenomenon. In the present chapter we trace the progression of the types of after-school activities from those characterized by spontaneous, child-directed play to those that become increasingly adult-organized, institutionalized, and professionalized. We discuss their role in the social organization of children's play.

We divide adult-organized after-school activities for youth into three broad categories—recreational, competitive, and elite—which vary in degrees of organization, rationalization, competition, commitment, and professionalization. These categories represent a developmental model, where young people progress through various kinds of activities, increasing their depth, fervor, and skill of involvement as they escalate their participation. Not all young people follow the progression of this extracurricular career; some remain at more recreational levels or retreat from intense types of after-school participation to more moderate and less demanding activities. However, these are exceptions to the norm, and the ensuing depiction represents the path followed by most young people.

Spontaneous Play

Traditionally, after-school activities were those planned and directed by children themselves. Beginning in earliest childhood, youngsters would come home after school, play in each other's houses, backyards, outside in the neighborhood, at the school playground or athletic field, and in child-organized games at any of these locations. Most often, this is the type of play engaged in by young children (Mead 1934), although it has always been a significant feature of all children's lives. Yet with the advent of early child care and day care, even relatively young children are engaging in child-centered play less often than previous generations. Still, this type of play continues to be prevalent and offers children several fundamental advances in their socialization.[7]

Spontaneous play requires that children master myriad organizational skills. For instance, they have to plan what to do, where and when they will meet and play, set up parameters of how to play, establish rules and roles for participants, and set handicaps to ensure equitable and enjoyable play (see Coakley 1990). In one regular neighborhood backyard game we observed, elementary school boys played various seasonally appropriate sports. Trees and sprinkler heads were transformed into bases and sidelines, throws or hits into the surrounding street or bushes were designated as in play, home runs, or ground rule doubles, and teams were formed depending on who showed up to play on a particular day. Involving people of different ages (a fundamental characteristic of spontaneous play) was handled by handicapping older, more skilled players (they had to "play down," bat other-handed, give a running start) and making things easier for younger, less talented players (they could have more swings, one-handed touch tackles, more leeway). While some rules were standing, set by the regular, local participants, others could be established anew, such as special multigame series with fixed teams or plays.

Negotiation is another skill learned through spontaneous play. Children had to routinely reconcile competing desires, settle different interpretations of what occurred and what it meant, select among competing plans, and make adjustments when things were not going well. In negotiating inevitable impasses in play, they could take turns doing what the other one wanted, they could demand acquiescence from the host ("I'm the guest") or the guest ("It's my house"), or they could invite another person over to get out of a disagreement. Negotiations were a prevalent form of child-directed interaction when sharing was involved, such as playing with certain toys or building joint baseball card collections. Further, any rules that were established prior to the start of play could be subject to renegotiation at any time if a participant so demanded: They might have to drop what they were doing and settle once again what was agreed on to do next, where the ball landed, whether the pitch was a ball or strike, and whether their teams, handicaps, or sorted piles of toys were really fair.

Finally, spontaneous play involved a considerable amount of problem solving. People got hurt feelings, became injured and angry, got into arguments, broke off their play in a fight, and got back together again. Issues arose that were not always possible to solve amicably, such as differences in age, size, strength, and personality. Participants therefore had to reach beyond simple negotiation and learn how to work out problems that ruptured the peace. This involved significant power dynamics, compromise, and communication. For example, we observed Trevor, who would often quit the game, without warning, when things were not going as he desired. The other children learned ways to deal with him, ranging from ignoring him to begging him to return, depending on their needs and his mood. Invariably, after this grandstanding behavior, he would reluctantly return to play. As managers of their own spontaneous events, children became sensitive to the delicate balance involved in negotiating the vastly complex issues that arose in pair and group play.

As several researchers have noted (Coakley 1990; Devereaux 1976), spontaneous, child-directed after-school activities taught participants a wide range of important interpersonal skills, from communication to cooperation, negotiation, compromise, improvisation, goal setting, malleability, teamwork, independence, and self-reliance.

Recreational Activities

Recreationally organized after-school activities varied widely in scope and character. They could be fundamentally centered on the *social* functions of companionship and play, such as those offered by established bureaucratic organizations (YMCA, local rec or community centers, and other private groups that offer "drop-in" services for working parents). Explicitly, these programs presented themselves as "excellent alternatives to staying home alone or just hanging out at the mall" (YMCA brochure). Second, these recreational activities could be centered on *fitness*. For instance, the Kidsport Fun and Fitness Club, a private business whose clientele is children who need after-school supervision, promoted its "Fun to be Fit" program for eight- to twelve-year-olds, emphasizing the health, nutrition, grooming, and fitness advantages of participation (Kidsport flyer). Third, recreational activities focused on extracurricular *learning*. Schools, seeking to capitalize on the after-school market, offered a variety of (paid) programs designed to keep children on the grounds after the traditional day has concluded. Program for After-school Learning (PAL) and After-school Adventures offered cooking, art, creative writing, and computer skills. Finally, the greatest number of after-school activities involved *skill development*. These involved the range of private and group lessons available to youth, ranging from offerings in the arts (dance, acting, singing, music), crafts (cooking, sewing, needlework), and individual sports (horseback riding, skiing, martial arts, tennis, skating).

In recreationally organized team sports, scoring was deemphasized. The youngest group of children usually engaged in games where no score was kept. For example, the YMCA, following its philosophy of "putting Christian principles into practice through programs that build a healthy body, mind, and spirit for all" (YMCA brochure), organized its youngest T-ball league so that players batted through the lineup once on each team per inning, until it was time to stop playing. Dean, a third-grade boy expressed his feelings about this orientation: "Yeah, it's fun. Me and my friends, we all play on the same team. Jack's dad is the coach, and he's pretty nice. But sometimes it's not so fun, because everybody has to get an equal chance to play every position, no matter how good or bad they are. And some of those guys out there can't even throw or catch the ball. And he puts me in outfield and them at shortstop, and if I catch a fly ball, I can't even throw it in to second base for the double play, because they can't catch it."

The Little League also offered a noncompetitive "midgets" league for seven- and eight-year-olds. No scoring was overtly kept by coaches, leagues, or parents, but children measured scores meticulously. As the father who managed the midgets Little League for seven- and eight-year-olds that was officially "noncompetitive" noted in making his report to the board, "Yeah, it's noncompetitive, but every kid out there on the field knows that the score is twenty-eight to twenty-six." Thus, despite an official adult recreational ethos, an informal undercurrent of competitiveness often surfaced among participants.

Two second-grade boys recounted their experience in the Y league where their team had just outscored another squad:

> KIP: We just finished the game, and we were lined up to do the team handshake. Lots of our friends were jumping up and down and yelling because we had won them, even though nobody said it.
>
> ALAN: Yeah, we scored eight runs in the first inning and nine in the second, and they only scored two in the first one and one run in the second.
>
> KIP: Everybody got up to bat every inning, and the only way they got us out was we all got up to bat.
>
> ALAN: Yeah. They couldn't even make three outs. They were lame.
>
> KIP: So we really creamed them bad, even though the coaches don't write it down.
>
> ALAN: Yeah, and so one kid spit on his hand for the high fives, and he got spit all over us.

Past the youngest ages, recreational teams kept score and acknowledged a winner and loser. However, there were no league standings or playoffs at the end of the season. Trophies, if distributed, went to all participants. At these levels the rhetoric of team spirit and fun was espoused. All players were mandated to participate equally and, if possible, in all positions. Children, especially boys, who valued displays of domination (Best 1983; Thorne 1986), might still undercut this by infusing hierarchy. Often dissatisfied with such egalitarian leveling, they preferred to have clearer distinctions drawn. In a football league for nine-year-old boys, one team kept its own record of all the teams' victories so that it could track league standings, and taunted players on losing teams.[8]

Coaches, here, were generally players' parents who had little or no specialized training. The leagues were usually arranged by generalist organizations, such as YMCAs or rec centers, that had broad interests in many fitness and extracurricular activities yet were not tied to the organizational culture of a specific activity. One parent touched on a main theme of recreational activities: "Right now we'd like to see Ken have fun, get some exercise, and begin to learn about lots of different things. Karen and I want to expose him to as much as we can. That way he'll learn the basics, and he can go on in the ones that he likes best later. It's her bag that all of the kids have to take a musical instrument, and I go along with that as long as they get to play some sport each season."

This philosophy was echoed by Mary, a fifth grader, who decided to go out for a sport she had never played before: "Some of my friends have played soccer for a year or two, and they must be good by now. I'm a little scared to sign up and play, since they've had a few years more experience than me, and maybe I won't be good enough to play. But it's supposed to be a just-for-fun league, and everyone gets to play. So maybe it won't be too hard, and I'll learn how to play."

The emphasis at this level, then, was on children forming broad interests in many fitness and extracurricular activities, without becoming particularly enmeshed in any specific activity.

These types of programs had several defining characteristics. First, they were adult organized and supervised. Adults brought with them a set of rules and regulations for how, when, and where things should be done, introduced a teacher-student style relationship, and established a clear situation of authority and hierarchy (cf. Coakley 1990; Eitzen and Sage 1989). Second, these programs were located outside the home or neighborhood/yard, in institutional settings, where adults were responsible for decision making and safety. The adult leaders might have been credentialed by graduate degrees or accreditation programs and brought a set of formalized procedures for running the activity. Third, in contrast to child-directed play, where participation might be exclusive, these programs were geared toward democratic acceptance of interested parties. The ethos held that everybody who could afford it was entitled to these "enrichments." Finally, the programs were guided by a philosophy of noncompetitive structuring (although participants might compare themselves informally to each other). There were no institutionalized contests, rankings, or other forms of hierarchical rating. Young participants were socialized to value acceptance and fairness, team spirit and camaraderie, knowledge acquisition and skill development, and submission to adult rules and authority.[9]

It is noteworthy that children's participation in these activities was often dictated by their parents. Young people might not have chosen or even liked a particular activity, but they often found themselves engaging in it because their parents believed it was something culturally edifying.

Competitive Activities

Succeeding this recreational base were after-school activities organized on a more competitive plane. Most recreational activities were capable of being performed competitively. For example, gymnastics lessons gave way to membership on gymnastics teams, young people moved up to competing in local martial arts meets, horseback riders participated in shows, music lessons led to competing for positions in the band, extracurricular academic enrichments led to participation in the Olympics of the Mind (an international competition where teams from various schools compete in trying to creatively solve learning problems), and even recreational "skip-its" (a rope-jumping club) had a championship structure. Other activities, such as team sports, were inherently competitive in nature. These progressed directly from informally organized children's games to an institutionalized league structure. In moving from the recreational to the competitive, these activities took on a different philosophy and character, emphasizing goal orientation, winning, and meritocracy. They also brought the presence and stigma of losing (Devereaux 1976).

Although universal participation was initially held as an ideal, this progressively diminished as competition escalated. Along with the formalization of the activity's structure, children were ranked and placed in skill levels. A hierarchy was established, where children who did not measure up were progressively excluded, ostracized, or denigrated. A continuum can be outlined, from an initial philosophy of democracy to one of increasing meritocracy, accompanying the increasingly competitive nature of children's play. All of the accompanying factors—such as seriousness, commitment, bureaucratization, and professionalism—shifted as people moved from the lower end of this continuum toward the top.

DEMOCRATIC PHILOSOPHY

At the democratic end of the competitive continuum, activities were structured hierarchically, yet the rhetoric of recreation was still espoused. Scores and tallies were kept and league or divisional standings recorded. Playoffs at the end of the season were provided within each league, although these did not extend beyond the league to a regional or greater playoff structure. In contrast to the recreational arena, volunteer coaches, unrelated to any team member, began to be seen. Drawn primarily from individuals in the community with experience and interest in the activity, these coaches imparted an element of professionalization and seriousness to the play.

Organizations responsible for coordinating and offering such after-school activities were usually specialized and tied to a single enterprise. They might have had some combination of volunteer and paid workers and a board of directors seriously committed to advancing the activity at the youth level. Many of them held democratic philosophies resembling this one stated in a letter to the coaches of a girls' softball association: "The key message is that the program or activity must be fun if the participants are going to get something out of it and continue to play. We have tried to structure the program on that basis and our #1 goal is that the girls have fun."

One of the seventh-grade girls participating in this league, Amy, described her feelings about playing at this level: "I've played more competitive sports, soccer and basketball, where I was really into it, and we practiced a lot, took it really seriously, and played against tough teams. But for softball I don't really want all that pressure or commitment. I want to have a good time, be with my friends, stay in shape, and keep my skills up. So that's why I went out for C Level [the recreational league] again this year. I don't want to ruin my whole summer by having to play softball. I want to be able to leave for summer vacation and not feel guilty that I'm letting the whole team down."

Yet sometimes young participants received mixed messages about goals from adults in various positions in these programs. Organizational administrators might have felt that developing a well-managed, educational, and professionally run operation was their main goal. They chafed at parents' efforts to foster social or recreational aspects of the sport as they promoted its seriousness and professionalism. In a soccer league office at the beginning of the season, as mothers thronged to switch their children onto teams with their friends, one administrator sardonically remarked to another, "What do they think this is, a social club? This is a soccer club." After overhearing this, another mother whispered, "They may not think it's a social club, but I sure do."

Other times it was the parents, more than the administrators, who took the activity seriously. They stood on the sidelines and admonished players to try harder and coaches to push the weaker players out of the critical positions. Others complained to coaches that the team should be managed differently. Attending a soccer game of a friend's fourth-grade son in another state, we made the following observations in our field notes: "The parents were all running up and down the sidelines screaming and shouting at the players and coach. While this looked fairly typical to us, several of the parents felt the need to approach us during the game and offer accounts for their behavior. 'Oh, you'll have to excuse us, we get kind of carried away.' Or, 'We hope you don't mind how we act, we hope Franny warned you about us. We just get very carried away.'" Their words suggested that they perceived their intensity, involvement, and competitiveness as deviant relative to the league.

Other times, parents leaned toward the democratic side and invoked that rhetoric. Josh, a fourth grader, described what happened at a soccer game: "It was the championship playoffs, and I wasn't getting to play too much. . . . [The coach] just put me in for half a quarter in the first half and half a quarter in the second half, and everybody else was getting to play three or four times that. We had two overtimes, and he kept me out the whole time. When I complained to him about wanting to play more, he told me that he couldn't put me in anywhere because I wasn't fast enough, I would hurt the team. Well, boy, when my dad heard him say that to me, did he go off! He lost his temper and started yelling at the coach right there, during the game, about how this was supposed to be more fair, and everyone was supposed to play more equal, and that he wasn't going by the rules of the league."

Attending another game with a friend, we noted a further interaction where the coaches pushed the group to a more competitive level of play. As our field notes document: "As soon as we arrived at the game the coaches pounced on our friend and his son. They were concerned about how to keep their winning team together next year when half of the boys would have to move into the higher age level. The coach tried to convince the parents of the younger boys to move their sons into the older age level even though they did not have to. The pressure was especially acute for our friend, whose young son was the main scorer."

While more talented players found the increase in competition satisfying, those with weaker skills were often unhappy. In one democratically geared competitive league, William, a fourth-grade baseball player, described his dissatisfaction with his coach's philosophy and practice: "My coach wants to win too much. It's not fun for me. I'm not getting enough playing time. . . . I never get to start. . . . He only puts me in to play in the outfield. I can play other positions; it's not fair. I want to get a chance to pitch. I can do it."

Coaches, thus, often found themselves caught in the pull between competition and recreation. On an eleven- to twelve-year-old girls' softball team, one coach had a postpractice meeting with the team and outlined his goals for the season. After talking about teamwork, hard work, learning, fitness, and fun, he added, "But let's not forget, we'll have more fun if we win." Looking over at one of the mothers who was an assistant coach, he saw her blanch. She quickly added, "But don't forget, the important thing is to have fun." She later talked to him about how important it was in their "democratic" league to emphasize participation and having fun. Yet once the games began, she was the most aggressive and competitive of all the coaches and had to be physically restrained at times to keep her from exclaiming her frustration to the players and umpires.

Thus, at this level, differences became more apparent between the stated ideals of the program and the actual practices of the participants. Adults usually espoused the commonly held notion of democratic play and skill development, but in practice often emphasized winning. Children had no such ambiguities. Despite the admonitions that "it's only a game," they were quite aware of performance differentials. They easily noted that in crucial situations, the rhetoric of democracy was abandoned and unmitigated competition came to the fore. The lessons communicated to youngsters through this level of after-school participation included a beginning awareness of inequality in talent and the legitimation of how this affected opportunity, as well as a new focus on competition and winning.[10]

MERITOCRACY

Organizations sponsoring after-school activities progressively detached from the vestiges of recreation and democracy as they became more competitive and professionalized. Skill and performance, criteria associated with a meritocracy, were increasingly rewarded, while effort and fairness diminished in centrality. Although the feeling still existed that fun was a desired outcome, talent and effort received greater acknowledgment, and democratic decision making declined, leaving coaches and directors less hampered by parents and official rules or rhetoric in making policy.

Emily, a seventh grader, explained the advantages of being in a performing dance company: "Having tryouts cut out all of those people who can't really dance, who aren't coordinated, and who just don't pay attention. For so many years my dance classes were filled with those kids, and they dragged the class down, made us go slowly when they couldn't get the steps or they forgot them. Now we learn much more because we can move faster, the classes are tough, and the rehearsals are serious. The people with the solos are the ones who are the best and who work the hardest, and you don't have someone's mother complaining to [the director] that their daughter should have a solo, because they know it's based on who's best."

Augmenting the previous competitive features were such elements as rank and stratification (the performing dance company had an A and a B troupe), posted, running standings, all-star games, and a national playoff structure. Individuals and teams competing in meritocratic systems could progress beyond the local area to compete in regional, statewide, and national tournaments. At this level we also began to see greater interest on the part of local businesses in sponsoring teams whose members wore the firm's name on the back of their shirts. Participants who excelled in their activity saw, for the first time, their name in the sports section of the local newspaper.

One of the prototypical organizations representing this level of institutionalization and competition was the Little League (see Fine 1987). Firmly en-
trenched throughout the United States, this association received regular
newspaper coverage and utilized upgraded playing fields. It had an extensive
support network, a widespread fund-raising arm, and a committed group of organizational directors at the local, national, and international levels. Within
the Little League (as with other activities such as soccer, ice hockey, dance, acting, and gymnastics), there were several strata of play through which youngsters could advance as they became older and more skilled.

The shift in character associated with the move from democratic to meritocratic deterred some participants from continuing to advance in the activity. One boy dropped out of his quiz bowl team when the level of competition
exceeded his abilities. Another quit the debate squad when the preparation time
for competitions became excessively demanding. The funneling process also led
young people to abandon some activities while concentrating on others. As Josh
(whose father yelled at the coach when he was in fourth grade) commented in
fifth grade: "I'm not going out for soccer this year. It was boring last year because I didn't get to play enough, and I also had a problem because I was in a
play and there was an overlap between the play and soccer. Like, I had to miss
part of tryouts because of soccer practice, and I didn't get to know if I'd gotten
in or if I'd gotten a good part. And sometimes rehearsals were on Saturday mornings when we had soccer games, and I had to leave games to go to rehearsals,
and my coach yelled at me. So I think I'll just stick with acting this year. I don't
have any friends in it, but I like it more and I'm better at it. It's more *me*."

The funneling effect of youngsters dropping out of extracurricular activities was associated with the rise in commitment these activities required, so that
they had to choose the one to which they would dedicate themselves. These
choices represented a deliberate move on the youngsters' part (as opposed to
their parents signing them up) and usually reflected their developing identities.

Beyond whole leagues organized at the more competitive level, coaches or
parents occasionally pushed individual squads into a more competitive posture.
One football team we observed was run by such a coach. He had worked with
a group of youngsters for two years, when they were in first and second grades.
The year that most of the players moved into third grade, he was faced with
having to move them into the next (third- and fourth-grade) age bracket, possibly losing their dominant position in the league. He discovered, however, that
there was one loophole through which he could keep his team at the first- and
second-grade level: if the players weighed less than fifty-one pounds. As it
turned out, most of his boys weighed in the low fifties, from fifty-one to fifty-
five pounds. So, with the parents' cooperation, he put them on a strict regi-

men: for several days prior to the weigh-in, he "sweated them down." He wrapped their torsos and legs in plastic bags, ran them vigorously, made them spit, and, on the last day, put them in the sauna for several hours to shed their excess water weight. With this plan he was successful in keeping them in the younger bracket.[11]

Another more competitive coach wanted to field a successful soccer team. Scouting teams around the city, he approached talented kids to recruit them. His became an informal all-star team. Unlike other teams, his squad sported team jackets and other vestiges of more competitive levels of play. They also practiced more hours weekly than the league guidelines permitted. On the day of each practice, he would take his van and drive all around the city, picking up his players and taking them to the field, returning them home afterward. His goal was to turn his squad into an international travel team when the boys were old enough.

Most youngsters enjoyed participating in some of the more competitive after-school activities. These demanded greater concentration and effort, and drew a greater sense of self-involvement from them, making children feel challenged and important. Moreover, such activities received greater attention from the surrounding adult world. Moira, an eighth-grade ballet dancer who had been with the performance company for several years, explained: "It's much more enjoyable when your skills get better. You learn harder steps to work on rather than the same old boring class everyday. Once you get to a higher level there's more, there's things that you can audition for, things that make you want to try hard in class. It hurts, but you keep going because there's still so much to learn. At each level there's something you have to learn so that you can do the next, so it's like you progress through, and it's much more fun when you get older because there's much more fun steps, like the jumps and the lifts. And you've got your technique in place, so you don't have to worry about that; you can just concentrate on what you are thinking. . . . And then when people find out about what I'm doing, like last year my teacher announced to the class that I was going to be in the *Nutcracker*, and so they said, 'Wow, that's cool.' And so I guess it feels good to be more involved at a higher level."

Youngsters also noted that the more competitive activities were for older and more talented participants, and appreciated the greater status they derived. Part of growing up, for these middle-class youngsters, involved being exposed to a variety of extracurricular experiences and acquiring many skills. However, they also learned from their climb up the ladder of extracurricular participation that adults and society valued in-depth involvement. Recreation and breadth, then, were less notable than competition and depth. Other values associated with advancing to this level of after-school activities included the stratification of hierarchy and ranking, exclusion, seriousness of purpose, and identification with participation in the activity.

Elite Activities

Almost all competitive after-school activities could also be performed on an elite level.[12] Children could progress from school plays or local dance troupes to participation in adult theater or dance performances, from the school band to the junior symphony, from local competitions to regional and/or national meets, and from competitively oriented leagues to elite leagues.

The decision to pursue an elite activity meant allocating it a greater amount of time, making it a priority ahead of other activities, and eliminating other projects. Not everyone wanted to make this commitment, as Rick explained when he was in eighth grade: "There were some acting things that I didn't try out for, that I felt were too hard for me, I guess because I didn't really want them that much. Like they had some children's parts at the dinner theater, but those plays run for three or four months. I guess that's what they are like, and grownups like that, but I would get tired of it before then, so I didn't try out for it. Like, the plays that I do are only five days, on two different weekends, and that's enough for me for right now. I like that and I can handle that, but I'm not ready for more."

For those who chose to make the commitment, not only their time, but their families', had to be shifted and other activities rescheduled around the elite activity. Moira, the ballet enthusiast, regularly took a lighter scholastic load so that she could spend several hours every day in the studio, while Brenna left school during the day to attend art classes at the local university. Many families planned their vacations around the demands of their children's activities, postponing, shortening, or eliminating out-of-town trips, or making their vacation a trip to the place where the child's team was having a competition. Samantha, a tenth-grade softball player, whose team played 120 games a season, traveled to out-of-town tournaments every weekend, all summer. Her parents came on every trip, renting a hotel room and putting a sleeping bag down on the floor for her younger sister. Even the extended kinship network was affected by her softball; they had to schedule their family reunion for July fourth, the one weekend her team had a respite. In addition, parents had to transport their children to and from these activities daily, adjusting their work, mealtime, and family schedules to accommodate these demands. One mother expressed her concerns: "Ever since my son started to play hockey seriously, my days have been ruined. He has to be on the ice at 5 a.m., and then he has practices after school. My husband and I haven't had a free weekend in months."

The accoutrements associated with elite after-school activities were superior to those at the organized and competitive levels, featuring enhanced, often personalized, uniforms, better equipment, better arenas, gyms, or fields, and upgraded transportation. All of this cost more money, which usually came from a combination of higher fees to parents and a more sophisticated fund-raising operation. One girl who tried out for cheerleading in junior high school was required to sign, along with her parents, a statement committing herself to pay five hundred dollars for the year's outfits and activities, to accord cheerleading a higher priority than all other activities (including academics), and to raise additional money for traveling to national cheerleading competitions. Another family, with two teenage daughters participating in elite after-school activities, took out a second mortgage on their house to support the girls' endeavors. They pooled all the money the girls received as Christmas and birthday gifts to save for travel and extra training, which included summer instructional programs and a private pitching coach. The support and dedication of adults, then, was a major component of elite after-school participation.

Concomitant with these changes, exclusiveness became salient in elite activities. All remaining vestiges of democratic participation were replaced by a philosophy of selectivity. The funneling effect operated strongly here, as more widespread participation at the recreational and competitive levels gave way to reduced numbers of involved youngsters in elite after-school activities. Tryouts were highly competitive, with limited slots going only to the most talented. Participants in elite activities therefore tended to be older, having progressed through the rudimentary learning levels before acquiring the skills associated with a highly competitive level of play or performance.

This unconcealed exclusiveness hurt young people who did not qualify for participation. Denise, a ninth grader, recalled her experience in fifth grade: "I will never forget how bad I felt when I didn't make the performing dance company. They called the kids who made it before school one day, and when I got there all my friends had gotten calls except me. I cried and cried. And so now I don't try out for things I may not make. I never want to feel that way inside again."

Others were more sanguine about their failures, putting them aside and turning to other activities, as we saw with Josh, the soccer player who switched over to acting. The range of after-school activities available was so expansive that most youngsters could find something to do that aligned more closely with their talent and interests. Moreover, by the time they got to this level, they could only afford the time to participate in one activity.

Once selected for the squad, participants soon discovered that adults treated elite activities seriously and expected that adolescents and preadolescents would impart the same degree of commitment. Practices moved from weekly or twice weekly to almost daily and required strenuous concentration. Coaches demanded strict attention and allegiance, subordinating not only participants but their families as well. Although recreational and competitive after-school activities were regarded as ends in themselves (cf. Coakley 1990; Eitzen and Sage 1989), elite after-school activities incorporated a different attitude; many participants and parents regarded elite activities as a track into some future enterprise. One mother described the reason she withdrew her third-grade son from elite ice hockey and enrolled him in a competitive soccer league: "There was no future in it. We had spent all those years getting up at five in the mornings on weekends and taking him to practice, and he was real good, but after next year there were no more leagues that he could advance to. So what was the point? He wasn't keen on the idea, but we switched him into soccer because there is the [elite] league he can get into after this, and he can continue with it all the way through high school."

Individuals aspired to play on their high school team, to compete in the Junior Olympics, or to win a college scholarship. Many young sports enthusiasts dreamed of athletic careers in college and the professional ranks. Nurtured by their parents, coaches, and friends, they sacrificed and worked hard to achieve these goals. As Samantha, the tenth-grade softball player, remarked: "My goal is to get more speed on my fastball and to stick with softball through the teenage years, which are the tough ones. Then I want to get a scholarship to college. My coach has already told me that I can get one; it's just a matter of how much I improve that will make the difference of if I go to, say, Arizona State or end up at Western Kansas. And then after that, there's no professional softball for women right now, but maybe by the time I get out, there will be." As the youngsters stayed on the professionalization path (Vaz 1982), the funnel continued to narrow.

Some have suggested that participation at the elite level also meant a shift from individual to team orientation. To function at the highest caliber, they argued, team members had to subvert their self-centered orientation and work for the welfare of the group (Berlage 1982). Yet their other-directedness was not strong enough to overcome the focus on individual development, mastery of skills, improvement of individual performance, and the concern with competitive abilities and outcomes (see also Coakley 1990; Eitzen and Sage 1989). Although elite participants made sacrifices for the team, they never abandoned their focus on developing their own careers. As Frank, a ninth-grade elite basketball player, remarked: "It's for the team, but it's for *me*. I mean, I want to help the team, because I'm on the team, and we're, like, one, but then inside of the team, I have to do better than this person or that person. The competition is razor's-edge sharp. I've never totally given myself so that all that I'm sacrificing for is the team. I'm always thinking about myself and my future."

Individuals also held this relationship to the coach, according the coach authority but never abdicating their own decision making completely. Although the coach made decisions for the competitive advancement of the group, overruling parents' authority, participants stayed with a coach only as long as it suited their best interests. This reinforced a combination of independence and interdependence, and a respect for authority, discipline, and loyalty.

Decisions were no longer made on the basis of fairness or ethical values, but on merit, pragmatics, and outcomes (Berlage 1982).[13] Coaches and leaders fostered a mentality of winning. Strategies and tactics to win that became more acceptable in the elite subculture included encouraging and hiding minor encroachments, glossing over umpires' favorable mistakes, and favoring shrewdness over integrity (Berlage 1982). Water polo players were taught to hook opponents' legs under the water, softball pitchers intentionally hit players on the opposing team, and, according to Vaz (1982), ice hockey players learned tactics for playing dirty, such as knocking their opponents' skates out from under them, hanging onto their pants, holding their sticks, and slamming them up against the boards. Pooley (1982), Smith (1978), and Underwood (1975; 1979) also note that cheating in sport is associated with a "win at any cost" attitude. Finally, young people were introduced, through their participation in the adult-modeled culture of elite activities, to some of the other less idealistic and "fair" aspects of society such as politics, favoritism, and financial considerations.

Berlage (1982) suggests that the meanings and values embedded in elite after-school activities are those of the corporate world. These values socialize children to the attitudes and behavior they will encounter in corporate jobs. They are predominantly transmitted through the specialization of roles, the subjugation of individualism and family for the team, the emphasis on sacrifice and self-discipline, the structuring into well-defined units, and the processual model of advancement. Other values associated with the elite level include subordination, interdependence, deferred gratification, professionalism, commercialism, and a strong focus on winning. While these characteristics define the elite level, as time progresses, the characteristics of each tier of after-school activity diffuse down to the developmentally preceding stage.

IN ASCENDING the developmental ladder of extracurricular activities, children progressed through various stages as they aged and their skills and interests unfolded. In early play, they spontaneously created the character of their activities themselves. But as soon as they became eligible, they were enrolled by their parents in a variety of adult-offered after-school "experiences" considered developmentally appropriate and enriching. Within these organized activities, children learned skills and enjoyed their recreation. A display of talent, interest, or the simple fact of getting older sent most children to participation at the more sophisticated competitive level. The nature of their involvement also changed through the introduction of a performance criterion, where participants were critically evaluated on the outcomes they achieved. Within the competitive sphere they learned the norms, rules, skills, and culture associated with higher-caliber participation in each activity. Eventually, some participants escalated their involvement to an elite level. Such individuals achieved a more meaningful extracurricular experience: they made sacrifices, but they sharpened their abilities and immersed themselves in their activity.

Their pathway along this extracurricular career moved them through a series of exponentially progressive experiences until they encountered the up-or-out dilemma: eventually the more recreational versions of many activities were phased out, and either children had to become more involved, building their physical, strategic, and/or mental skills and making a serious commitment, or they had to give up the activity completely. Societal expectations embodied within the structure of after-school offerings simultaneously built on and generated this developmental model.

Chapter 6

Friendships: Close and Casual

OVER THE LAST quarter of the twentieth century, the role of children's friendships has risen in import. People have come to recognize that children are capable of socializing earlier than previously thought, and have lowered the age at which children commonly begin their formal and informal education.[1] This has thrust children into peer groups from the age of toddlerhood, so that many children trace their earliest friendships back to the preschool years. Preadolescent children's friendships form one of the most important reference bases and sources of primary group attachment, coming to rival the importance of families (Bowerman and Kinch 1959; Savin-Williams and Berndt 1990). Friends provide children with a means of entertainment, a source of feedback, a feeling of belonging, and a foundation of identity.[2]

Children's friendship patterns are structured by their demographics, supporting the formation of certain types of friendships and restricting the development of others. Scholars have broadly explored these issues, noting, with some exceptions, the circumscription of relationships within the parameters of race, class, and gender homogeneity.[3] Not all friendships, though, are comparable, with relationships showing different degrees of contact and intimacy. Considerably less has been written about the types of friendships children form, other than to mark their existence. Grant and Sleeter (1986) provide a typology for adolescent friendships, including "friends one does some things with," "friends one does things with," and "best friends" among same-gender peers, and "boy/girlfriends" and "nonromantic boy/girlfriends" among other-gendered peers. Psychological researchers have also posited the existence of a range of adolescent relationships, including "acquaintances," "just friends," "good friends," and "best friends."[4]

In this chapter and the one that follows, we closely examine the different types of friendships preadolescents form, the people with whom they form them, and the characteristics that define them. Children's friendships can be differentiated quantitatively and qualitatively—by the number there are and the amount of contact they involve, and by their closeness and intensity. All the children we observed were involved in relationships that varied from the most intimate and frequent camaraderie to more remote and situationally lodged acquaintanceships. These friendships held certain social meanings in the peer group and displayed patterns of occurrence connecting them to other social factors and processes that we discuss in chapter 7. This discussion informs the role of friendships in both the peer culture and society.

Close Friendships

Primary in importance were children's close friendships, which they defined by several key factors. Close friendships were forged through significant, meaningful contact over an extended period. People usually shared interests with these friends and liked to spend their time engaged in or discussing similar pursuits.[5] This generally implied some overlap of life worlds that brought them together and gave them overlapping experiences on which to draw. Close friendships were also anchored in a base of intimacy and trust, where participants could share deep feelings with each other and feel secure that these would be held in confidence. Close friendships originated and were maintained through several critical venues, although there were intersections among these.

SCHOOLMATES

The vast majority of preadolescent children met and maintained their closest friendships with other children who attended their schools, the place where they spent the bulk of their social time.

Composition. Close friendships that were rooted primarily in school contacts tended to be age and gender homogeneous.[6] This was for partly structural and partly cultural reasons. Structurally, schools placed a premium on age stratification, tightly separating children into age-segregated groups.[7] Not only were children placed in age-grouped learning units, but they were also shuffled through the cafeteria at lunchtime and through the playground at recess according to their age-linked grade schedule. There was hardly any time during the school day, then, when they would have time to interact socially with someone who was not their age. Culturally, children brought their own preferences for interacting with peers of the same age and gender. As we discuss in chapter 8, peer-enforced cultural norms of separation as well as differences in the types of activities in which boys and girls engaged kept children of different genders from developing close friendships. Age separation was also reinforced by the status hierarchy inherent in the peer subculture. Children looked up to and gained status from playing with older people, while they derided and lost position for playing down. Damian, a fourth-grade boy, offered his views on forming close school friendships with children of younger ages:

> Q: *Are you ever friendly at school with kids who are a different age from you?*
> DAMIAN: No. I consider them lower life forms. Outside of school I play with them because they're my neighbors, they're there. I don't have to call anybody. I wouldn't call anybody from a lower grade.

When asked about their closest friends, children readily identified the circumscribed area within which members of their friendship pool were located.[8] Ellen, a fairly popular fourth grader, described her close friendship group: "All of my main friends go to my school. They're all girls, and they're all in my grade, except some of them are in one of the other classes." Nancy, a girl from the fifth grade, told about her friendship group, and how it formed and re-formed with the shuffling of students into different homeroom configurations at the start of each year: "Mostly all my friends I have are girls who are in the fifth grade. Like, Laura's one of my friends, and she's in this class. My other friends are in the other classes. Because we were friends in fourth grade, and in fifth grade they tried to split us up. And so when Laura and I got in the same class this year, we didn't really know each other. The only way we knew each other was through Jennifer, which is another one of my friends, 'cause we were both Jennifer's best friends, but this year we were together, so we decided we liked each other, and decided to be friends."[9]

Activities. When people got together with their close friends, they engaged in a variety of activities. Some elements were common to all close friendship play, while others differed by age, interests, weather, and gender. Older preadolescents covered a wider terrain than younger ones, traveling around town on their bikes or rollerblades, going to playgrounds out of their neighborhoods, innertubing down local creeks and streams, and going to shopping areas and malls. Younger people stayed closer to home, playing indoors or in the neighborhood.

Although girls did go outside sometimes, when they got together with their friends, they tended to do more indoor activities centered in their bedrooms, living rooms, and kitchens. Alli, a fifth grader, mentioned some of the things she and her best friends did, noting that they "have sleepovers and go to movies, and get together after school. At sleepovers we rent movies and make popcorn, stay up late, that kind of thing." Sara, a third-grade girl, described her activities with her friends as involving the following: "After school, usually we bike, get [rent] movies, go to movies, play games, watch TV, make cakes or something, play outside."

Craig, a third-grade boy, talked about the activities he and his close friends often pursued: "Well, sometimes we invite each other over and I have a Genesis [video game] and we play Genesis, and we play basketball, and we jump on our tramp that Morgan has, our next-door neighbor has, and they let me jump on it. And so we just do stuff sort of like we do at school, except sort of like we jump on the tramp and all that stuff."

Sean, the middle-level fourth-grade boy, described the things he did with his close friends, noting how the activities varied periodically: "Jump on my trampoline, just talk, all sorts of stuff. I live by the school, so if it's a weekend we can go over and play by the school, and they have a place at the park so we can go to the park and stuff. We like sports a lot. We have different things. For two months we might be into playing cards, and in another two months it might be something else like trading cards, so we do different kinds of stuff like that."

Danny, in fifth grade, echoed the theme of cyclical variation, tying patterns of activities to the season: "Well, let's see. It depends on the season. Usually when it's hotter outside, we'd be outside most of the time, playing sports, and if it's not so nice, rent a movie, go to a movie. Even if it is nice, we may go to a movie, later at night. And maybe go to the mall, play at the arcade sometimes."

Overall, boys were more apt to play with computers and video games or to engage in loosely structured sports, whereas girls played board games, cooked, or played with clothing. Common to both genders were renting movies (the most universal activity pursued on overnights), talking or just "hanging around," and playing outside in the neighborhood.

Making Friends. People made close friendships in different ways.[10] They often picked up friends individually, meeting and befriending one person at a time. This was especially common in the lower grades, before the larger friendship groups that became cliques began to form. Younger children tended to have fewer close friends overall, and so only sought to make one or two new friends at a time. As they aged, and were shuffled around from class to class, they were thrown together with new combinations of people and added new friends to their list. As a result, older children were more apt to have a larger number of people whom they considered close friends.

Chuck, a fifth-grade boy introduced in an earlier chapter, described the progression through which he picked up friends: "There's one that I really like in my class, and right when I moved here I met him, 'cause he was in my kindergarten class, and we did a lot together. And he was my only friend 'till first grade, and then I met some other kids, and they started being my closer friends, like David, who is in my class, and John, who is in my class now. And then later on in second, third, and fourth grades I met some other friends like Casey, Jack, and Rob, and Travis, and then all of them. Now I have a lot of friends. I've been here for a really long time."

Another way to make friends was to acquire them through other people who had friends, picking them up all at once or sequentially, as the other friend made them. Becky, a third grader, described how she made her close friends through the help of her primary, best friend: "Well, my core, main friend, I met her in kindergarten, and then there're some I consider my good friends, really good friends now, because they're a friend of the first friend I really had. This first friend, I met her in kindergarten, and we haven't been in the same class since, but we have so much in common that we have just stayed friends. So as she made friends, they became friends of mine too."

Finally, some people acquired a collection of friends all at once when they transferred into preexisting friendship circles. This happened when individuals moved into new neighborhoods and schools, or when they changed social groups, being invited in by one or more members of the group (such as we saw in chapter 3). A change in social group could be the result of upward, downward, or lateral social mobility.

Individuals often liked some of their close friends more than others or interacted with individuals differently, depending on the length of their close friendship. They tended to play more frequently and in a greater variety of ways with people who had been their close friends for a longer period, only gradually bringing new friends into broader patterns of interaction. Often this was due not to intentional differential treatment but to the lack of established play patterns such as they had already forged with longer-term friends. Such people often owned toys or dolls that were compatible with their friends, facilitating their joint play, or had ways of doing things that they knew were compatible. As Kyra, a third grader, noted, "Me and Sara usually play with our stuffed monkeys; she got one for her birthday, and I got one for my birthday!"

Children also found it easier to arrange things with friends they had known longer because these relationships had informal "institutional" ties: their mothers knew and liked each other, their families had carpooling relationships into which they could easily fall, they had shown that they could spend long periods

together without fighting, getting bored, or getting homesick, and their families knew that they could call on each other for child-care favors when they
were busy or taking a trip out of town.[11]

Damian, the fourth-grade boy who noted the importance of age to the stratification of close school friendships, discussed some differences in the activities he pursued with his two closest friends. These were due, he noted, to the
variation in longevity of the friendships, one older and one more recently
formed:

> Q: *Do you guys ever spend the night?*
>
> DAMIAN: One I haven't spent the night at, and one I have a lot.
>
> Q: *Why the difference between them?*
>
> DAMIAN: Because one I've known since first grade, and the other I met
> this year. And he's come over to my house a few times and we always
> hang out during the day and play and stuff, just we've never gotten
> really around to hanging out with each other at night. I don't know
> why, because we've been friendly almost all year now. We will, but
> we just haven't. Same thing with doing homework projects together.
> Me and my newer friend I haven't done work with, but my other
> best friend has, I have done work with him. It just takes a while, I
> guess.

Number of Friends. Children varied considerably in reporting the number of
close friends they had. Some claimed to have as few as one or two, citing individuals in their grade or class. Dan, a fourth grader who described himself as being
"unpopular," talked about his paucity of friends: "Well, really because I started
later, first I started in a different school and switched to this school all of a sudden, and it wasn't in the beginning of the school year so I didn't have a chance
to meet them all, all the kids. So I started somewhere else, in the first of the year,
then I transferred over here, and not knowing anybody here, I didn't make many
friends that fast. So it usually takes a while and it's best to meet them in the beginning of the year, so what I have here is like one or two friends, that's it."

Paul, a third grader, also discussed his friendship situation: "I'm not like
every kid in the world, okay? I don't really have a group of friends. I have a best
friend and I have a next friend, and they're both in my grade, but neither of
them is in my class." Like Dan, Paul was not a member of a group or circle of
friends but had select individuals whom he considered his closest friends. These
people were not necessarily close friends with each other.

Below individuals like Paul and Dan were the social isolates, discussed in
chapter 4, who did not have any close friends among their schoolmates at all.

At the other end of the spectrum, the largest number of friends that any-one reported or that we observed was around fifteen. Ellen, the popular fourth grader introduced earlier, said she had "about fourteen or sixteen close friends. Most of all of my friends are close friends. Well some of them are closer than others, but they're all fairly close friends."

> Q: *How long have you been friendly with most of these people?*
>
> ELLEN: Some of them really long, some since just this year, some since third grade, some since second, some since first, and some since kindergarten.
>
> Q: *And are most of them friendly with each other as well as with you?*
>
> ELLEN: About two of them no, but the rest of them are in one big friendship group.

Ellen's description characterizes the gradual formation of her popular clique. It arose from a smaller friendship circle and kept adding members over the course of several years until it grew to a fairly large size.

Most people identified a group of closest friends that ranged in between the two extremes.

A number of factors contributed to this difference in the quantity of peo-ple's closest friends. First, the size of friendship groups varied considerably be-tween the popular clique and the smaller, nonpopular friendship circles. Nonpopular children might have groups that ranged between two and five members, while popular cliques sometimes got as large as fifteen. Second, size varied with age, as the popular clique began to form in around third grade and progressively picked up members each year. It was smaller in third than in fifth grade, and popular people were likely to have fewer clique members in the ear-lier grades than the later. Finally, as noted earlier, boys' groups sometimes tended to grow to larger sizes than girls', since they functioned to form teams for sports play in addition to social intimacy, and sports play required larger num-bers of participants than social interaction.

Intimacy. The most critical feature of close friendships, beyond membership, social activities, and compatibility, was the support and intimacy people derived from them. All children spoke of the trust they felt toward their closest friends and the things they could talk to them about that they could not discuss with others. Sociologists have speculated that girls' friendships display this intimacy, but have regarded boys' relationships as more superficial, forming sites for roughhousing and play (see Dweck 1981; Fine 1980; Lever 1976).[12] The boys and girls we studied did display some of this difference, with boys leaning more toward sports and girls toward intimate interactions, but that did not exclude boys from engaging in intimacy altogether. For example, boys shared confidences with their friends, confronted each other about attitudes or behaviors they questioned or did not like, and engaged in relationship talk. Chuck, the fifth grader with many friends, discussed the nature of his close friendships: "We tell each other our secrets, and we talk about our feelings. We respect each other a lot. Sometimes we just argue for the fun of it. It's fun to do everything with that type of friend." Eder and Sanford (1986) note that while the level of intimacy often deepens in this age group, care has to be taken so that individuals do not appear sexually intimate.

FAMILY FRIENDS

Children formed close friendships with the children of their parents' friends, with whom they spent quality leisure time on weekends and holidays. These relationships were often rooted in children's very early years, preceding their entry into school. Such friends, with whom they grew up, offered a place of refuge where they could escape from the social hierarchy and dynamics of the school peer subculture, into relationships that did not judge them the same way. These relationships provided continuity over time and were supported by the friendship of the parents. If things became troublesome between the children, parents were there to help work them out. Parents also facilitated these relationships by including their friends' children in specially planned activities and trips. These relationships were imbued with a special feeling because of the ties between the families. Friendly families also forged close bonds by meeting each others' extended kinship networks and by traveling out of town together. Close family friendships were influenced in character by the demographic correspondence between the children, by their relation in age, gender, and school attendance.

While the norm of close friendships supported age and gender homogeneity, some family friendships did not follow this pattern. Like relationships within the family, family friendships involved children forging friendships with older and younger children who were not necessarily of their gender.[13]

Tammy, a third-grade girl, discussed her close family friendships with children who were linked in multiple ways:

Q: *Do you have any other friends in the close friend category?*
TAMMY: Yeah.
Q: *Where do you know these people from?*
TAMMY: I know them through my parents, their friends have kids, like
some kids that are younger than me, and some kids that are older

than me, and they all are boys. And we go over to their house, or
they come over to our house.

Most youngsters who identified family friends as falling into their closest
friendship category, though, had at least one demographic trait in common with
these other children. Gender formed a stronger bond for friendship than age,
so that most people reported close family friendships within their gender even
if they were outside their grade.

Paul, the third grader with few school friends, spoke of a close family friend
who was his gender, although not his age: "Well, his name's Freddie Mitchell.
We go over to the Mitchell family a lot, and so I like the kids there. They're
all older than me." Freddie, Paul's friend, was one of the children he described
as "all older than me," probably the youngest of the group.

Betsy, a fourth-grade girl, talked about her relationship with Heather, a family friend who was an older girl: "I have two best friends, and they're like my
very, very best friends. And they're both named Kim, and the one Kim who
I've known for like very, very long, my mom used to be her preschool teacher,
and that's how we met, 'cause my mom got friendly with her mom, and she's a
year older than me. She's ten, and she goes to Banks [another elementary
school]. And we're really, really good friends, and she comes over here on Fri-
days 'cause her dad has to work in Smithhaven [a neighboring town], and we
go to dance class together. And we're really close; she tells me a lot of secrets.
And we play really weird games; we don't play like house, we play like we're
animals and trolls, and we make big forts, and we usually, I have a lot of makeup
and sometimes we get into my makeup, and we put perfume on, and my mom
says we stink, and I have these ball gowns, and we get out each of them, and
sometimes we use them as, we throw them down on my dog beds and make them
into beds, and we usually do like that kind of stuff."

The strongest family friendships occurred when children overlapped in age
and gender. If the families lived nearby, this often meant that the children also
attended the same school. Kyra, the third-grade girl, explained how she met
her best friend at school: "Well, Shelly I knew since my mom adopted me, and
well, actually Shelly was my first friend because my mom knew her mom and
when Shelly's mom adopted her, then my mom was just thinking, and so she
adopted me so Shelly was my first friend. And now she goes to my school, so I
see her every day."

Children whose parents had extensive friendship networks of their own,
or who had older siblings who gave their parents access to other adults with
children in their age range, often found that their parents were friendly with a
group of people who had children their age. Matt, a fourth grader, described

the overlap between his school and family friends: "I've got a big group of my closest friends. Around seven guys. They're all in my grade."

> Q: *Have you been close friends with them all for a while, or are they newer friends?*
>
> MATT: I've been friends with most of them for a while. Like, I started being close friends with them around first grade and kindergarten.
>
> Q: *How did you become friends with them?*
>
> MATT: I just made 'em from my mom, because they were her friends' kids. And then we became friends. I met them at home before I met them at school. Like at soccer and a bunch of sports, mostly, where our moms all signed us up.

Overlapping family and school friendships generated a base of intimacy and trust that was strong and lasting. Sara, the third grader mentioned earlier, spoke about how she maintained her friendship with a family friend who had moved out of town: "I have a really close friend, her name is Sally Duffy. She went to this school last year, but now she doesn't anymore. She moved to Merrill [nearby town]. I don't get to see her very much, but I write letters and call her a lot. And when we were babies my mom always talked to her mom and we always played, and then we grew up as friends."

> Q: *So do you still have sleepover dates with her?*
>
> SARA: Yeah. I have sleepover parties a lot with her. And I had a birthday in April, and I invited her. And she spent the night, just her. 'Cause I never see her a lot.

RELATIVES

Preadolescents' interactions with family members, such as cousins, could be as frequent as those with family friends, especially when the parties were thrust together on weekends and holidays or did special things together. This was limited to relatives who lived in the local area, however, where the contact they generated could be regular. Yet most families that we observed did not spend the amount or quality of time with their relatives that they did with their friends, possibly because these associations were chosen by birth rather than selected on the basis of compatibility. Fewer relatives than family friends, then, fell into children's closest group of friendships.

Jack, the fifth-grade boy discussed earlier, described the close friendship that he had with his two male cousins:

Q: *What about your cousins, do they live in town or out of town?*

JACK: They live in Smithhaven [nearby town].

Q: *So how often do you get to see them?*

JACK: About once a month, maybe twice a month.

Q: *How old are they?*

JACK: One is twelve, and one is eight.

Q: *Tell me about your relation with them.*

JACK: We, I barely ever talk to them on the phone. I can't see them at school because they go to school in Merrill [nearby town], and I just see them on weekends and it is always sleepovers because they live in [nearby town]. So that's just about it.

Q: *So what do you do with them when they sleep over?*

JACK: We watch movies. We barely ever talk, except about sports and everything.

Even though Jack considered these cousins close friends, his lack of daily or regular contact with them reduced the potential for intimacy in their relationship. As a result, they interacted on the basis of family and culturally shared topics, and common interests in music, television shows, and movies.

NEIGHBORS

Because of their propinquity, neighbors offered a pool from which preadolescents could forge close friendships.[14] Children could spend time with their neighbors easily, getting together with them, without the encumbrance of parental assistance, after school, on weekends, on holidays, and during the summer. Unlike school play, neighborhood play occurred within a setting that did not structure interactions by age. Neighborhood friendships crossed age boundaries more readily than school friendships. Without the framework of the peer subculture and its stigma on boy-girl interaction (see chapter 8), these friendships were also more likely to cross gender lines. Of all relationships, those from the neighborhood, then, were the most likely to be diverse in composition. Yet since children often formed the strongest bonds with individuals who were the closest to them demographically, they were less likely to develop their most intimate friendships with neighbors, unless they were of their age and gender.

Children who cited people from their neighborhood as their closest friends often had difficulty making friends in school. Dan, the fourth-grade boy who blamed his lack of school friends on coming into the class after the start of the school year, found both of his closest friends in his neighborhood. One, Sam, was in his grade, and the other was Sam's eight-year-old brother, a third grader. Dan said he usually played with the boys separately: "They don't go along together. It's pretty much one or the other or something they'll both agree with."

Q: *So are you like the man in the middle here between Sam and his brother?*
DAN: Well, usually I stay out of their way, but yeah, I usually am in the middle to do whatever I can.

Two other people who found their best friends in their neighborhoods were Roger, the third-grade social isolate (introduced in chapter 5) who spent a lot of time with the two-year-old next door, and Meredith, the third-grade girl who also had hardly any friends, and who spent most of her time playing with the seven-year-old girl next door whose parents home-schooled her. Meredith's home-school neighbor, lacking the daily social contacts found in school, was happy to play with Meredith anytime she was available. These neighborhood best friendships exhibited a common element of desperation and descension.

When children found neighbors who were in their grade, they often attained the enhanced intimacy found among children whose family friends attended their schools. They could see their neighborhood friends daily at school and also play with them after school and on weekends. Tammy, the third grader introduced earlier, spoke about her neighbor, classmate, and close friend Jimmy: "I have a friend named Jimmy, and he's one of my best friends because he lives close. And I go over to his house a lot, and we play with his dogs and sometimes we go to the park and take hikes and we watch movies, and we don't do as much as I do with my other friends 'cause there's not as much I can do with him 'cause I can't play dress-ups, but sometimes he'll let me dress him up as a girl, and he doesn't care, he just puts on dresses and high heels. And he'll go downstairs and say, 'Hey, I'm a girl!'"

Overlaps between neighborhood and school that involved common age and gender were capable of generating similarly close friendships, such as the one between Sara and Kyra, two third-grade girls. They played together every day, and if either of them had another friend over, they were likely to invite each other over as well. Sara identified her circle of close friends: "Well, Sally Duffy's my very, very, closest one, and Kyra and Iris are my other really close ones."

Q: *What kinds of things would you do with Kyra or Iris?*
SARA: Well, a lot, Kyra and Iris. We usually decide on games, because I usually have Iris over and then I invite Kyra over because she lives next door, and we usually just either play in the snow or the backyard, and just figure out games we like to play. See, she will

invite me if she has Amanda over, and I will invite her if I have Iris over, or sometimes the four of us play together, or sometimes it's just Kyra and me. So either way, I usually see Kyra every day.

Casual Friendships

Beyond their inner circle of close friends lay a wide range of others with whom preadolescents maintained more casual friendships. Children saw, played, and talked with their casual friends, and generally liked them, but interacted with them less frequently and with less intimacy. These were people who could be counted on for situational assistance and support, to whom children would turn for companionship in a group, and who held common interests and attitudes, but whom they liked somewhat less than their core friends. Unlike close friendships, which were a part of most children's lives, casual friendships were less common; some people had many, others had few, still others had none. This varied with children's position and group membership, social skills, and general inclination. Like close friendships, casual friendships could derive from several kinds of social environments.[15]

SCHOOL FRIENDS

Character. For some children, casual school friends were similar in kind to their close friends, but not in quantity. That is, they liked their casual school friends nearly as well as their close school friends, but they never quite got around to socializing with them outside school, in the afternoons or on weekends. These people did not see a significant difference between the kinds of interactions they had with members of the two different groups.

Amy, a fourth-grade girl, talked about the relationship she had with one of her casual school friends, Lauren: "We've been trying to get together to play [outside of school], but we don't. We play at school, and she's really nice to me and I'm really nice to her."

Casual friends could be people who were members of the same large social group, but who belonged to a different subgroup within it. This was a common structure in the popular group, where no more than five or six people associated intimately in the most core unit. Craig, the third-grade boy mentioned earlier, cast the difference between close and casual school friends as a matter of quantity rather than quality:

> Q: *And what would you say would be the difference between your more casual friends and your close friends?*

CRAIG: Well, my more casual friends, they like have more close friends
that they play with more. And so, and my more close friends I play
with a little more. 'Cause I barely get to see the casual friends, 'cause
I haven't known them for a long time 'cause they've been in the
different classes. So I don't get to see them a lot. And so we each
have our own set of closer friends, but we're all friendly.

More commonly, however, people went beyond the quantitative difference
in time spent together to carefully delineate a qualitative distinction between
the types of relationships they had with close compared to casual school friends.
Tucker, a fifth-grade boy, explained both the similarities and differences between
these types of friendships:

Q: *What would be the difference in your relationship between your more
casual friends and your closer friends? Are there things you do with your
closer friends that you wouldn't do with your more casual friends?*
TUCKER: Yeah. Oh there's nothing different. There's no difference. I just
probably don't see them quite as often.
Q: *But you're not closer friends with some, there's not more intimacy or
talking with some than others?*
TUCKER: I mean, I might talk to my closer friends more openly than I
would to some of my friends. 'Cause I trust them more maybe. Than
some of the friends that aren't as close. I mean, most of my friends
are really close, but some of them are just different than others; you
know a person, and you can tell them certain things.

Josh, another fifth grader, went slightly beyond Tucker in delineating a
qualitative divergence in these "minor league" relationships: "I usually don't
play with them as much, like I might goof off with John or Blake and invite
them over a bunch. I don't talk to them a lot about things. I think I am less
willing to share my feelings with them than I am with close friends. I don't know
quite why, but maybe it's because I don't have as much trust."

Finally, Jennifer, the fifth grader, drew the strongest difference in talking
about these two kinds of relationships. Of casual friends, she said: "We're just
on a friendly level. We sit together at lunch, we talk together, we're just mainly
sort of friendly."

Q: *What types of things would you not do with them that you would do with
your other, closer friends?*
JENNIFER: Well, I wouldn't exactly work together with them. I also
wouldn't really invite them over. 'Cause they're not exactly close
friends, they're just friends. I also wouldn't, I don't really have any

secrets but I sort of know other people's secrets, but they told me I shouldn't tell anyone but my real friends, so I make sure these don't get out by not telling people like them.

Composition. Like close school friends, casual school friends were still mostly a homogeneous group. People rarely crossed the age/grade boundary to befriend other people because of the status chasm and the lack of opportunity. Cross-gender friendships were somewhat more common. These varied by grade level, as children in the middle years of elementary school had fewer interests in common with members of the other gender than they did toward the later years.

Mitch, a third-grade boy, admitted to having a girl as a casual school friend but was hard-pressed to think of anything they could do together:

Q: *Are there many boys and girls who are friendly?*
MITCH: Some, not many.
Q: *What kinds of things might you and Eve do together?*
MITCH: Well, not much. I usually play with my friends that are boys, and she usually plays with her friends that are girls.

Most third-grade boys would agree with this statement. Casual friendships, though, did not require as great a commitment or as broad of an overlap as close friendships. By fifth grade there were more boys and girls who considered each other casual friends. Kenny, a fifth grader, described the way boys and girls started becoming friendly: "Well, we hardly ever talked to any girls last year, but this year it's different. We know more things about them. I don't know, we just like to hang out with them. They come to us, and we'll ask them a question."

Increased friendly contact between boys and girls derived not only from a growing maturity but from areas of shared interest. Homework and schoolwork formed the major source of common ground where both parties could relate to each other. Girls also made forays into boys' activities, notably sports. As we discussed in chapter 5, the girls' subculture broadened during the 1980s and 1990s, opening the way for girls to participate in a variety of athletic endeavors without stigma.[16] During the same period, the boys' subculture did not make such modifications, and boys rarely came over to play with girls on the monkey bars, on the hopscotch courts, or in their circles of play.

Soccer was the cross-gendered sport that drew the participation of more elementary school girls than any other. Organized leagues abounded, and many girls at levels beginning in around fourth grade played on teams, both recreationally and competitively. To a degree in third and fourth grades, and with greater numbers in fifth grade, girls entered the playing fields at elementary school recess and played soccer with the boys, not as individuals but in groups. At one school, teams competed every soccer season at recess. One fifth-grade team was composed of boys only, the other was a mixed team. Boys who played on the latter referred to it as the "girls' team." At another school, there was a similar situation, where a rotating all boys' third-grade team played against a mixed-gender team from the same grade. Names were used to describe these teams. The boys' team was alternately called the Huskies or the Wolverines; the mixed boy-girl team was called (by the girls) the Hamster Poops. Josh, one of the boys who played on the Hamster Poops, discussed his relationships with his female teammates: "At soccer, girls play and boys play all together, and I play on the girls' team, but there's a bunch of boys who play on the girls' team. They do that just to make the teams fairer. If I am doing defense, and there's lots of girls playing goalie, always, a whole bunch at the same time, so we are talking and stuff when the ball is down the field but no, I wouldn't consider them friends."

Danny, in fifth grade, discussed both the extent and limits of his casual friendships with girls:

Q: *You have any girls that you are friendly with?*

DANNY: There are some girls here that I play soccer with. They are on my team. There are three girls who are on my soccer team which I got to be friends with.

Q: *Here at school or outside?*

DANNY: Outside of school. They go here too. That's Beth, Karen, and Ann. They are all very good soccer players.

Q: *Aside from playing soccer with them, do you ever talk with them?*

DANNY: Sometimes.

Q: *What kinds of things do boys and girls talk about at your age?*

DANNY: Homework. That's basically it.

Mariah, a popular, athletic fifth-grade girl, also identified homework and sports as the common ground on which boys and girls established friendships:

Q: *In what situations might you have an opportunity to chat?*

MARIAH: When we're like working [on assignments in class], sometimes we do that when we're supposed to be working. Or we don't. That doesn't happen that much, but it does happen.

Q: *Do you ever do anything else with boys of a friendly nature?*

MARIAH: Oh, yeah. Sports, all the time. Basketball. I'm not a big athlete, but I like basketball a lot. I like soccer too, but it's not my favorite sport. No other girls like to play basketball, although a lot of them like to play soccer.

A smaller group of boys and girls moved beyond these circumscribed areas to engage in actual socializing. This was more likely to occur with members of the popular boys' and girls' cliques, and to be limited to fifth graders. In fifth grade, Brad, the clique leader, and some of his friends interacted in less structured domains with girls. He explained that "there are some girls that are really nice to boys. To some boys, but they can't stand being around other boys, and it's the same way with girls."

> Q: *So there are some boys and girls who are friendly across, and there are others who totally stick to their own sex?*
>
> BRAD: Because I'll talk to girls and stuff, and sometimes we let girls in on our practical jokes because it makes it even funnier. It's easier to fool people if you have two sexes anyway.

These kinds of interactions fell within the framework of a growing interest in boy-girl sparring that had romantic overtones.

NEIGHBORS

Although preadolescents did not form as many close friendships with people from their neighborhood who were not similar to them in age, gender, and school, such individuals often made good casual friends.[17] Children from the neighborhood became casual friends if they were played with inconsistently or seasonally, not as the first choice for daily play, but on an intermittent basis or when other, more desirable, people could not be found.[18]

Neighborhood casual friends could overlap in age and gender if they were not in people's core friendship circles. Several boys and girls had such neighborhood friends whom they called up and got together with, either individually or in groups, when they had extra time after school or on weekends.

Josh, the fifth grader, described his relationship with Will, a neighborhood friend who was in his grade: "Will is a minor majorish friend. Of the minor friends, he is one of the closest ones. He is, he used to live just down the street, he just moved."

> Q: *He is in your grade?*
>
> JOSH: He is in my class. He is still pretty close. We didn't get together too much because I would go home and do homework and he would go home and play, and then I would go out and play and he would go home and do homework. Kind of opposite there. We would have snowball fights, we would do that kind of stuff. I had a treehouse that is now falling apart, and we would go over there and play stuff.

Aside from unsynchronized schedules, neighbors remained only casual friends for other reasons. Kevin, a popular fifth grader, explained why the boys in his neighborhood who were in his grade were not friends of the closest rank:

Q: *What kinds of things do you do with your main friends?*

KEVIN: We play sports, which is a lot, and then we just talk, hang out in a clique, so-called.

Q: *What about after school? Do you ever see them after school?*

KEVIN: Not really, unless they're like coming over to my house for a birthday party or something. Or they're just spending the night. Otherwise I have a whole different other group of friends.

Q: *And who are they?*

KEVIN: They're the ones who aren't as popular at school, like maybe they're too rough at school, or maybe they're always quiet, and they're like still into all these action heroes and stuff, but they play basketball or something and I like to play basketball with them. So they're kind of my friends at home.

Q: *And where do you find them?*

KEVIN: Sometimes I just go over there. Just to hang out and play.

Q: *So you are more friendly with these kids outside of school than in school?*

KEVIN: Yeah. Like one kid, I might say hi to him once a month or something in school, but after school we go play basketball, we talk, it's just like we are really good friends, you know.

Q: *And why is it you have so little contact in school if you are so friendly outside of school?*

KEVIN: Sometimes they're in different classes. Sometimes they hang with a different clique.

Q: *Would your friends in your clique not like it if you were friendly with these nonclique members?*

KEVIN: Sometimes, yeah, you can ruin your reputation by hanging out with somebody.

Kevin's remarks illustrate the existence of a stratification system, where kids valued others by how outgoing and fun they were to be with, how athletic they were, how close they felt to them, and the group to which they belonged. They preferred to have certain kinds of friends, those of the same age, same gender, and same school. But when they could not get these kinds of friends, such as in the neighborhood (as well as with the family), they would settle for other friends: those who they didn't like as well, those who were immature, those who were younger, or those of another gender. These kinds of people formed the basis for casual friendships. When same-age or same-gender people were not available, people readily sought out neighbors with whom they might pass the time. Sean, the fourth grader, summed this up when he said, "Ned is just a kind of friend you meet occasionally where he's under your age, but he's still fun to play with."

Sara, the third grader with the close friend who lived next door, described her casual friendship with a neighbor, Kyra's younger sister Chelsea: "Down a notch from my close friends would be, well, Kyra's little sister, she's four, and that's my brother's really close friend. And her name's Chelsea, and she's really cute and fun to play with, and when Iris is not home, 'cause Kyra and Chelsea are sisters, then I just go over to Kyra's house 'cause she's my next-door neighbor. We [my brother and I] play with both of them and make shows for her dad." Like Dan, the fourth grader who became close friends with his best friend Sam's brother, Sara included her close friend Kyra's little sister into her friendship circle, although at a lower notch.

Kyra also mentioned neighbors when asked about casual friends: "Like yesterday, Sara called me and asked if I could play in the snow with her and her brother Zack and his friend, Tommy, who was over. And sometimes Lucy and I play with Zack and Tommy a lot."

> Q: *And how old are Zack and Tommy?*
> KYRA: Zack is ten and Tommy is ten, and they're really pretty good friends.
> Matt, the third grader, laid out a whole cross-age and -gender neighborhood play group to which he belonged. These were all people whom he classified as casual friends:
> Q: *So in your neighborhood, you guys play together across different age groups?*
> MATT: Yeah, I do. I have friends that are in different grades. My next-door neighbor is in fifth grade, and he has a brother and a sister who are in kindergarten and the sister is in third grade.
> Q: *And do you play with all of them?*
> MATT: Yeah. And then, there's a baby that lives across the street that's maybe about one.
> Q: *And you play with the baby?*
> MATT: Um hum. And there's also a someone in preschool, our next-door neighbor, and that's all.
> Q: *And what about girls? Do boys play with girls in your neighborhood?*
> MATT: Sometimes.
> Q: *What kinds of things would boys and girls play together?*

MATT: Well, my little brother, he plays with Alyssa, the third grader, and they jump on our tramp.

Q: *And how old is your little brother?*

MATT: He's six.

Q: *But even though Alyssa's in third grade, do you play with her?*

MATT: Yeah.

Q: *So what other kinds of things do you do?*

MATT: We play Nintendo, and we play the computer, and we play Bar Games.

Casual neighborhood friends could come as individuals, clumps, or whole groups. On snowy days, people might call each other to organize sledding parties. On nice days, large groups might be recruited to form teams for neighborhood games. If these games were successful, they might even be extended to last over several days.[19]

FAMILY FRIENDS AND RELATIONS

Like neighbors, family friends and relations who lived in the general vicinity often offered better casual than close friendships. These people were not freely chosen, like school friends, but, like neighbors, were there. Like neighbors, they might fall into different age or gender categories, or might have annoying traits that would diminish their standing in the school social hierarchy. Away from the eyes of their status-conscious peers, preadolescents could play contentedly with these nonchosen others and manage to enjoyably pass the time. Regular contact even brought a degree of closeness that elevated people who might not be otherwise chosen as friends at all to a casual friendship level.

Heidi, a nine-year-old fourth-grade girl, discussed her friendship with the daughters of a family friend: "My mom has a friend who has two daughters, and they go to another school. They live up in Merrill [nearby town]. When our parents get together, I go up and see them. We go to movies together and stuff, 'cause one's like seven and the other's eleven, and so we do stuff that we all are kind of used to doing, but we, like the youngest, might have different ideas, and Kate has different ideas of games, but we all figure out games."

While Heidi's decision to accompany her parents to their friends' house was elective, Sean, a fourth-grade boy, did not have that choice. He was taken on a regular basis to family outings with his cousins, who lived within half an hour of home. He described the progression of their relationship: "As far as the next level of friends, in that category I would also put my cousins in [nearby town]. They have three boys, one ten, one twelve, and the other sixteen, that I see pretty often.

> Q: *Do you get along with them?*
>
> SEAN: Yes, we have gotten to be pretty good friends. At first we weren't. Our families used to get together and we'd fight. There was a lot of competition between our mothers and between me and the one my age, he's kind of a braggart. But then our moms worked it out, and so we kind of had to too. I wouldn't say we are the best of friends, but we get along better. We see each other once a month, usually for a sleepover, and then we also usually take a family trip together in the summer. When you spend that much time together for so many years, you kind of get closer. And we know all the same family and stuff.

Sean's experience was the reverse of Nicole's. A sixth grader, Nicole had been closer friends with her local cousins when she was younger. During the early years, her parents had gotten together with their family members and brought the children along all the time. However, as the cousins began to get older and decided that they would rather be with their friends than with their cousins, they applied pressure to be turned loose. Although her parents continued to visit their relatives, Nicole had to do so much less frequently. Her relationship with her cousins, which had been casual at best, then faded to weak.

Family friends' and relatives' children most often served as a source of casual friendships when they lived close by and were seen often. These friendships were imbued with both the positive and negative aspects of family and pseudofamily relationships: regular or frequent interaction, but lack of voluntary selection. Age and gender overlap elevated some of what might otherwise be nonrelationships to the casual level, while age and gender diversity brought some potentially close friendships down to the casual level. Other relationships were just comfortable floating at the casual level, consisting of friendly but not intimate close camaraderie, based on regularity of contact.

Chapter 7

Friendships: Compartmentalized

U<small>NLIKE CLOSE FRIENDSHIPS</small>, which were fairly intimate in nature, and casual friendships, which were somewhat less frequent in contact, less intimate in nature, and often less voluntary in selection, compartmentalized friendships were not characterized by their degree of intimacy. Compartmentalized friendships could span the gamut from the importance and intimacy of close friendships to the relative distance of friendly acquaintanceships. Compartmentalized friendships were characterized, instead, by how and when they happened, as they were located in particular niches in children's lives. Friendships were compartmentalized if they remained within a limited domain and did not cross over into other spheres of people's social worlds. This might entail people being located at a distance where they could not be seen except at certain times of the year, or it might mean that they were tied to certain activities or behaviors that did not overlap with other ones. Compartmentalized friends were ones that might easily be available for interaction at only certain times and places. As a result, compartmentalized friendships were often *role relationships*, involving individuals in specific types of interaction and dealing with only certain aspects of their complete selves. As such, compartmentalized friends might have access to a different part of people than what they presented to others, from their most intimate and reflective selves to their most situation-embedded or superficial selves. Compartmentalized friendships, then, were somehow constrained, restricted, or confined, by location, setting, time, season, dimension, or role.

Activities Friends

As we saw in the discussion of after-school activities (chapter 5), preadolescent children engaged in a plethora of enterprises. Some of these were more social than others, bringing children into contact with other people. When children found themselves in the company of other participants, they tended to gravitate more strongly toward some and to be less drawn to others. With these people, they might become anywhere from "situationally friendly" to extremely close. The nature of activities friendships was influenced by the organization of the activities in which children engaged.[1] This could include solitary activities (piano, horseback riding) or those involving organized teams and leagues, activities overlapping with other arenas or those that remained distinct, activities occupying a distinct season of the year or those that were available year-round, and activities in which children dabbled or those to which they were seriously committed.

ORGANIZATION

Over the course of the preadolescent years, many youth activities evolved organizationally. This did not affect solitary activities as much as group ones. Becky, the third grader who had made most of her core friends through her first, kindergarten, friend, talked about her friends from dance, tennis, and swimming lessons: "Well, I have one friend in dance that our moms signed us up together. I have one that I went to tennis with, but then she switched to another school and we don't talk very much anymore. 'Cause it was just me and her in tennis lessons. It was like a private, and I haven't taken swim lessons in a long time, and 'cause I've also taken private swim lessons with just me and a couple of other girls. But I haven't tooken them in a while. Plus I have another friend, Ava, who's from my dance class, but I only see her in dance class."

These activities, popular among girls, were not always as conducive to generating friendships because they lacked the numbers found in team (especially boys') sports. Yet team sports evolved over time. When boys were young, their athletic teams were often set up, by the sponsoring organizations, into teams composed of people from the same school. This meant that children participated in athletics with a group of others that they already knew from their school, usually from within their grade. When asked if he had any friends that he had made through his participation on the soccer team, Mitch, a third-grade boy, replied: "No, they are mostly from my school. I play on the "Holland" team so all my friends on that team go to Holland."

Even by the latter years of elementary school, Travis, the fifth grader introduced in chapter 6, described the overlapping nature of his athletic and school activities:

> Q: *And do you do any organized activities outside of school?*
> TRAVIS: I'm on a baseball team and play sports all year round on

different teams, and most of my friends are on these teams. My sports teams are filled up with kids from Zenith, mostly they have a Zenith team. Zenith soccer team, Zenith basketball team, Zenith football team. Baseball is the only sport where it's not like that, where they split you up and you get to meet new people.

As we showed in chapter 5, by sixth grade, most team sports began offering competitive programs featuring tryouts, where participants came from a variety of school backgrounds.

SITUATIONAL FRIENDSHIPS

In contrast, activities where individuals were mixed with people from other schools offered the opportunity to make new friendships. Some of these were situational friendships that did not extend beyond the particular activity. Melanie, a fourth grader, discussed the friendships she made in the weekly ski program in which she was enrolled: "Well, I go with my family, but they have this Avalanche ski thing, and I go there, but I don't really have any friends, because I make friends in there, but they're just sort of 'for the moment' friends."

Q: *And what do you do with "for the moment" friends?*

MELANIE: Nothing really, they're just friendly to me, and that's it. Just the other girls in the program. There might be different ones who go up there every week. We don't really hang out together when we're skiing down the mountain. We ride the chairlift together and eat lunch together. So I'll sit next to the ones at lunch that I like, and we'll talk about the lessons and what we can do and what we can't do, and who we like and who we don't like.

Tucker, the fifth grader who explained the difference between his casual and close friendships, talked about his compartmentalized friends from baseball:

Q: *Do you have friends from baseball?*

TUCKER: I have friends like when I see them, they're like my friends, when I see them and everything, but we're not close enough to actually get together.

Q: *Okay, let's talk about your when-you-see-them friends. What kind of things made the difference between these and your closer friends?*

TUCKER: Difference is a matter of closeness, like when somebody, like the people on my baseball team, like I like to talk with them and goof around with them and stuff like that, and we like to hang out together when we're at games, or baseball, but we just don't see each other as much and we don't, you know, we're just not as close, basically.

SEASONAL VARIATION

Many people made the kinds of activities friends just described, suitable for associating with during practices, rehearsals, lessons, and/or games. The next step would be to get together with these people in another setting. Many such excursions into friendship lasted only for the duration of the season, tapering off after the activity stopped bringing individuals together.

John, in fifth grade, described the way a relationship he had with another boy was built around the schedule of their joint enterprise:

> Q: *Do you have any other friends who are not in your grade?*
> JOHN: No. Not close friends. I have Cal Brown, he's on my soccer team and he's in the sixth grade.
> Q: *When do you mostly hang out with him?*
> JOHN: Soccer days, Monday, Wednesday, and Fridays, and soccer games, Saturday.
> Q: *So you might have a date with him after a soccer game or something like that?*
> JOHN: Yes.
> Q: *And is he a good friend?*
> JOHN: No, I just know him from soccer.

Josh, the fifth grader, noted how the casual friendship he had with Will, his neighbor who was usually too busy doing homework to coordinate schedules with him, escalated into more contact during the basketball season, when they were both on teams:

> Q: *So would you say you play with Will more during basketball season?*
> JOSH: Yeah. 'Cause we're always over there practicing. When we're not doing homework, then we're over there playing on his driveway.

Depending on the nature of the activity and the length of the season, individuals spent differing amounts of time with compartmentalized friends. People who participated in year-round pursuits such as music and dance did not experience these seasonal fluctuations in friendships. Others, who rotated from one seasonal activity to another, moved from one friend or set of friends to another over the course of the year. Blake, a fifth grader who was involved in several competitive-level sports, had a group of activities friends with whom he spent a lot of time during each season, in addition to his coterie of close and casual friends at school. His degree of involvement in each of these sports required that he spend considerable time in practices and games, necessitating a great deal of contact with these teammates. Individuals who were only moderately involved in their extracurricular activities did not spend nearly the same amount of time with their coparticipants as did those who were more deeply committed.

This high level of contact and connection sometimes led individuals to develop very warm relationships with activities friends. Kenny, in fourth grade, talked about the closeness and seasonal fluctuation in his friendships with his swim teammates:

Q: *You say another really good friend is on your swim team?*

KENNY: I've got four really good friends from swim team, that I met through swimming.

Q: *Do they go to your school?*

KENNY: No, they live out in Merrill and Smithhaven [nearby towns], and I only see them in the summers.

Q: *During the summer when you are doing the swim team stuff would you say that that's who you mostly hang out with?*

KENNY: Yes.

Q: *What do you do with these guys other than swim with them?*

KENNY: We rollerblade, hang out, have sleepover dates, make plans on the phone. And we're on the relays together, we do stuff like that.

Q: *Do you ever see them in the off season?*

KENNY: No.

Q: *Do you think there is any difference between your friendship with those guys and the guys that go to your school?*

KENNY: No, but I see more of the kids in school. Than summer friends. 'Cause I never get to see my swim friends in the winter, and 'cause summer is only three months and school is nine months. And actually I like my swim team friends more than my school friends. I think that the time we spend together in the summer is closer than the time I spend with my friends in the winter 'cause we're all together a lot more. And we really get to talk.

Ironically, although Kenny saw his swim team friends only during the competitive season, he considered his relationships with these individuals more meaningful than those that he had with his close school friends.

EXPANDED FRIENDSHIPS

Some activities friendships broke through the boundaries of their compartmentalization and moved into the core of individuals' lives. Such friends might see each other outside the days on which their activity occurred and on a year-round basis. They remained rooted in their activity but extended beyond that.

Matt, the fourth grader with the extended neighborhood network, spoke about one of his best friends whom he met through an after-school activity: "One of my really closest friends, Alex Reese, I met at baseball. He goes to Lincoln [another elementary school]. We were on a team together in first grade, and we liked each other, so we started to see each other outside of practices. Then we started to have sleepovers. Now he's one of my best friends. Then last year he wasn't on my team, but this year he is again, and I'm really happy. He's not the only friend I've made in one of my activities, but he's the closest one."

Friendly relations for children in after-school activities progressed from "hanging around" together during practices and trying to get paired together or placed near each other so that they could talk and work together, to making plans to get together at other times and places, to having more frequent and long-lasting arrangements together. Heidi, the fourth grader, mentioned a friendship that she had made through an after-school activity that she was hoping would blossom: "Well, actually I have one person I'm meeting that I think will be a good friend, and she's from a different school and I met her in instrumental music."

Kyle's experience shows that extended activities friendships can even arise on a cross-gender basis. He talked about a friend he made at ice skating lessons: "I ice skated for three years. Figure skated. Then I stopped 'cause I just didn't like it anymore, I wasn't passing any of the tests. I went up to freestyle two, and I just couldn't pass for freestyle three. But we were very good friends, and she's still one of my best friends. I met her through ice skating."

Q: *So she's not your age?*

KYLE: She's like a few years older, like three or four years older.

Q: *When you were friendly with the ice skater, what kinds of things did you and she used to do?*

KYLE: We went to a concert, she likes to come over to my house sometimes, and we like to go to Sandy's Drum Shop together, and things like that.

Q: *So she likes music too?*

KYLE: Yeah. She's a drummer like me. We have a lot in common.

Neighborhood Friends

Some children had compartmentalized friends from the neighborhood whose lives overlapped with their own but who did not even rank as casual friends. They saw and interacted with these others in only limited ways and at circumscribed times. For example, when children were thrust together on the school bus and at other times of obligatory contact, they would often select certain people with whom to associate.[2]

Allison, a fourth grader, mentioned friends with whom she primarily interacted on the trip to school and back: "[They are] not people I would really play with, 'cause we're not really friendly. But we just sort of like to bike to school together and talk. That's about it. Sometimes we pick each other up on the way to school together with our bikes. We sort of just call each other and say, 'Do you want to bike to school?' Otherwise I just take the bus. I sort of like taking the bus. But if the weather is nice, we might bike. But if I take the bus, Samantha, Jenny, and Lorraine are usually on it with me, because they're in my neighborhood. So they're my bike friends, and my bus friends."

Other times individuals made neighborhood friends whom they held to a compartmentalized relationship because they didn't really like them that much. They interacted with them when they were thrust together in the neighborhood or when brought together by other people, but problems in the relationship kept their association from growing beyond its compartmentalized scope.

Becky, the third-grade girl, spoke about a neighborhood girl with whom she had such a relationship: "There's a couple of girls who live on my block. One's Cindy. We play and she's really nice. And another's Kaley. We have a friendship relationship, but sometimes she just turns away from me, 'cause we walk to school together, like this morning, I just, we were talking about flowers, and I said, 'Can a flower get darker than this car?' And she has this really kind of weird personality, and she just turned away from me. And she's done it many times before. And then she tells her mom a whole 'nother story. And so we're friends and so sometimes she just does that, and so sometimes me and Cindy just leave her. And my other friend Katy she walks with us. And they all live close by in my neighborhood."

> Q: *So really, this one that is kind of strange, you mostly see her walking to and from school?*
>
> BECKY: Yeah, sometimes we play, but just sometimes out of the blue she thinks that just she knows everything and she's just a person of the world, like she's the president. She knows everything. And she's done that maybe six times, and she hasn't really, she just does it all the time, and we get really mad at her. 'Cause she just turns away from you and goes like *that*, like she's all, she's just the best. And she's younger than us, and she doesn't know, 'cause we've done that, and we know it's not right. Then when she tells her mom another story, her mom thinks that we're the bad guys. So I try to keep it

down, the amount of time I play with her, 'cause you never know what's going to come of it.

Telephone Friends

Preadolescents varied in their use of the telephone. Some made phone calls only to make arrangements with friends for upcoming activities or to check on their homework. Others, even at a young age, were telephone chatters and would use the phone as a means of contact and entertainment. They called their friends when they were bored and discussed the events of the day, or they played on the phone by calling each other and leaving messages. Sometimes telephone use went through cycles, with children finding it fascinating for a few months and then getting tired of it. The telephone provided a medium, however, through which people could come together who did not feel comfortable associating on a face-to-face basis, or who were not able to be that close. In these kinds of cases, people developed friendships that were compartmentalized to telephone use.[3]

Local telephone friendships often cut across gender lines. Girls and boys found it more comfortable to talk to each other on the phone than to talk in person, despite the greater difficulties of finding things in their immediate surroundings to discuss. Telephone interaction afforded them privacy and confidentiality. They could approach someone of another gender and make plans, inquire about their and others' relationships, and just gab. Maintaining a relationship on the telephone took people away from the potential gossip and ridicule of the peer group, so that they would not be teased about interacting with a boy or a girl. They could also talk for as long as they wanted, without anyone prying into the conversation. Boys and girls often spent their time in the evenings and on weekends, especially weekend nights, talking to each other. This was a way to get to know each other better, and to meet new boys and girls who might be friendly with boys or girls they knew but who attended other schools. Thus, before they were old enough to date, boys and girls engaged in pseudodating on the telephone. Friends even arranged telephone blind dates for each other. Some boys and girls found themselves tongue-tied around members of the other gender in person but were able to ease their anxiety on the telephone. This also afforded them the opportunity to use a variety of conversation-enhancing props, such as preconstructed scripts and silent ghostwriter friends who stood by in the wings to help them through rough spots in the interaction. Telephone relationships between boys and girls stood in a liminal middle point between the casual relationship of platonic friendship and the major commitment of dating. This enabled them to put feelers out to members of the other gender to see if they were interested in them, and if they could carry on a conversation together.

Kevin, a popular fifth-grade boy, talked about the nature of this type of interaction:

> Q: *Do you ever talk to girls on the telephone?*
> KEVIN: Uh huh. I do. Yeah. I have. Actually, in school and on the telephone, that's the only time we conversate [sic], unless I do have a crush on somebody and they like me, then we might do something together. But it's a lot easier working up to that by doing the phone thing for a while first.

Boys took a variety of roles in talking with girl telephone friends. Aside from directly pursuing romantic relationships, and often as a precursor to these, boys approached girls in several less forthright and dangerous ways. Some tried to be a "confidante" to one or more girls, listening to their tales of trouble in their relationships with other girls or boys. They responded sympathetically, gave sensitive advice, and served as friends. Others took on the role of "mediators," going back and forth between one or more people, trying to give advice to both, and helping them work out their problems. Still others played the bon vivant, entertaining large groups of friends, keeping themselves talking on the phone to many different people. Eventually they hoped to work themselves into the kinds of more intimate relationships about which they were counseling, but they planned to move into this more gradually, after they had prepared themselves through these other roles. These types of relationships, platonic and flirtatious, were especially subject to swings and fluctuations, lasting for a few months and then possibly fading out, sometimes replaced by new telephone flirtations, but other times not.

If boys and girls were not talking to cross-gender telephone friends, they were often talking to same-gender friends about individuals of the other gender. This provided endless fodder for conversation , also in the evenings and on weekends.

Tucker, the fifth grader, talked about one such telephone relationship:

> Q: *Are you a big phone guy? [Nods.] Are there any people you talk to on the phone whom you don't play with or see that much?*
> TUCKER: Alex. I don't see him that much, but I talk to him on the phone a ton. More than anyone else.
> Q: *What's so great about him and you on the phone?*
> TUCKER: Because we just joke around. We have forty-five-minute phone

calls, and we just sit and talk because we are bored. Like when we are home alone, we just sit in there and talk because there is nothing else to do.

Q: *What kinds of things do you talk about on the phone?*

TUCKER: Girls.

Preadolescents formed their other main type of telephone relationships with people who lived too far away to be seen in person. These people were not contacted as often, since communication involved long-distance telephone rates, but the calls served to keep a relationship begun in person active and current. Telephone friendships were often maintained with people who had once lived in town but subsequently moved away. Betsy, a fourth grader, mentioned two of her departed telephone friends: "I talk on the phone with my close friends who moved, and I have two really close friends who don't live here any more. With them I talk on the phone because I can't get together with them." Their moving relegated Betsy's friends to the "telephone zone," which became the only place where she was able to reach them.

The other type of out-of-town telephone friends were individuals who never lived in the same town, but whom people met while they were out of town traveling, or who came through town on their travels. These people had always been relegated to a compartmentalized time and place, and the telephone became an extension of that. Tammy, a third-grade girl, discussed the content of her conversations with a telephone friend from another state, with whom she talked every weekend: "We talk about what we're doing at school and what we're kind of doing [with] activities. If we're reading a good book or something like that. If it's getting close to a visit, we talk about that, or a visit that we just had."

Vacation Friends

Summer and holiday periods might offer preadolescents the opportunity to form other types of compartmentalized friendships. Freed from the temporal and spatial commitments of attending school, children had the opportunity to engage in broader kinds of local relationships or make new friends during travels to other locations. Preadolescents extended the range of their activities by taking in-depth lessons, attending camp, visiting friends and family members, and taking vacations. Any of these had the potential to generate new friendships, some of which might carry over into individuals' regular lives, while others remained compartmentalized.

OVERLAPPING FRIENDS

For some children, new friends and activities were not a feature of their non-school periods. With working parents who could not afford to travel or send their children to camps, holiday intervals greatly resembled school lives. They might be sent to day care, fostered with friends or extended kin in the local area, or enrolled in the programs offered at the local public schools. The people they encountered in these activities tended to overlap with those they saw during the school year, offering them the opportunity to extend their network of regular friendships, but not to make compartmentalized ones.

Ellen, the fourth-grade girl, came from a divorced family and explained how one of her close friendships was formed during a summer program at her school: "I met Karen at summer camp in between third and fourth grade."

> Q: *What kind of summer camp?*
> ELLEN: It was a day camp summer camp, you know, like when your parents have to work and you have no where else to go. It was at our school; you sign up one week at a time, but I went for the whole summer. We had already met, and on the first day of summer camp I remembered seeing her on the playground in third grade and I knew we were in the same grade, so we kinda came together 'cause we kinda knew each other, and we just turned out to be really good friends.

Another common pursuit for younger preadolescent children, especially boys, was attendance at week-long sports camps focused on skill development, playing games, and socializing with other youngsters. These camps were fairly stratified by age and gender, so that people were in homogeneous groups. When children were sent to these camps, their parents often coordinated their enrollment so that they would be with known friends. This was a very important feature to younger preadolescents, who were nervous about signing up for things alone and reluctant to take the chance of being caught without guaranteed companionship.

Josh, the third grader who played soccer on the girls' team, discussed the composition of his summers: "[I] go swimming, play baseball, football, do a bunch of sports."

> Q: *Is that something that is organized, or do you just do it casually?*
> JOSH: I go to camps. Some soccer, some baseball, some football, and that's about all.
> Q: *Do you ever meet any kids there?*

JOSH: Well, not really, although there are always kids there that I don't know. But I usually don't meet them because I always sign up with friends of mine from school, and we just hang around with each other.

When children's summers included activities that were structured like year-round activities, the friendships fostered were apt to be age and gender stratified, just as school friendships were.

LOCAL FRIENDS

Preadolescents also pursued other kinds of unstructured activities in the local area over summers and vacations that put them into contact with a demographically wider range of people. For individuals who were not enrolled in weekly camps, neighborhood friends, who could be seen without parental transportation or assistance, rose in prominence. Members of these cross-age and gender groups emerged from their homes and found other similar groups with whom they might join for more complex and challenging play. This could be spontaneous, involving bike riding, exploring, playground games, fantasy or role play, or other types of "hanging out," or it might entail organizing a sports game.

Local neighborhood games sprang up in particular locations that were conducive for use as playing fields, and people who wanted to participate wandered down there when they saw individuals starting to assemble. Other people often joined in as well who were sleeping over, who could ride their bikes over, or who were called and invited over for the purpose of a game. One group of mostly boys became so engrossed in their daily summer game of baseball that they decided to organize a series. They chose up teams to last for the whole series (adding newcomers who arrived to play on different days only if they could substitute for regulars who were absent) and kept track of the scores in all their games. This running baseball game, which lasted in one incarnation or another for the duration of one summer, was composed of boys spanning a four-year age range and included several girls as well. Another group of neighborhood boys, a mixed-age group who had not previously bridged their age boundaries for any amount of serious play, bonded over the summer into a larger community of friends, any of whom could collect and assemble for play, depending on who was available. For the summer period the norm discouraging younger boys from phoning older boys was suspended, boys of different ages had overnight dates together, they invited each other to birthday parties, and the boys played freely together, in the large group or in smaller groups of twos or threes. At the end of the summer, when school began, they separated once again into their age-segregated boundaries and withdrew from their summer relationships. Both of these groups offered people a range of compartmentalized friendships with others whom they would not normally befriend during the school year and whom they ceased to associate with once the school year began, even as neighborhood friends. When the summer returned, they turned to the neighborhood once again to seek out those compartmentalized friendships.

LONG-DISTANCE FRIENDS

Compartmentalized vacation relationships existed among people who lived in different cities. Time away from school afforded people the opportunity to reconnect with former friends who had moved out of town.

Marsha, a fourth-grade girl, described the way she resurrected the closeness of her friendships with two friends who had moved, one to a nearby town and the other to another state (Florida): "Well, I try to [keep in touch with them], but it's kind of hard because it's a long drive and it's hard to do a lot of stuff. But usually in the summer time, during the school year we're not real close, but in the summertime we get better acquainted. We play a lot together and do a lot of overnights."

> Q: *And your friend from Florida, do you ever hear from her?*
> MARSHA: Yeah, whenever I go down there, 'cause I visit Florida a lot, 'cause a lot of my family's there. Like cousins and stuff. Yeah, I call her up and sometimes we see each other. So, when we see each other we're friends because we always write to each other. We send each other letters.

Such friendships could be resurrected not only when people traveled to visit their friends, but when friends came back to visit their former homes. People who came from out of town to spend their summers in the local areas might also be befriended as well. Children met these visitors through friends and relatives, at local camps and structured activities, in their neighborhoods, and at local parks or out in public.

Individuals also formed compartmentalized friendships with new people they met while traveling or attending camps or other programs out of town.[4] Some met children of or near their age when they went on family vacations to resort areas, keeping in touch with them over the rest of the year. Families who annually returned to the same vacation spots might regularly see other families and their children with similar patterns. This particularly applied to families who had vacation homes or time-shares near other families with children. Some families returned to their extended kinship area for long summer visits or sent their children without them for protracted periods, where children might form summer friends. Emily, in fourth grade, discussed how she kept in touch with the summer friends she had made while staying at her grandmother's house in Connecticut: "By phone. I write letters to them too. And I go out to Connecticut where my grandma lives most every summer, and so I can see them when I go there." Many children were offered the opportunity to see their summer or vacation friends every year, and to form deep friendships. Several children had close circles of friends that they spent their summers with year after year, growing up together. Like local summer friends, these compartmentalized relationships were apt to stray across age and gender boundaries.

Older preadolescents often graduated from spending their summers at home, hanging around the house and playing with local or neighborhood friends and going to local week-long camps, to attending summer-long camps or going on travel trips. Some went to dude ranches in the upper plains, others went to camps in the mountains where they learned camping, river rafting, horseback riding, and other mountain pursuits, others went to more traditional sports or multipurpose camps, while others attended camps focusing on one specialized pursuit such as drama, a sport, or service to a community. Rhonda, a sixth-grade girl, indicated that she planned to take such a trip with a long-distance family friend: "This summer I'm actually going to go on a trip with a friend. A friend from my parents that's younger than me."

In these environments, people forged deep, compartmentalized friendships. A summer spent away from home, in the primary company of peers, for an extended period, offered older preadolescents the opportunity to explore their feelings about themselves, their developing awareness of feelings about members of the other gender, beginning feelings of independence and self-sufficiency, and relationships with adults who were neither teachers, nor coaches, nor parents. Such programs were often geared toward preadolescents developing skills and experiences that promoted feelings of self-sufficiency and self-esteem. Participants drew on the friends they developed to explore these changes within themselves.

Denise, in sixth grade, explained why her summer friendships were particularly important to her: "The summer trips that my parents have sent me on have been really important to me in my life. For me, they're an opportunity to get away and get enough distance on my life here, and that takes a while, it doesn't just happen the first week that I am out there. But usually by about the middle of the summer I am away from my regular life and my regular friends enough that I can get some distance on them. And that gives me a chance to think about my regular life. What kind of person I want to be, what kinds of friends I want to have. And I get into long talks with my summer friends about all these kinds of things. So we get really close. And then when I get home, all my regular friends never get into conversations like the ones we had in the summer. They seem so shallow. All they talk about is school or people. And it takes me a while to get back into that."

These time-out periods provided safer havens for people to share secret feelings about themselves and their lives than they found in their regular home environments. The friendships they developed on vacations were predicated on such reflectiveness and were often more intimate than everyday ones. Holding such friendships in an idealized state of closeness was consequently easier over the remainder of the year, where they were not subject to the wear and tear of normal pettiness, and where they could be maintained by occasional phone calls or letters. Vacation relations varied greatly in character from casual to very close.

Family Friends and Relatives

Family friends and relatives who lived distant could become compartmentalized friends, often very close ones. Family trips took on a special quality because of the precious resources they expended in time and money. These trips were not made frivolously, then, but taken only to visit people with whom the family felt very close. All members of the families visited could become preadolescent children's friends, whether they were adults or children, but children established special bonds with one another. Distant family friends and relatives were likely to be age and gender diverse. The closest relationships usually formed, however, among children of the same gender, with closeness in age being a secondary factor. Children who were distant family friends or relatives could keep in touch regularly, writing to each other, speaking on the phone when their families called, and seeing each other on visits. They often had friends or family members in common that they saw more frequently, who conveyed news about them to each other, thereby enhancing the link.

Becky talked about her compartmentalized friendship with a girl who was a year older than she: "My mom, her best friend, she has a daughter, but she lives in New Jersey, and of course she goes to another school.

Q: *So do you ever see her?*

BECKY: Um hum. I'm going to go and visit her this summer. And she came to visit me last summer.

Q: *And so do you just play with her when you see her, or do you write to her or talk to her on the telephone?*

BECKY: I write to her and I talk to her. And we play when I see her.

Some children had even closer compartmentalized friendships. Mark, by sixth grade, had known Jamie, the son of his parents' close friends, who was a year younger than he, for five or six years. Jamie's older sister, Marcie, attended college near where Mark lived and came by his house to visit. When Mark's parents went out of town, Marcie usually moved in to take care of his sister and him. They talked about Jamie a great deal, and about the kinds of things Jamie was doing. When Marcie went home for visits, she often carried notes between Mark and Jamie. Mark usually went to visit Jamie in the summer for a week, either by himself or with his parents. Sometimes they enrolled together in basketball camp there. When Mark's family went on vacations, they invited Jamie to join them. Although Mark had other friends at school, he considered Jamie his best friend. He made it clear that if anything ever happened to him, he wanted Jamie to get his sport card collection. Mark and Jamie's relationship occasionally had some difficulties, especially when they were visiting each other at their homes and had to deal with other local friends, but Mark's and Jamie's parents usually intervened to help make sure they smoothed over the rough spots and got things worked out. Their friendship, although compartmentalized to the times they could see and speak to each other, was familiar and trusting.

Relatives could constitute the same kinds of friends, when families visited regularly and the children liked each other. Mariah, the popular fifth-grade girl who was involved with sports, described one set of her cousins as close compartmentalized friends:

Q: *Have you visited enough with these kids that you know them fairly well?*
MARIAH: Yes, we really know our cousins; we go over there every
    Thanksgiving.
Q: *Where do they live?*
MARIAH: In Nebraska. We have five cousins there, Andrew, Jason,
    Keeny, Naomi, and Sean. Sean's really old. He just graduated from
    high school, and he's going to go to college. Naomi's in high school.
    She's about my sister's age, one year older. Keeny's my age. And the
    rest are younger. Andrew's small. He just started kindergarten. And
    Jason's in first or second grade, I forget which.
Q: *So you look forward to getting together with those cousins?*
MARIAH: Yes, a lot. Even though we don't see each other that much, we
    like each other. We go to places, we watch TV there, we do things,
    we talk.

CHILDREN THUS had the most complex and varied types of relationships with their compartmentalized friends, finding them both near and far, among family members and friends, of the same age and gender and different, and having anywhere from casual to best friend relationships. These relationships were special because they were not evoked everyday but were held in abeyance in people's minds and hearts.

Friendship Patterns

Preadolescents had various types of friends, ranging from their core, close friends to their more superficial acquaintanceships. Close friends tended to have age, gender, and interests in common, and to maintain regular and deep contact. Less close friends tended to drift away from these commonalities, yet they occupied children's lives, providing substance and contact. The most idiosyncratic relationships were the segmented ones, falling into the overlapping circles of children's lives and varying enormously in their quality and character. Examination of these diverse sets of relationships and the patterns that connect and underlie them yields some further insight into their influence on the character of children's lives.

ADDITIVE NATURE

Children's lives overlapped each other in a variety of ways: temporally, spatially, by gender, by age, by interests, and by common friends and relatives. Individuals whose lives intersected with each other in only minor ways tended to regard each other only peripherally. Those with significant and multiple (at least two) overlaps—in such critical domains as school, residential propinquity, extracurricular participation, and familial friendship—were most likely to forge stronger bonds. These overlaps provided greater opportunities for contact and forged the commonalities in interest that gave people shared areas for interrelating.

STRATIFICATION

Preadolescents varied enormously in the amount and types of friends that they had. Some individuals were awash in friends, getting frequent calls for social activities and finding many avenues where they could turn for both intimacy and companionship. Others had a narrower range of choice. Still others searched more desperately for friends with whom they could either play or talk. Certain patternings existed, stratifying the children with greater quantities and qualities of friends from those in more lonely situations.

At the top of the hierarchy were those children who had ample numbers of close *and* casual friends. They never had to worry about spending their time alone when they wanted something to do. Ellen, the popular fourth grader with the large circle of friends, described the way she might cast about if she wanted to find a close friend to spend the night: "It just depends. There could be a bunch of people. 'Cause let's say you call one person and she can't make it; you can always call another person. There's always at least one person, almost always, that's available."

Tucker, the popular fifth-grade boy with many different types of friends, explained why he thought people in the popular group acquired an abundance and variety of friendships: "Well, some of the patterns are, most people, some people look up to me, I guess, 'cause I'm popular and I'm good at sports. And some people say that. I don't know. I guess people, if you're good at sports, or they see you're good at something, generally you'll have more friends I guess. 'Cause you'll have your good friends from your clique, and then you'll have the other kinds of people who look up to you who are your more secondary kinds of friends."

Tucker also explained how the top stratum of people acquired casual friends in addition to their close companions: "Well, I really don't know. Probably get them, I've gotten a lot of casual friends 'cause my friends introduce me to other friends. And I've just every year, maybe there's just a couple of new kids, or somebody, I try, like if there's somebody that I haven't gotten along with, I try to make friends with them, make peace with them, because sometimes that works out and I have a good friendship."

Popular people were surrounded by a tight circle of close friends within their clique and a looser circle of casual friends. The latter included people they met through other friends or people who looked up to them because of their popularity. Mariah, a popular fifth grader, reflected on some of the problems associated with having such a large group of both casual and close friends: "I have so many different kinds of friends that I kind of have to measure myself out so that people don't get jealous. Like my friends might get jealous if I was hanging out with somebody that didn't hang out with the clique. Like if I was just hanging out with her all the time. Then that wouldn't be good or accepted, or whatever."

Beyond the popular people, who had many and varied friends, were those with *close* friends who occupied the next lower stratum. They did not have as many casual friends as the higher-up people, but they still had a core of close friends. Kyle, the fifth grader, analyzed these friendship patterns in the following way: "I would say more people that don't have as many friends have more good friends than casual friends. Because that's just the way life is. When they start closing down, the casual friends are the first to go, because they don't have as much of a following. You're always going to have at least one really good friend that you can talk to about anything. Practically."

Paul, the third grader who had only two close friends, compared his friendship situation to that of his favorite friend, Bruce. He often was unable to arrange to play with Bruce, who had many more friends than he, and who had a busier social schedule. As he put it: "[Bruce] has a lot of friends. I don't have much. Don't have the team friends." The popular Bruce thus had the outer layer of friends that Paul lacked, the team friends, who mostly likely were casual friends. Paul had his close friends but lacked casual friendships. This was the common pattern characterizing the people in the nonpopular middle friendships circles. This pattern was articulated by Becky, a popular third grader, and echoed by Kevin, a popular fifth grader:

> Q: *And what about the not-so-popular kids?*
> BECKY: It seems like they never have anybody to play with. They're always walking around alone or with one friend at recess.
> Q: *And what about the kids who are not as popular? Do they have the same kinds of friendships that you do?*
> KEVIN: A little bit, but they are a lot surer of them. Like they're the action hero thing, and talk about cartoons and stuff. And they have like two or three people and they just walk around and talk with them, basically. They have fewer number, but they still have as close and loyal friends.

Despite the belief of Kyle and many other people that everyone had at least one good friend on which he or she could rely, this was not necessarily true. People at the bottom of the friendship hierarchy lacked close friendships altogether and had to make do with only *casual* friends. They wanted, often desperately, to have close friends, but they were unable to make them. Often, they were able to form close friendships with one individual or were let into a friendship group, but these relationships did not seem to last. The friends they made dropped them and moved on to other choices, and the groups that had let them in at first demoted them to the lowest status, then made it so unpleasant for them that they withdrew altogether. These individuals were left with compartmentalized friends only, clinging to their vacation and family friends for closeness, and finding compartmentalized relationships with school friends, neighborhood friends, and activities friends, who would associate with them while they were there, but had no interest in seeing them outside those settings.

Matt, a popular fourth-grade boy, offered his view of the social situation of people that he considered "smart but nerdy": "They're not really liked, but they still play soccer or basketball or stuff. They don't really have a clique. All they have is situational friends. And then they try to get into the clique and stuff, and they say, 'Ah ho, ho' and they laugh and stuff, but it doesn't do anything. It doesn't matter; they don't get into the clique or anything."

Wes, an unpopular fifth-grade boy, explained what it felt like to be in this situation:

> Q: *And so does it make you feel bad that you don't have more friends?*
> WES: Yeah, kind of in a way, because I would like to have more friendships around here to make it easier in school in case I need help with other things. Of course Mr. Clark's always there to help me that way so I'm usually always taken care of, by myself. Or if I need help, I usually get it from my roommate in my desk group; that's my helper there. I can get help from them; it's just that I never really have any friendships in that way.

The hierarchy of friendship thus aligned closely with the hierarchy of status, enriching the well endowed and impoverishing the needy.

SOCIAL DIFFERENTIATION

Children's friendships evolved over time. Younger children tended to make friends with whoever was nearby. At the youngest ages, being a child was enough to qualify someone as a candidate for friendship. Preschoolers' best friends were the members of their play groups and the children of their parents' best friends. Such relationships were based on quantity of contact: they were the people whom children saw most. These early friendships carried over for a time and were especially reported by the third graders as salient. Over the course of the preadolescent years, however, the criteria for friendship tended to shift, with propinquity giving way to shared interests. No longer did children select their closest friends on the basis of quantity of contact, but they became increasingly discriminating, placing more importance on the quality of those contacts. Being nearby and being available diminished in importance, and having status, popularity, or shared interests rose to prominence. With these changed emphases, children came to gradually shed their earlier friends with whom they shared propinquity and family but not immediate currency, and to reformulate their circles of friends.

Concomitant with this trend was a rise in social differentiation (Simmel 1959). During children's early years, their circles of friendship were highly overlapped. Their close friendships tended to fall into the broad area in which school, neighborhood, and/or family friends and relatives coincided. Many of their relationships had these multiply additive characteristics. Just as their time and relationships were preoccupied in these minimally differentiated spheres, their identities were similarly encompassed: they saw themselves as the composition of these overlapped spheres. However, as preadolescents moved toward the latter years of this period, they increasingly branched out, separating themselves from their earlier groups and establishing new reference groups. They opted for more and greater participation in extracurricular activities, including those in which their school friends were not involved. They became more reluctant to attend family gatherings and maintain friendships with cousins and other family members with whom they did not particularly have anything in common. They met friends on summer vacations who were not part of any other reference group. In this way they separated and differentiated their social circles and established more distinct facets of their selves and identities. This increase in social differentiation reflects the increase in the peer orientation of children as they approach adolescence, and their overall rise in power over the same period.

The role of friendships in the peer culture was mixed. Friendships contributed to the status stratification of preadolescents, since having a greater quantity and quality (high prestige) of friends was associated with being ranked higher and feeling better. Yet, at the same time, friendship served as one of the great equalizers: having friends, no matter what their status, generated a positive social experience and made people feel good. Since nearly all children had friends of some sort, friendship was one of the great safety nets or levelers in the informal peer culture.

Chapter 8

Cross-Gender Relations: The Early and Middle Years

SOME OF THE friendships discussed in the previous two chapters reached across the gender divide, although many did not. Gender represents a fascinating theme in the study of preadolescence, for children react vehemently and differently to members of the other gender during the years leading up to this age period, during it, and during those leading away from it. In this chapter and the next, we trace the development of cross-gender platonic and romantic relations, noting both the dominant patterns and the significant variations. Most scholars have emphasized the separation of preadolescent boys and girls into discrete gendered cultures and worlds.[1] But while we note this gender divide, it is not the only form of boy-girl interaction we observed. Cross-gender relations were characterized by three distinct stages, during which girls and boys were alternately integrated, separated, and reconnected. Beyond these normative patterns, children thought about and made excursions toward members of the other gender in direct and indirect ways. These stages occurred during the three age periods we refer to as the early, the middle, and the later years, comprising (roughly and with some overlap) preschool and first grade, second through third grade, and fourth through sixth grade.

Gender Integration: The Early Years

Children began their early lives and their education with a much greater attitude of gender neutrality than they later developed. Although they experienced intensive gender socialization and labeling as infants, they remained fairly open to cross-gender friendships throughout the preschool and earliest of elementary school years (Oswald et al. 1987; Voss 1997).[2] As we noted in chapter 6, when children were very young, the primary determinant of someone's suitability for friendship was propinquity: a nearby child was acceptable as a friend. Young children thus readily acquiesced to forming play groups and to spending time with relatives, neighbors, and family friends selected by their parents based on their availability.[3]

FRIENDSHIP PATTERNING

When they entered into the preschool and early elementary years, children brought with them a strong gender awareness. They were learning the role parameters of their gender and experimenting with gender-varied clothing, role modeling, and identification. For instance, when Stacey was four, she cast off her jeans and shirts, and wore nothing but dresses for the whole year. Five-year-old Mark carefully noted aloud each time he encountered an occupation that seemed to be male- or female-associated, fixing these patterns in his mind. Yet children at this stage, ranging in age from three to six and educationally located between prekindergarten and first grade, were socially open to gender in ways that they might not be later. They were somewhat more likely to socialize with members of their own gender, but there was little stigma attached to cross-gender companionship. When Katy was in kindergarten she mostly played with girls, but she also had two friends from school who were boys. She and her male friends would spend time together at school, but they would also make arrangements to play together at home, after school, or on the weekends.

Other girls leaned more heavily toward cross-gender friendships. Betsy, in third grade, described her current attitude toward boys, comparing it with the way she used to feel when she was younger: "Brett, he and I used to be best friends, but then he sat on my stomach at my friend's birthday party, was squeezing me, like he was trying to kill me. And now we're just not friends. But we still talk. Or like Matt, we used to be best friends. There was a period of time in kindergarten and preschool where I only liked boys, and I wouldn't go hang out with girls, and then now I can't stand boys except my dad." As Betsy noted, the openness toward cross-gender friendships that predominated in the early school years was temporally bounded. Children's ease of interactions and lack of self-consciousness about playing with members of the other gender did not last.

Paul, the third grader with few friends, offered his recollections about the age demarcations that changed boys' and girls' friendship relations:

Q: *So do you think it's kind of common for boys and girls to be friends, or it's not that common?*
PAUL: Um, I don't think, it depends what grade you're talking about. Like this grade, it's not that common I don't think. Other grades . . .

Q: *Older grades or younger grades?*

PAUL: Well, mostly really old grades. Really old grades and really young grades, 'cause young grades it's just like a bunch of kids who really, like the whole class, like, likes each other, they just look for friends to call and play with. Sometimes that's what it's like with very small kids, they have girlfriends, a lot of people for friends. In the second grade I don't really think it's like that, but when you get really old I think you could have a girlfriend.

Preschool and early elementary school children's cross-gender friendships were thus mostly comfortable and unself-conscious, not rigidly marked by gender boundaries.[4] Children played along mixed lines, unrestricted by cultural roles or norms prohibiting such interaction.

ROMANTIC ALTERNATIVES

Young preadolescents did not usually interact with each other in a romantic or sexualized way. This was something they associated with their parents or older siblings, but not with themselves. There was not a complete lack of interest, however, and every group contained modes of behavior for selected boys and girls to explore this area. Some boys and girls were more regularly interested in dabbling with romance or sexuality, while others became drawn into it from time to time or seasonally, when such pursuits developed momentum. At times this romantic interest was held privately, without being shared among friends.

Nancy, the fifth-grade girl, recalled with embarrassment her early desire for a boyfriend and the way she simulated romantic attachment to one of her classmates:

Q: *Have you ever had any interest in boys, kind of a boyfriend type of thing?*

NANCY: Uh, yeah. In kindergarten I wanted to like somebody, and so I just picked somebody and said to myself, "Okay, I like you."

Q: *And so what kinds of things did you do with him?*

NANCY: Nothing. I didn't show it in any way, I didn't tell anybody about it. I just said, "Okay, I like him." And that was that. I have no idea why I did that. It's embarrassing now to think of that.

Marcia, when she was in kindergarten, decided she liked one of the boys in her class and told her friends about it. This was a boy with whom she was friends, and with whom she used to play frequently. She never spoke to him about these thoughts, though. She never allowed it to surface in their interaction, keeping it a secret.

Children rarely spoke openly of romantic feelings for age mates, generally acting toward their peers only as friends. The behavior that offered a generalized exception to this was the chasing and kissing games, which provided a way for children to more openly explore cross-gendered romantic expressions.[5] In these games, groups of boys and girls ran after each other and chased groups or individuals of the other gender. Such games varied in nature, but the object was to chase or be chased. When individuals got close to getting caught, they often turned around and reversed the roles, chasing rather than being chased. When people actually got caught, they sometimes were kissed, but usually the chasers lost their nerve and just backed away or pushed them. Other games were more elaborate, involving locking up the apprehended individuals in makeshift jails. Delivering or receiving an actual kiss, however, was the most exciting outcome to an exhilarating chase.

John, a fifth-grade boy, looked back nostalgically on his first kiss: "Some boys like some girls right now, and I think it started about first grade, that boys started liking girls. That's when me and my friend got our first kiss."

Q: *How'd that happen?*

JOHN: Um, Alex, a girl in our grade, she was one of the "kissing girls." She was always chasing the boys and trying to kiss them. Me and Travis thought this was fun. We would chase the girls too. But one day we wanted to see what would happen if we let her catch us. So we ran down behind the slides area, and we slowed down so she could catch us. No one else was around. So she caught us, and she gave us each kisses. Then we ran away.

Chasing and kissing games, then, were not practiced by all members of the grade, only the "kissing girls" and "kissing boys."[6] This ensured that people who were not willing participants did not get molested. People signaled their interest in entering the game through previous participation, or by running away and looking back or shouting and jeering at members of the other gender.

Kevin, a fifth grader, spoke of his experiences with chasing and kissing, offering his estimate of the extent of the participation:

Q: *When do people start getting interested in the opposite sex?*

KEVIN: It really depends. Like for me it started in first grade. Some I'm sure haven't started until third grade. But I definitely started in first grade.

Q: *And what were your early experiences?*

KEVIN: Boys chase girls, girls chase boys. And like, "You know who I have a crush on?" and stuff.

Q: *At that age is everyone into the chasing stuff and the liking stuff, or is it just a certain portion of them?*

KEVIN: Thirty percent or something, not very much.

Children in the preschool or early elementary school years generally interacted readily, then, both within and across gender groups for platonic friendship. More romantic interest and interactions were restricted by peer norms to games of chasing and kissing. Children participating in such games were generally the more precocious and popular individuals, those who had more friends and more visibility in the grade. Individuals did not feel free to express any other forms of romantic interest.

Gender Segregation: The Middle Years

Once they were firmly settled in elementary school, children moved into the stage of strict gender separation. This generally began in about first or second grade and lasted until fourth or fifth grade. Like Paul, who noted the difference between the way children interacted with members of the other gender at the "really young grades" and the "really old grades," most children were aware of this patterned movement into and out of contact with members of the other gender.

Kenny, the fifth grader, reflected back on the phases of gender relations through which he and his friends had passed:

Q: *Do you think that it is common that most boys of your age are not as good friends with girls?*

KENNY: Yes, we don't hang out with any girls. We are like a different race from them.

Q: *Thinking back when you were younger, when you were little, did you used to be friendly with girls?*

KENNY: Yes. I had a couple of friends who were girls.

Q: *When did you think that boys and girls separated out of the same race?*

KENNY: 'Bout second to fourth grade.

Kenny marked the main boundaries of the middle period, where boys and girls "separated out of the same race," noting that boys and girls were generally not friendly with each other during this time.

INTERESTS AND ACTIVITIES

One of the primary reasons boys and girls separated into different races and ceased to interact with each other on a friendly basis was that their interests sharply diverged.[7] Boys and girls moved into highly gendered worlds where their concerns and recreational activities were different (see Thorne 1986). Boys pursued sports, fantasy card games, sport card collecting, and rough-and-tumble play, while girls engaged in relationship building and intimacy work, dressing up, playing with dolls, and pursuing dance, art, and gymnastics.[8] Paul, the third grader, supported the notion of different interests as the source of the chasm between boys and girls: "Well in the middle grades boys have other friends, and they think that girls aren't that, they don't really like them all that much unless the boys like dolls or something." With few overlapping interests, boys and girls had little to do with each other, aside from school activities. They were engaged in developing gendered groups and identities that left little room for transgression.

Craig, the third grader, indicated the rarity of boy-girl friendships:

Q: *Are there many boys and girls who are friendly?*
CRAIG: Not many. I have one girl that I'm friendly with, Adair.
Q: *What kinds of things might you and Adair do at school together?*
CRAIG: Well, I usually play with my friends that are boys, and she usually plays with her friends that are girls.

ATTITUDES TOWARD THE OTHER GENDER

During this phase of gender segregation, boys and girls tended to lose the positive feelings they had toward each other. At best, they regarded each other neutrally. At worst, they moved into the "cooties" stage, thinking of each other as contaminated (Thorne 1993).

Kyra, the third grader, expressed the negative perspective that girls at this stage commonly held toward boys. This included a lack of interest in romantic attitudes as well as platonic ones:

Q: *Do girls of your age have any interest in boys?*
KYRA: Not really. We don't like boys.
Q: *Do you think any of the guys in your class are cute?*
KYRA: Um mum. They're more annoying.
Q: If they're annoying, what kinds of annoying things do they do?
KYRA: Well, Colin falls out of his chair purposely, they're always talking, so they could be called jitterboxes instead of boys, and they talk too much, and they're just annoying.

Like Kyra, most girls regarded boys as violent, uncouth, dirty, and mean-spirited. Boys were disgusting and had nothing that would interest girls in them.[9]

Seth, a third grade boy from the popular crowd at another school, reinforced Kyra and Brett's sentiments, expressing disdain for members of the other gender:

Q: *Do you have any friends who are girls?*

SETH: I used to have one back in second grade, last year. But she just like started to say well, "I don't like you because I want to be with my friends," and I bet her friends just started saying, "Oh my god, you're playing with him?"

Q: *What would be wrong with being friends with you?*

SETH: People would say, "You're friends with the opposite sex!"

Q: *But you're not really friendly with girls?*

SETH: They're okay. Sometimes they can be nice. Sometimes they can be just sort of dorks.

Q: *And so just as far as just liking girls, do you have a little bit of interest, or no interest?*

SETH: None of my friends has any interest. No interest.

Seth's remarks indicate the presence of a second factor influencing the contours of boy-girl relations: the peer culture. During this period, boys and girls began to frown on cross-gender associations and delivered informal negative sanctions to each other for violating these boundaries. Such attitudes were more powerful among the popular boy crowds than in the less popular middle circles, and in the middle girl friendship circles than among the more precocious girls, but they set the tone for the entire grade.

ALTERNATIVES: FRIENDLY CONTACT

While the predominant mode of social life involved gender segregation, there were patterned exceptions. Cross-gender relationships inside school were harder to maintain due to peer pressure, leaving middle elementary school students with more cross-gender family and neighborhood friends than those from school. Some boys and girls who had been close friends during the younger years managed to retain their friendships, however. In addition, there were times when groups of girls or boys drifted together for occasional play. These group interactions were usually oriented around play rather than relationships and were short-lived. More lasting cross-gender friendships were usually pursued on an individual basis. Several people indicated that they were the type who had kept close friends of the other gender during the years of segregation. This was often the case with girls who enjoyed playing sports. Yet playing with boys did not necessarily mean establishing friendships.

Lauren, a fourth-grade girl, talked about her friendships with several boys:

"I've always been a girl who's had boys as friends. My boy friends are all in my grade. I've known them since last year when I moved here. And also I don't keep in touch with my boy friends that are from New York, but I do have a few there." She had a hard time describing the basis for these relationships, however. When asked what kinds of things she might talk to her boy friends about, she replied, "Not much. I can't think of anything."

Meaningful relationships did exist among boys and girls during the years of separation, although they were rare. They were not found in every grade in every school, but rather more occasionally. These could take two forms: individuals with incidental cross-gender friends, or "crossovers," who lodged most of their friends in the other gender.

Tammy, the third grader, talked about one of her two best friends, a boy who displayed this crossover pattern: "I have a friend named Jimmy, and he's one of my best friends because he's in my class at school and also he lives close to me. And I go over to his house a lot and we play with his dogs, and sometimes we go to the park and take hikes, and we watch movies. And we don't do as much as I do with my other friends 'cause there's not as much I can do with him 'cause I can't play dress-ups. But sometimes he'll let me dress him up as a girl, and he doesn't care; he just puts on dresses and high heels. And he'll go downstairs and say, 'Hey, I'm a girl!'"

> Q: And does he have any other girl friends?
> TAMMY: Yeah, me, Annie, and him are like really close friends. Usually we're never apart, we usually all just play together.
> Q: And how is it for Jimmy to be friendly with you two girls, among the boys?
> TAMMY: Uh, he can't stand boys. He's really mellow, he's not wild, and he doesn't like playing soccer, basketball. And he's really weird, and we made up our secret language, we just say everything backwards. And he doesn't really care 'cause, well he's friends with other boys, but he just thinks they're too wild; he's really calm.

Drew, another third grader from the same school, spoke of a crossover girl who held a similar place in the boys' community as Jimmy did in the girls':

> Q: What sorts of things would be things that girls and guys could play at?
> DREW: Well, sometimes in PE, girls and guys do jump rope and play tag. Well, Cindy is sort of like the person on the boys' side, and Jimmy is sort of like the person on the girls' side. He likes to play with the girls a lot, and the girls like to play with him a lot.
> Q: And what do the boys think of Jimmy?
> DREW: We like him too; it's just he likes playing with the girls more than the boys.

Q: *So you don't think he's weird or anything because he plays on the girls' side?*
DREW: No. He's just regular.
Q: *And what about Cindy?*
DREW: She's just regular too.

While these platonic "crossovers" (see Thorne 1993) were accepted fairly nonchalantly, romantic cross-gender relationships constituted a more serious breach. Different friendship patterns could also be discerned between boys and girls. The higher-status boys were the most reluctant to form cross-gender associations, attaching a strong stigma to companionship with girls. Popular girls were not as adamant in their rejection of boys, although they generally had little to do with them. This may have been due to the romantic aspects of girls' gendered culture, generating some measure of acceptance for boy-girl connections. Less popular boys were freer to have a more positive attitude toward girls, since they had less to lose in status or in their friendship circles by associating with them. Lower-status girls had as little interest in crossing the gender divide as did the popular boys, being firmly rooted in their girls-only world.

ALTERNATIVES: CHASING AND TEASING

During the middle elementary school years the interactions between boys and girls were the most problematic. Beyond the large-scale gap were chasms of awkwardness and misunderstanding. Boys and girls were unsure of how to relate to each other, had uncertain spurts of interest in each other, and alternated these with strong negative feelings about each other. Part of membership in boys' and girls' gendered cultural worlds involved expressing and enacting hostility toward the opposing group. This happened between individuals and groups, involving teasing and deriding. The chasing and kissing games of the early years were replaced by a more mean-spirited gender play. Some of the excitement of the chase remained, but the outcome was more frequently tinged with hurt and injury.

Nancy, the fifth-grade girl, recalled that in first grade a group of boys tried to catch girls and make them eat grasshoppers. She viewed this behavior as cruel and degrading, with the boys taking advantage of the girls.

Betsy, the third grader, noted that teasing and negative interaction were not the exclusive domain of boys. Girls, too, acted mean to boys they did not like. She described one of her friends who teased boys a lot: "She'll just yell to them. Sometimes, even, to get on their nerves. Like when they're playing basketball, she likes getting on their nerves. And she does that very easily. She's very good at it, and sometimes, like, when I'm mad at somebody, like sometimes I get mad at Brett, and so I'll go up to him and I'll take his hat and throw it. And I do that a lot."

Q: *Do you mostly do these things to boys that you kind of like, then?*
BETSY: Well, boys that I can be around, but I don't really like them.

Many instances of chasing and teasing arose between boys and girls who disliked each other. At other times, this manifest dislike was tempered with a sexual tension or interest that lingered just below the surface. Finding no acceptable outlet in the peer culture, boys and girls channeled their feelings into the culturally approved chasing and teasing behavior.

Travis, a fifth-grade boy, reflected back on the chasing experiences of his friends during the middle years:

Q: *Did boys ever act differently toward girls whom they kind of like?*
TRAVIS: Yeah, they acted bossy. Like they were kings and stuff. Some boys I remember would tease girls, and they'd play this weird chasing game.
Q: *How did the chasing game work?*
TRAVIS: I think they'd chase girls and they'd catch them.
Q: *What would happen if they'd catch them?*
TRAVIS: I don't know. I think they'd put them in jail or something.
Q: *And did the girls ever chase them back?*
TRAVIS: I think so. I don't know.
Q: *Are chasing games mostly played by boys and girls that kind of like each other?*
TRAVIS: I don't know. I never was a chasing boy.
Q: *And so who were the chasing boys?*
TRAVIS: Some of my old friends in my other classes.
Q: *And would you say that these are boys who are more or less popular?*
TRAVIS: A little more popular.
Q: *And would you say these are boys who are more interested in girls or not interested in girls?*
TRAVIS: Interested.
Q: *What happened to the chasing games?*
TRAVIS: Well in third grade, I think in third grade there was a little. In fourth grade we didn't do it at all.
Q: *What did boys in fourth grade do toward girls who they liked?*
TRAVIS: I think they just thought they had cooties and didn't talk to them.

Travis's comments again raise the issue of status and cross-gender behavior. Popular boys, those who were the least likely to have girls as friends, were the most likely to participate in chasing and teasing games. They expressed their interest in girls, whether it came out as negative or positive, through this safe and acceptable venue, and it was accepted by girls as such. Although they were occasionally hurt, the popular girls continued to participate in these chasing and teasing games.[10]

Unpopular boys, in contrast, departed from these gender role norms and more readily expressed their romantic attraction for girls. As the case of Roger, the third-grade isolate, illustrates, this was often met with more severe reactions. Betsy explained: "Well, there is a boy, Roger, and he'd get on the girls' nerves, he'd be kissing our desks, and sneaking up on us and trying to hug us, and he'd chase us, and finally we just got fed up so there was a big mud puddle, so we said, 'Roger, we think we've found a part of a plane,' and so he stepped in the puddle and he got his shoes wet. So he's looking down, and then we started doing what he did to us, 'cause we got really mad 'cause he's been doing it, and it really got us mad, and a couple of other boys were doing it with him."

At times, recognizing the difference between chasing and teasing games that were based on liking or not liking was problematic. Many boys and girls fluctuated between liking and disliking members of the other gender. In addition, some people who played these games liked members of the other gender while others did not. Children were drawn to this activity because it could be a fun and exciting game, and because others were doing it. There were often multiple motivations driving the participants, leading boys who disliked girls to mix in with those who liked them. This served to accentuate the ambiguity of this form of cross-gender interaction. Less popular boys often lingered in this midstage elementary school behavior into later grades than those who were more socially advanced.

ALTERNATIVES: FLIRTING AND LIKING

Despite the prevailing feeling that boys and girls had no romantic interest in each other during the period of segregation, there were people who departed from this norm. In contrast to the clear patterns relating social status and types of behavior noted thus far, individuals who flirted with members of the other gender or who developed a crush on someone could come from any rank of the stratification hierarchy. Quiet and shy people who were not popular could like someone of another gender as readily as those who were outgoing and highly visible. Whether they had the courage to act on those feelings was another matter.

Josh, the fifth grader, offered his view of the factors influencing cross-gender romantic interest during the middle elementary school years:

Q: *A lot of sociologists think that in those middle years, like second, third grade, that there's no interest of boys and girls in each other.*

JOSH: That's not true. Well, I have one friend who's always been like, second grade I guess, a couple of friends that have always liked girls, I guess. Sometimes people who have older brothers and sisters like the other gender more. Because they see their older brother or sister doing it. And, or they have older friends. So I would say there's a small group of people who go through those grades liking members of the other gender.

The first step toward more active romantic interaction involved moving beyond the negative gender play found in chasing and teasing games. Putting aside this veneer of dislike, individuals interested in members of the other gender began to engage in subtle flirting. Flirting risked rejection and ridicule, for it violated both the platonic and romantic prohibitions of this developmental period.

Yet Matt, a fourth-grade boy from the popular group, indicated that he was aware of occasional flirtatious behavior occurring between boys and girls of his age:

Q: *How do they flirt?*

MATT: They would usually just start talking. Like, we'll be talking and then, like, one of the girls or boys would come up and then just say like, "What are you guys talking about?" And then we'd all start talking.

Q: *So it looks a lot like regular hanging around? ["Uh huh."] So how can you tell it's flirting?*

MATT: I just can feel it. I can feel that it's because they like somebody.

Sometimes flirting was less subtle, involving more overt moves toward members of the other gender. Strong advances tended to scare people away, however, leaving the initiator rebuffed. As noted earlier with Roger, when overt moves were made by unpopular people, they were usually unappreciated. Overt moves by popular people might arouse a more positive reaction, even if indirect or delayed.

Betsy, the third grader, described the actions of one of her more daring friends: "Cindy, she does go crazy sometimes. She's more like Annie, she's becoming boy-crazy."

Q: *And does she flirt with boys?*

BETSY: When we went on our break, she was having fits for Matt and Brett. But she just jokes [with] them because she just thinks they're cute, and sometimes she'll be yelling for them and I'll go over to them and say, "Oh boys!" And that's asking them to run away. And, like, Annie jokes around with boys a lot too. They go talk to boys more than most people.

People who attempted flirting were usually either rejoined or ignored; in either case they rarely encountered social damage. If nobody responded, they had not exposed themselves significantly. A few people confessed to having secret liaisons, where they liked someone who liked them back, but where both parties agreed to keep their affections private, not sharing knowledge of them with their schoolmates. They saw their boyfriends or girlfriends, or talked with them on the phone, only outside the school setting, away from the prying eyes and ears of their classmates. Only a very few individuals in the middle years had the nerve to be direct about their affections, approaching the people they liked and not hiding their feelings from others. One third-grade couple liked each other and talked on the phone a great deal. They tried to hide their relationship from others, and to diminish the effect of others' opinions on them when a few people learned of their feelings. Eventually this strain became too much for them, and they broke up.

More commonly, however, people who liked members of the other gender failed to act on their feelings. The uncertainty was too frightening, and the potential negative consequences too strong. Travis, a fifth-grade boy, spoke about hiding his long-term romantic interest in girls:

Q: *When do you think boys start first getting interested in girls?*
TRAVIS: Well, I liked girls a long time ago. A lot of my friends did, but really we were just scared to talk about it because we didn't know if other people did. We didn't want to be embarrassed.
Q: *How long is a long time ago?*
TRAVIS: Third grade, fourth grade.
Q: *Did you like any specific girl?*
TRAVIS: Just if they were pretty.
Q: *Did you ever tell anyone about it?*
TRAVIS: Just my best friend, Bo.
Q: *What do you think would have happened it someone else would have found out?*
TRAVIS: Well, like right now no one really cares, because there are a lot of people that go on dates. Back then I didn't really know what other people thought. But it was just kind of scary.

Travis's remarks highlight that while people were intimidated by the danger of exposing their feelings to individuals of the other gender that they liked, they were more afraid of the reactions and behavior of other members of their peer group.

PEER REACTIONS

The power of negative peer reactions was enough to deter most people interested in romantic liaisons from acting on these interests. Children were concerned with fitting in and being accepted, fearful of ridicule. The elementary school years were characterized by acutely fierce ridicule, untempered by the gentility of politeness that comes to cloak most interactions later in life. When boys or girls latched onto an item that violated peer norms, their reactions usually followed a predictable pattern.

Kenny, the fifth grader, recalled an incident of ridicule that he experienced in third grade, after placing his only phone call to a girl:

> Q: *Was it a serious call or kind of a prank?*
> KENNY: Both. I asked her if she liked me, and she said not really.
> Q: *Sounds like a serious call.*
> KENNY: Then she told everybody that I called her.
> Q: *So what happened?*
> KENNY: Everybody knew that I had called her.
> Q: *Did they make fun of you?*
> KENNY: Really badly for a while. It was horrible. But then it died down.

During the period of ridicule, most people suffered severe anguish. Some tried to avoid problems by isolating themselves from people, waiting for the storm to blow over, while others were so engulfed by it that they never saw an end in sight. Their distress, and others' perceptions of it, was vivid, as Seth, a popular third-grade boy, described: "Most kids, if they're interested in a girl, they won't tell anyone. They'd just keep it a secret, because people now make fun of them. Like, 'Oh god, you like her!'"

> Q: *Has that ever happened to anyone in your grade?*
> SETH: Some people, yeah.
> Q: *What happens when people get made fun of?*
> SETH: Usually they just walk away and look like they feel bad. They try
>   not to let it show, or people will just lay it on more, but they look
>   bad. You can just tell.

Very few people were willing to submit themselves to the anguish and humiliation of public ridicule. They had seen it inflicted on others and understood what it was like. Paul, the third grader, explained how this unfolded: "If you'd really like to be friends with a girl, you know why you don't usually? 'Cause they say, 'You're friends with a girl?' And 'Blah blah blah, blah blah blah.' And they make fun of you. And I realize that usually I don't tell people that I like them until I think it's the right timing."

LIKING IN SILENCE

Fear of the fallout from peer reaction led most people in the middle years to keep from approaching individuals they liked and revealing their feelings. People who did not realize what might happen if their secret got out to the wrong crowd quickly learned the hard way. Kenny, the fifth-grade boy who called a girl in third grade and told her that he liked her, only to have his deed turned into fodder for class ridicule, spoke about the consequences of that event for him: he did not stop liking her, but rather "liked her in silence." Kenny thus moved into the great morass of secrecy in which most preadolescents held feelings or experiences that they thought would be mocked by the peer group.

Like Kenny, Chuck, a fifth-grade boy, moved his feelings toward girls into the closet after a bad experience:

> Q: *When did you first start being interested in your first girl?*
> CHUCK: Second grade. Early first grade.
> Q: *Even during those years that sociologists think that boys and girls don't get together?*
> CHUCK: It was just like a crush.
> Q: *So you first had a crush back then. And did you ever talk to girls that you might have had crushes on?*
> CHUCK: Oh no. It's harder to talk to girls that you have a crush on than to girls that you don't have a crush on. You just crush from a distance.
> Q: *Did you ever tell anybody?*
> CHUCK: Yeah. My best friends. But then my best friends told their best friends, and it kind of went out and there was a scandal for about a week.

Kenny and Chuck liked in silence because they made the mistake of coming out with their taboo emotions. Most people did not have to experience this shame firsthand to learn what would happen: they learned from the experiences of others. It was common, then, for people, even during the gender segregation years, to like members of the other gender; they just could not tell too many people about it. Damian, a fifth grader, described his experience as "basically like little crushes, like she's cool, and like it was like one of those secret crushes that you never told anybody." Like boys, girls held secret crushes on which they were afraid to act. Mariah, the fifth grader, indicated that one of her best friends had "held a crush on a boy for like the longest time, I can't remember, since like kindergarten. And she's still holding it."

Paul confided that he had always liked girls and described the way he protected those feelings:

Q: *Are you friends with any girls?*

PAUL: Um, ah, well I used to be really active, but now, not really. I like some girls.

Q: *Is it a secret?*

PAUL: Yup, sure is. It's a secret. [whispering] I really like this one girl. She's not in our class.

Q: *And did you ever mention this secret to anybody?*

PAUL: Um, my friends that I can trust, yes.

Q: *Did you have any girls that you liked last year?*

PAUL: Um, last year, well Katy I used to like.

Q: *So would you pretty much say you've always liked a girl, or is that just a recent thing?*

PAUL: Um, well I'd say that I've pretty much in every grade liked a girl. But this grade, um, I like girls but it's not like we're friends.

Paul's remarks illustrate that in some way it was easier to like girls in silence during the middle years than to be friendly with them. Both romantic and platonic interest became socially stigmatized during this period and faded from public sight. That does not mean, however, that it actually disappeared. Contrary to both popular and scholarly belief, cross-gender interest continued to flourish. Ironically, cross-gender platonic friendship may have suffered more during this stage, even though it was less stigmatized, because it needed open contact to survive. Romantic interest could subsist in secret, unnourished, for much longer.

Chapter 9

Cross-Gender Relations:
The Later Years

After the years of segregation, cross-gender contact began to reemerge. Throughout this later period, comprising fourth through sixth grades, people initiated cross-gender relationships for two purposes: friendship and romance. The movement back toward members of the other gender was fraught with excitement, tension, and danger, however. Many less sophisticated individuals chose to remain within the relative safety of their own gender group, letting others forge this path. During these years, then, children engaged in the widest diversity of cross-gender contact patterns, with some firmly rooted in the separated mode of the middle years, others beginning tenuous platonic friendships, and others testing the romantic waters.[1] We consider the range of feelings and behaviors along this continuum.

Separation

A significant portion of the boys and girls, nearly one-quarter of those in this age range, showed little or no interest in bridging the gender divide. These people had spent so many years holding divergent interests that they found it difficult to socialize casually with each other. Their preoccupations did not overlap enough to support platonic relations, and they did not feel comfortable pursuing romantic attraction. Some individuals made attempts at reintegration, but these were often uneasy. Early forays into the cross-gendered world tended to be furtive; boys and girls made "gender jabs" at one another.

Kenny, the fifth grader, spoke about the extent of his interaction with girls:

Q: *Are you friendly with any girls?*
KENNY: Some.

Q: *What kind of friends are they? How good of a friend are you with them?*
KENNY: We talk to each other. If they forget their lunch or if they need
  something, I'll give money to them if they need it.
Q: *Do you ever see any of these girls outside of school to do something with?*
KENNY: No.

School-related topics, such as doing homework assignments, eating lunch,
and paying for lunch, were areas where boys and girls were the most compatible, where they could safely converse.[2] When boys and girls played together on
athletic teams, they often kept their cross-gender relationships compartmentalized; that is, they interacted in shared activities but did not develop friendships. Many individuals, even those with structural overlaps, continued to have
little or no interaction with members of the other gender.

Friendly Interaction

In contrast to the middle years, a sizable number (roughly one-half) of boys and
girls developed friendly relations. Early boy-girl platonic contact continued, as
it had during the gender segregation phase, to flourish primarily when girls
played sports with boys.

Tucker, the fifth grader in a middle friendship circle, described the nature
of the boy-girl friendships he observed:

Q: *What about friends who are girls?*
TUCKER: My world is more filled up with boy friends. I mean, there are
  some girls that have been my friends since first grade, ones that play
  sports and stuff, but I don't hang out with them and talk to them.
Q: *Do girls have to come into boys' sports worlds for boys to play with them?*
  Do boys ever go into girls' activities to play with them?
TUCKER: Yeah.
Q: *Like what kinds of girls' activities do boys participate in?*
TUCKER: I don't know. Jump rope, hopscotch maybe, I haven't seen
  that, but um, that's what they could do.

Tucker struggled to think of ways that boys moved into the realm of girls'
worlds because this crossover was decidedly more rare. As we noted in chapter
2, girls' gender roles expanded during the 1980s and 1990s to a much greater
extent than did boys'. Consequently, it was more likely that a girl who liked to
play sports could count boys among her friends than a girl who did not, and
there were not many boys who ventured into the activities described above.

Ben, another middle-rank fifth grader, discussed three girls on his soccer
team who became his friends:

Q: *[Are you friends] here at school or outside?*

BEN: Outside of school. They go here too. That's Sandy, Leslie, and Kim. They are all very good soccer players.

Q: *Aside from playing soccer with them, do you ever talk with them?*

BEN: Sometimes.

Q: *What kinds of things do boys and girls talk about at your age?*

BEN: Homework. Or when we're like working, sometimes we goof around when we're supposed to be working. That's basically it.

Outside of sports, boys and girls found other bases for friendships. Some who had been friendly years before revived their shelved relationships. Others forged cross-gender friendships that grew out of shared school interests. The incidence of cross-gender neighborhood and after-school activities increased. But not everybody pursued platonic boy-girl relationships; some people preferred to keep their distance. Those who were willing to move beyond their segregated spheres had to take the risk of getting teased or feeling awkward.

Romantic Interest

Slowly, and more tentatively than for platonic friendships, boys and girls began to put out romantic feelers.[3] This began with very few individuals and increased in fits and starts.[4] Everyone watched with riveting interest as the frontrunners made their romantic forays. Some were quickly rebuffed, while others received more tentative response.

Individuals developed greater interest in members of the other gender and got up the courage to speak openly about these feelings. Kevin said the turnaround in boy-girl relations occurred in fourth grade: "We no longer had boys chase girls and stuff. It just wasn't that immature any longer. It became, like, cool." Chuck, the more popular fifth-grade boy, offered a more differentiated view of individuals' transitions out of the segregation stage into cross-gender rapprochement. He talked about the range of grades at which people began to make this passage: "Early starters, I guess you could call them, in around third or fourth grade. Late starters, not until fifth grade. By now it's big. There's four people going out. Four couples. Going on a date, serious."

A fifth grader, Mariah, described her first encounter with boy-girl activity as reflecting a simultaneous rise of boy-girl interest: "All of my friends all of a sudden just kind of had an interest in boys. All of the girls in my class." This rapidly changing dynamic might reflect either the tendency for groups to swing from one set of interests to another, or the sudden release of people's pent-up romantic interests when the constraining social norms loosened. Many preadolescents reported that they waited eagerly for other people to break the ice before they felt free to discuss or act on their interest in members of the other gender.

Laura, a popular fifth grader, saw her friends' increased interest in boys as a more gradual phenomenon: "Fourth grade is when we really first started. We'd be just like walking around and talking, but in fourth grade we didn't really do much. In fifth grade is when we just, kinda, started talking about like the dating crowd and stuff."

Multiple patterns—with people moving into romantic interest individually, by friendship group, or in a swing encompassing a whole crowd—were thus possible. While different groups of boys and girls began moving toward romantic integration at different times and at different speeds, by fifth grade enough people had become interested in the other gender that it attained a foothold of legitimacy in the peer culture. Many individuals still held no interest, but the more popular groups were definitely aroused. Less popular people watched this behavior and commented about or ignored it, but they knew that it had begun. Roughly one-third of the people we observed had made romantic overtures by the end of this time period.

TALKING ABOUT BOYS AND GIRLS

The rise in romantic interest was accompanied by increased talk about members of the other gender. Boys' and girls' groups gossiped about specific individuals, discussed who liked whom, what these people did, and what everyone thought about it.[5] Conversation about romance blossomed on the telephone as well as in person, and both boys and girls spent their evenings and weekends engaged in gossip and speculation. Like romantic interest, boy talk and girl talk was primarily popular among certain segments of the population. Those who became interested in members of the other gender were more likely to seek out others with similar interests as friends. This dissolved friendships that had existed for years and led to the formation of new ones. Often, cross-gender romantic interest was spurred by the early onset of puberty. Hormonal shifts and physical changes generated not only an interest toward the other gender but an interest from the other gender as well. Boys whispered to each other about which girls might be members of the "Bunny Rabbit Association" (BRA), and girls talked about boys whose voices were changing.

Laura talked about the prevalence of "boy talk" and attempted to answer the question of which gender first became interested in the other: "Oh well, my friend Erica had a crush on somebody last year, I hope she doesn't mind if I tell you, but . . . We both did, and there was another girl who also liked a boy last year, so I don't know if girls do or boys do, because I've never really been a boy or been to boys' sleepovers and I don't know what they talk about at sleepovers. But like at sleepovers we always talk about who everybody has a crush on. Kind of gossipy stuff."

Not only did talk about boys and girls become more open, accepted, and frequent, but as Kevin, who was popular, explained, it changed in character: "Well, we went from saying that 'she is gross,' or 'I don't like her,' and we started talking about, 'Do you think I should ask her out?' and stuff like that. Or, 'Do you think she likes me?' And then you start worrying about if they like you, and not just if I like her or if she likes him. Now you worry about if they like you."

Boys and girls tried to figure out if others liked them by how they acted. They carefully watched each other at recess to see if someone they liked paid attention to them or talked to them. They discussed minute behavioral innuendos in detail, analyzing them for the slightest inflection. They especially looked for gratuitous interaction, begun for no apparent purpose than to create an excuse for conversation. By far the best way to find out if someone liked them, however, was to hear about it from one of his or her friends.[6]

Jake, a fifth-grade boy, discussed one route to this kind of information that several people pursued:

Q: *What kinds of things do you talk about on the phone?*

JAKE: Girls. That that would be the main topic of telephone talk.

Q: *Do kids hang out with girls or go with girls at this age?*

JAKE: Very much, I would say. You don't notice it that much unless it's one of your friends, but Laura, she's the girl that I am just friends with, we really talk about who likes who. So because of that, I know who a bunch of girls like and that they are going out with boys, but if you are somebody else who doesn't have a friend that's a girl, you don't know nearly as much.

Q: *Why, do girls talk about kids more than boys?*

JAKE: No, no, I know a lot of boys, and she knows a lot of girls, and so she will tell me all the girls she knows and I will tell her all the boys I know.

The platonic friendships that boys and girls were beginning to form or to deepen paid off richly in this important area: when faced with the uncertainty of romantic attraction, they could see whether their interest or feelings were reciprocated.

ATTRACTIVE CHARACTERISTICS

Before they began flirting, boys and girls had to decide whom they liked. They used different criteria to determine what they found attractive in members of the other gender. For boys, the preeminent determinant was appearance: they had crushes on girls they found cute.[7] Girls, in contrast, followed a more complex and intangible set of criteria.

Mariah, a popular fifth grader, described what she looked for in a boyfriend:

Q: *So when did you first start developing a crush on a boy?*
MARIAH: Like two months into the year.
Q: *What kinds of things is it based on?*
MARIAH: They have to be nice to you, or else forget it.
Q: *Is there anything else you look for in a guy?*
MARIAH: How intelligent the person is. Because if the person's not very smart, then, I don't know, that can get kind of annoying. 'Cause they're always asking questions, and uhhhhhhh! You're supposed to know this stuff!

Joanna, another popular fifth grader, elaborated further on similar concerns:

Q: *What are girls or boys looking for in each other?*
JOANNA: Usually it's because they're nice, and mature. Not like embarrassing like, "You have cooties." Like, Eric [was] always really embarrassed and stuff. And that was one of the reasons I decided it wouldn't be a very good idea to go to the movies and stuff with him. But Rob is ten times more mature. He doesn't get embarrassed. Sometimes he gets embarrassed, but it's like me. Sometimes I get embarrassed, but not usually.

These girls, then, were more concerned with boys' intelligence and maturity than their appearance. What they left unsaid is that social status represented the first-cut factor in their romantic selection. Popular boys and girls, who were the people primarily involved in cross-gender relations at this age, restricted their focus to other people of similar position. As we noted in chapter 2, being friendly with, flirting with, or going with people who were less popular than they would lead to a diminution in individuals' own status; making a connection with people in the popular crowd would increase their status.

It was not only popular people who were romantically attracted to members of the popular crowd; everyone was. Popular boys attracted the attention and interest of girls who were popular, unpopular, and socially isolated. The same was true for the popular girls. This was a common pattern, where a small segment of the population was sought after by the entire population of the other gender. It led to many people lingering, frustratingly, around individuals who were chronically "over their heads." Attractive characteristics, then, were a relatively elite commodity.

Nancy, a fifth-grade girl, described a popular boy whose attention was desired by many girls: "We kind of expected him to ask Alice out. But then he just surprised everyone and asked Mariah out. Because, we knew he would ask somebody out."

Q: *How'd you know that?*

NANCY: Well, because all of the other girls like him. And some of my
   lower-down friends that are not as popular like him too.

Q: *So there are a lot of girls who like this one guy?*

NANCY: Yeah.

SEXUAL INTEREST

Boys and girls often had different goals in a preadolescent romantic relationship. While they were both spurred by the excitement, status, and aura of maturity inherent in a romantic liaison, their divergences were rooted in differences between male and female culture.

For boys, a status preoccupation centered on sex.[8] Kevin was the first to introduce this topic:

Q: *Do you think that boys get interested in girls first, or that girls get*
   interested in boys first?

KEVIN: Boys get interested in girls first.

Q: *What makes you say that?*

KEVIN: I don't know. Uh. I think it might be sexual attraction at first. I
   know one thing, is some guys, if they see a nice girl, they kind of
   want a kiss from her. And then, a lot of boys, not myself, but a lot of
   boys, 'cause they've been sexually attracted to a girl, they wonder if
   the girl wants to have sex or whatever it is. And I used to wonder
   about that. It is kind of an interesting question. I think that's really
   interesting.

Not only were boys interested in sexual exploration for its own sake, but they sought it to enhance their social status. Boys derived peer prestige for "scoring" with girls and talking about it. It is at this age that the "baseball" analogy of sexual exploration (first base, second base) surfaced, leading boys to talk about sexual matters that they barely understood.[9]

Girls, however, were socialized to derive their status from having boys pay attention to them, from having boys do things for or give things to them, and from resisting sexual pressure. When Joanna was asked whether she thought girls were interested in boys "for sexual attraction," her reply was typical of the prevailing attitude in the girls' culture: "No. They kind of want a boyfriend, but just to hang out with, you know, watch good movies. Usually it's a boyfriend thing."

Parties, either in private or out in the open, facilitated group sexual behavior, but most preadolescent girls initially resisted the pressure to participate. As noted in chapter 2, at one party, Matt, a sixth-grade boy, yielded to persuasion from his friends that he "put the moves" on his girlfriend, Amy, and get her to kiss him. Amy was dismayed by Matt's repeated insistence, coupled, as it was, with the threat that if she did not kiss him they would have to break up. Confused and dismayed, she ran from Matt crying. Amy's friends rallied to her support and left the party with her.

Flirtation

Once interest in members of the other gender became established as legitimate and people could openly speak to their friends about it, they felt freer to begin flirting with the people they liked. Flirting had always occurred, but because boys and girls were uncomfortable with each other or with their own sexuality, it had been done in a subdued or disguised manner. As boys and girls started to think of themselves as sexual beings, they began trying out their sexuality on peers of the other gender.

Kevin talked about the way people flirted: "There is a lot of teasing, with the very popular guys. People tease them. You flirt so much, that's why people like you, and stuff. And I think that the popular boys are not always the only ones doing the flirting. It's the girls flirting with us. There's a lot of flirting where guys are always wanting to talk to some girl, and you can tell, and girls are always wanting to talk to some guy, but girls will do that. If they like someone, you find them saying, 'Oh that math project is so hard.' And stuff that really isn't a conversation; they just want to start a conversation. It's not for the sake of having a conversation. It's for the sake of talking, or having that person recognize you."

> Q: *Aside from just starting up a casual conversation with somebody, is there another way that people flirt?*
>
> KEVIN: Yeah, kind of. A boy might break into a girls' soccer game if they like one of the girls. Or if all of the girls are cute there. Boys will

always play the same game that they're playing. So like if a girl is playing wall ball, then the boy will play wall ball, and try to get that girl out, and stuff like that.

Q: *What about physical roughness, like roughhousing?*

KEVIN: I think sometimes boys try to show off, like if a girl is there. They might try to act tougher than other guys.

These kinds of cross-gender interactions were often very difficult. Not everyone could think of clever things to say to members of the other gender that would make them look funny and interesting. Boys and girls found it especially difficult to interact with people they liked. They often had little to say, and tried to form bonds or connections on a weak base. Unsure of how to behave around members of the other gender, individuals often acted awkwardly. One boy traded on his double-jointedness, twisting his body into pretzel-like positions at parties. To attract interest, boys often emulated the macho image, while girls assumed the demure posture. In attempting to appeal to members of the other gender, children aligned themselves with the most socially common gender role norms. In this way, they gravitated toward the most traditional aspects of those gender roles.

Another form of flirtation was practical joking. People played practical jokes on individuals they liked and disliked. Sometimes girls called up boys they liked, pretending to be someone else, and asking them who they liked. If they found out it was them, they would admit to being themselves. This backfired when the boys recognized their voice and got mad at them for the prank. Other times preadolescents got together with others to pull pranks.

Jake, a midlevel fifth-grade boy, spoke about practical jokes that involved girls who had spurned him: "Like, sometimes we will disguise our voices as girls, call up our worst enemies who like that girl, and say, 'Do you want to go out with me? Oh, I can't, I am absolutely your worst enemy,' and say stuff like that."

Q: *How does having a girl who is a friend help you do something like that?*

JAKE: Sometimes when you can't disguise your voice very good, like sometimes you can't make your voice like a girl, then if Laura, if she was over, then it would be easier to make a prank. Sometimes it is hard for me to disguise my voice anyway.

Q: *Some of your practical joking involves teasing?*

JAKE: No. They mostly involve girls, and when we find out who likes who, then we will probably make a prank that night on one of them. Like when I found out who the person I was friends with for so long, who she really liked, I tried to disguise my voice as him and call her up.

Boys and girls moved into more advanced forms of flirting at boy-girl parties or other out-of-school situations. These often took the form of games. Just as the youngest children had expressed their sexual interest through chasing and kissing games and children in the middle preadolescent years expressed their sexual interest through chasing and teasing games, older or more socially precocious preadolescents engaged in exploratory sex games. Preadolescent sexual games took traditional forms like "spin the bottle" and "seven minutes in heaven," as well as newer forms such as "truth or dare." Some girls derived popularity and attention from being "fast," from being willing to kiss boys, to engage in extended "making out" sessions, or from participating in sexual touching games such as "trust me." Girls who were fast might attain temporary popularity, but they ultimately were viewed by both boys and girls as "cheap" or "sluts."

Josh, a midlevel fifth-grade boy, described a religious retreat where he watched this occur: "Rumors are starting to happen about things that are starting to happen like making out and stuff like that. I was at this overnight with my Hebrew school where there was. This year there was all boys upstairs and all girls downstairs. Last year there was a whole bunch of rooms. Boy rooms. Girl rooms. All next to each other on different floors. The girls would come into the boys' room and play truth and dare and stuff, but that's like the closest thing."

> Q: *How do you play truth or dare?*
> JOSH: I didn't participate in it because I didn't want to. What you did was somebody would start and they would ask somebody else if they wanted truth or dare. If they said truth, they would ask them a question probably about relationships and they would have to tell the truth. If they got a dare, they would dare them to do something.

These games suspended the usual restrictions on boy-girl interaction, allowing both genders to venture further in expressing their sexual interest. Like the chasing and kissing games, they were practiced by only certain segments of the population: the kissing boys and kissing girls. Flirtation generated popularity for boys and girls by commanding attention from members of the other gender. It indicated to people that they were moving out of the realm of childhood and becoming more mature. Precisely when individuals were ready to make such a move depended on their physical maturity, their family background (sexual attitudes and behavior), their relation with older siblings (if they had them), and the popularity of their social group.

Approaching the Opposite Gender

Even more frightening than liking someone or participating in sex games at a party was openly committing oneself to tell such people of one's interest or asking them for a date. Although this was risky and scary, some individuals eventually approached each other more directly. These mavericks were the trailblazers, who faced the most uncertainty and censure while having the least social support and established groundwork on which to build. Those who waited until dating became a more established practice found it somewhat less traumatizing to approach the people they liked. Preadolescents were especially concerned, here, with gender-appropriate norms. While girls have traditionally had to wait for boys to make the first move, these patterns have become somewhat moderated, so that girls were occasionally the first to approach boys.[10] Consistent with our discussion in chapter 2, girls' assertiveness in romance was accepted in the peer culture. Yet, at the same time, the norm remained that boys were ultimately responsible for the assertive role. Other girls cleaved tightly toward the demure demeanor and would not think of being the one to make the first approach. With positively sanctioned exceptions, then, boys generally found themselves in the role of approaching girls whom they liked.

Kevin, a popular boy in fifth grade, explained this pattern:

Q: *Can girls go after boys, or are girls still sitting around waiting for boys to make the first move?*

KEVIN: I think mostly boys make the first move. Boys ask a girl out, girls don't ask a boy out. It happened with me and Nicole, that she asked me out first, but I don't think it happened with anybody else.

Q: *How do you feel about that?*

KEVIN: I think it's fine. It's just everybody's used to the other way. But I think it's like, *dang*, because it's hard to ask somebody out. I've asked a girl out, and it's hard to walk up to someone and say, like, "Would you like to go out sometime?" It's hard. It's, like, I'm the one that's always going to be going through all that pressure.

INDIRECT APPROACHES

Beyond considerations of gender, people approached individuals they liked in both direct and indirect manners. The safer way was to do this indirectly (see Eder and Sanford 1986), inquiring through intermediaries if one's approach would be positively received. If the answer was no, the would-be approachers avoided the pain of direct rejection, enabling them to save both feelings and face. People usually used their closest friends as intermediaries. It helped if the intermediaries were friends with the intended contacts, but this was not a requirement. If intermediaries were friendly with the desired targets, they might feel those persons out more discretely, avoiding having to admit that their friend liked the person. When the envoy had no particularly close relationship with the target, a more unsubtle approach was necessary.

Mariah described the intricacies of one indirect girl-to-boy approach: "Well, first, you get your friend to go up and ask the boy, like ask them if they like the person who you're asking for, so like I had to do that for my friend. She asked me to go up and ask him if he liked her."

> Q: *How'd you do it?*
> MARIAH: Just directly, straight to the point. It doesn't even have to be a boy that you're friendly with. If you're on a mission, you can just go right up to the boy and ask him.
> Q: *So what happens if you say that to a boy, do they get all embarrassed, or excited, or what?*
> MARIAH: Sometimes they get embarrassed, but not always.
> Q: *Was he alone, or was he with his friends when you asked him?*
> MARIAH: With his friends. And I went with her other friend, not alone, but the two of us.
> Q: *And so then what'd he say?*
> MARIAH: I think he said yes, right on the spot. And so then you go back to tell your friend, and then the friend would get the guts to ask the guy out. Or he would ask her out.
> Q: *And how do they do that? Do they do that in front of other people as well?*
> MARIAH: Well, Joanna went up and asked the guy out, right in front of other people, but most of the people didn't pay attention. Some people do, but not really, and so then you say go away, and they go away.

Sometimes people received an immediate response to an indirect inquiry such as Mariah had arranged. At other times the response was not as quickly forthcoming. Joanna spoke about an indirect approach she had initiated that took longer to come to fruition:

> Q: *So who made the first move on each other between Rob and you?*
> JOANNA: Actually it was kind of the same time. 'Cause he knew because Mariah had asked him if he liked me and when he said yes, she told him that I liked him too. She called him and asked him, "Do you like Joanna? 'Cause she likes you." And I never really thought that

he would like me. And he went, "Well, I have to think." No one
really thought that I would like Rob. They thought that Mariah
would, because they were really good friends and stuff. But then he
said that he liked me. She called him Thursday night, and then he
gave her the answer on Friday morning at school.

Q: *So you had to wait all Thursday night 'till Friday morning to find out?*
Was that nerve-racking?

JOANNA: No. Because he told her on the phone that definitely he would
tell her the next day. And he hadn't said no yet.

DIRECT APPROACHES

The indirect approach required less courage on the part of the approacher, because the responsibility for talking to the target was passed on to a friend. Yet
there were advantages associated with the direct approach as well. Kenny described how the direct approach could generate peer status:

Q: *Do you know of any boys who actually got up enough nerve to tell girls*
that they liked them?

KENNY: Yes, it happened in fifth grade.

Q: *How did he do that?*

KENNY: I was standing real close to him, and he asked her.

Q: *He asked her directly straight out?*

KENNY: Yes, and everybody, after he asked her, everybody was patting
him on the back.

Q: *What happened? What did he say?*

KENNY: I don't know. That he liked her, he thought she was cute, that
he wanted to go out with her, stuff like that.

Q: *And why were they congratulating him?*

KENNY: Because she didn't outright reject him, so that's a victory.

The boy in this case gained the respect of his peers because he had the
courage to make a direct approach and because his tender was not immediately
rejected. Other reasons people chose to make a direct approach included their
ability to present themselves in their best light and their ability to safeguard
their privacy. If the girls rejected them, there was less chance of other people
knowing or talking about it.

Getting Rejected

Not everyone who made a direct or indirect approach received a positive response. People tried to manage others' reactions to them, increasing their chances of success by limiting their approaches to targets they thought would receive them positively. This was risky business, however, and people's feelings and status were fragile. Rejections stung more intensely than acceptances felt good. The safest way to manage an approach, in the event of a possible rejection, was to employ both indirection and discretion.

Jake spoke about a rejection he received that was managed so well by the intermediary that the target never even knew she was rejecting him:

> Q: *Do people ever keep it a secret if they like someone or are going with*
>   *someone?*
> JAKE: A lot. I'd say 70 percent. That's the thing, I like this other girl
>   now, and I have Laura for a friend, so I had Laura talk to her about
>   me. So you get somebody to pull a plan or something.
> Q: *So what happened when she pulled this plan?*
> JAKE: It didn't work very well. The girl I like, she likes this boy named
>   Ian, and Ian doesn't like her, and she knows that.
> Q: *So she said she liked somebody else?*
> JAKE: Well, not really. Laura asked her what if somebody else liked her,
>   was there somebody who she would like back if they liked her.
>   Nobody was on the list. The only person that no matter what, was
>   going to be on the list, was Ian. So then she came back and told me.
>   She was very cool about it because she did it in a safe way that didn't
>   embarrass me by not mentioning my name.

People who tried to avoid the stigma of rejection in front of their peers used the personal approach. When their advances were spurned, they had to figure out some way of saving face, but they were the only ones to know. John, a fifth-grade boy from the middle friendship circles, recounted the way he approached a girl that he liked: "I just walked up to her when nobody was around and talked to her and told her I liked her."

> Q: *And so what'd she say?*
> JOHN: She said she had a crush on one of my other friends. She said she
>   liked him and she didn't want to go out with me.
> Q: *So how did that make you feel?*
> JOHN: Not bad. Because we were still friends and stuff.

John was able to salvage his feelings, at least to himself, by telling himself that he still had the girl's friendship. Not all rejects were this lucky. The tenuousness of romantic relationships, especially among the less precocious individuals, made people particularly sensitive.

Dating

For people who successfully approached members of the other gender and got them to agree to "go" with them, the next issue was dating. Not all "going together" couples went out on dates, but it often happened. Preadolescents were very excited about the possibility of dating. Dating was one of the first things people talked with each other about, after they confirmed a mutual romantic interest. Early daters attracted greater attention due to the unusual nature of their activity. As time passed, this ceased to be as unusual, and they were joined by other courageous souls. By fifth grade, significant numbers of people in the popular circles were dating and "going with" others (see Merten 1996d), and this behavior was accepted as less shocking.

Uncertainty about dating behavior made individuals nervous, even though they saw their prospective dates every day at school. Cultural lore was passed around about what to do on a date. Jake discussed what boys and girls might do together when they were involved in a "going with" relationship: "Mostly go shopping or go to movies. A lot of times if you have an activity, you will get the other person to go to that activity and watch."

Q: *Like a sporting event?*
JAKE: I got invited to go to a play, so I went.
Q: *Would you take them to something that your parents took you to?*
JAKE: Yes, or a lot of times you might have a soccer game and you might ask them to come and watch.
Q: *What else would you do with a girl that you were going with?*
JAKE: Just about nothing else.
Q: *No talking on the phone?*
JAKE: Not really. That's just, I think we're still nervous to talk on the phone with a girl or something.

These kinds of contacts provided opportunities for boys and girls to spend time together outside the school setting without the pressure or formality of a peer-structured date. They involved preadolescents' placement in commonly frequented, natural settings that were therefore safe. At the same time, they acknowledged the specialness of the boy-girl relationship, separating it from interactions with other groups of boys and girls, and creating some space, although temporary and small, in which the couple could interact privately.

Boys and girls also went on more formal dates, where they made plans to go out together without their parents or teammates. These might be alone or in the company of other dating couples. Kevin gave some examples of good "date activities" for preadolescents: "You go to the movies; the movie thing is like really strong. Or like you might, maybe, go to like the Rock Creek Festival or something."

> Q: *How about the mall?*
> KEVIN: The mall you don't want to go to because you don't want to just go shopping. The reason you don't go to a mall is because people don't want to think that they have to entertain the other person. Just go to a movie, which is very easy.
> Q: *Because there's that awkwardness of what are you going to do together?*
> KEVIN: Yeah. And what are you going to talk about and stuff. I mean, if you go to a movie, you get to talk in the car, too. It's just perfect timing. When you're running out of talk, the car stops.

By carefully planning their time on dates, boys and girls managed the interaction to maximize the excitement and minimize the anxiety. Conversation was somewhat strained, for boys and girls felt uncomfortable talking about the things they normally discussed in school. Unable to rely on topics of conversation revolving around their routine activities, they gossiped about other people, discussed their plans, and talked about what to do. Avoided at all costs was emotions or relationship talk.

Dating interactions were guardedly separated from boys' and girls' daily lives. Because relationships were so sensitive and uncertain, boys and girls did not know how to interact at school with the people they were going with.[11] They talked about their dates with their girl and boy friends, but they felt awkward talking about them with each other. They knew how to be platonically friendly with members of the other gender and how to flirt with them, but they were unsure about how to engage in more secure romantic behavior. Dating preadolescents, then, often limited the scope and nature of their interaction with each other, especially in school.

Ben, the fifth grader, discussed the sensitive nature of in-school relations among dating couples:

> Q: *What about hanging out more at school?*
> BEN: That's really hard too. I only know one couple who act like they are going together when they're at school. The rest of them just stick with their boy friends and their girl friends. Hanging out in person, in front of other people, is really hard.

Dating behavior was not scattered aimlessly throughout the grade, but concentrated in the elite, upper strata. Only the most popular boys and girls felt comfortable leading the way into active romance, and their advances in this area represented a component of their high social ranking. Chuck expressed this connection between dating and popularity:

> Q: *Is there any pattern to the kids who are into the dating thing?*
>
> CHUCK: Well, it seems like the shyer ones, they either don't admit it, or they don't have a crush on anybody. And then also the ones that are new at this school are not involved.
>
> Q: *Would you say that the dating thing is confined more in the popular crowd? Or is it just by people that are less shy?*
>
> CHUCK: Probably more in the popular crowd. I don't know the girls' stuff, but just from the boys, it started with the more popular group. Definitely the more popular people are going out first.

Peer Reactions

When the first "daters" embarked upon their activities, they often faced gossip and social stigma. Ben described the kinds of rumors that led to embarrassment among early romantically linked couples: "They start calling them names like loverboy. Make fun. Start a rumor and everybody would find out." Although curiosity still abounded, social embarrassment diminished as romantic relationships became less novel and people got used to them. Individuals could still face humiliation for some kinds of romantically linked situations, but these no longer encompassed all romantic encounters.

Joanna explained how her embarrassment level abated over time for some kinds of situations but not for others:

> Q: *So is it embarrassing to let people know that you like a guy now, or is it okay?*
>
> JOANNA: Yeah, I really don't care. Just as long as they don't come up to me and tease me and stuff.
>
> Q: *What if you liked someone and they didn't like you back? Would that be different?*
>
> JOANNA: That would be very embarrassing. But I'd probably, when I'm with Rob, I wasn't sure if he liked me, so and Mariah knew his number or something, and Mariah and Rob are friends, and so she called him and asked him, and I found out that he did, so then I wasn't embarrassed.

This lessening of embarrassment, then, was related to the development of romantic and dating peer norms. As such norms arose or were learned and accepted from older friends and siblings, preadolescents had firmer ground on which to base their activities. Peer norms were structured and serious. Departures could bring on the tyranny and shame of social censure. One universal norm was romantic monogamy. The peer culture had no concept of individuals "playing the field." It was absolutely forbidden, from elementary through high school, to be engaged in romantic relations with more than one person at a time. Any person who conceived of him- or herself as not completely attached and free to romantically experiment on a multiple basis encountered fierce negative sanctioning.[12]

Chuck recalled the type of reaction one girl received when she tried to go out with two boys at one time: "That was a big scandal, I guess you could call it."

Q: *What was the scandal?*

CHUCK: Some sex rumors, and like, that someone was cheating on another person.

Q: *So you're only allowed to go with one person at a time? There's no such thing as playing the field?*

CHUCK: Well if you go on, like, a first date and you try someone out and you don't like them, and you want to see somebody else, you can probably tell the person.

Q: *So you have to break up with them before you can try somebody else? One at a time is the rule?*

CHUCK: Absolutely. You never see it any other way.

Kevin elaborated on some of the dimensions of the monogamy norms: "You don't go out with two people at once. It takes a *long* waiting process after you break up with someone before you can ask somebody else out. You can't jump right into another relationship. Like Karen, she used to go out with Rob. I think it took her a year before she could do things, before things were okay."

People seriously considered the effect of peer reaction before they engaged in any romantic behavior. Such behavior constituted the most serious fodder for gossip and might generate rumors that could wreck individuals' self-esteem and social standing. When queried about more advanced romantic activities, like kissing and holding hands, Kyle indicated how this was inhibited by the norms and sanctions of the peer culture: "Not around school. Definitely not around school. If anybody got caught, they'd be like out of school in a second because it'd be so embarrassing. 'Cause people in our school, some people are very vulgar and mean and really twisted and they are big jerks and most people hate those kind of people, but if any of those people caught people holding hands or kissing, they'd tell, immediately, and they would tattle, and spread it around school."

Peer reaction could cut both ways. While it focused potentially hurtful attention on people, it gave them a visibility that boosted their popularity.

Liking in Silence

Paralleling the trend seen in the middle years, many boys and girls were hesitant to express their romantic interest in members of the other gender. They developed an interest or crush on someone, but they were afraid, for several reasons, to bring it out into the open.

One motivation for liking someone in silence was the fear of rejection. Kenny expressed his reason for not approaching the girl he liked:

Q: *Is there any girl you like at the moment?*
KENNY: Yes.
Q: *Mention anything to her about it?*
KENNY: No. She's very popular.
Q: *So what difference does that make?*
KENNY: She's more popular than me, so she probably wouldn't like me.

In this case, his assessment of the low likelihood of the girl's returning his feelings made Kenny decide to restrain his advances. Boys and girls were acutely aware of the status hierarchy in the grade and the consequences of moving beyond their group. Thus, although they often liked someone outside their strata, they were unlikely to approach people at higher levels.

A second reason people remained silent about their romantic interest in others was their fear of ridicule from their peers. Especially during the transitionary period, when boys and girls were first starting to develop romantic feelings or to come out into the open with them, the romantic stigma remained strong. Cross-gender interaction was still regarded by many as distasteful, problematic, and gossipworthy. This was particularly the case among the less popular groups. Kenny showed that even fifth-grade boys could be reluctant to express interest in girls because of anticipated peer reaction:

Q: *Do you know of any girls who like any boys?*
Kenny: Yes.
Q: *Who tells you that kind of stuff?*
KENNY: Other girls.
Q: *How secret are these secrets really?*
KENNY: They don't want this to spread around the school. I don't want
    it to spread around the school that I like a girl.
Q: *So you do think that these things stay pretty secret?*

KENNY: Yes.

Q: *And do you ever tell the people that you like them?*

KENNY: No, not usually. It's too risky, still.

The group of people who silently and unobtrusively held romantic interest remained a presence in the later preadolescent years. It is difficult to compare the size of this group at later preadolescence with the middle years since
it remained relatively closeted. Some of the people who liked in silence during the middle years were the first to make a move during the later years, while
people with no cross-gender romantic interest moved into the silently interested category. The silent romanticizers thus became more numerous during the
later years, as more people developed romantic feelings and the climate became
somewhat more hospitable for having, if not expressing, them.

THE POPULAR PEOPLE set the normative tone for the entire social spectrum
throughout their preadolescent careers. While they held cross-gender friendships, these remained socially accepted. When they moved away from cross-
gender interaction, it became stigmatized. When they reforged platonic
cross-gender relationships, and later became interested in romance, these became not only accepted but status generating. They were the ones to break these
grounds first, and although they suffered initially for it, they benefited socially
over the long run. Individuals who lagged in the cross-gender game were eventually labeled nerds and faggots.

The peer culture opened the pathway for platonic and romantic cross-
gender relations slowly and grudgingly, defined the forms that these could take,
retroactively accorded participants elevated status, defined the outer limits of
romantic behavior, and ultimately diminished the social status of those who did
not participate. This culture normatively traced a single acceptable route
through the progression of boy-girl relationships and negatively sanctioned,
through censure and ridicule, those who deviated from it. There were boys and
girls, from the popular crowd down through the pariahs, who desired to stray
from the normative path and cultivate romantic relations out of the approved
sequence. Most of them were inhibited by their knowledge of the censure they
would encounter if they breached these informal constraints.

The character and progression of relationships between preadolescent girls
and boys, as shown here, are not as simple as most have described. The pattern
dominating both the cultural wisdom and the scholarly literature, of preadolescent boys and girls living in discrete, gendered cultures and worlds, was not
exclusive. Throughout these several stages of cross-gendered relations, there
were always people who desired to violate the normative behaviors. Although

a few had the courage to breach these norms, the majority did not. Most individuals were held in check by the sanctions embodied in the peer culture and the consequences individuals faced when they departed from the normative track. Freed from this constraining model, preadolescent boys and girls might have more freely intermixed platonic and romantic interactions throughout the elementary school years, adopting a range of behaviors that blended the traditional gender roles to a greater extent. They were discouraged from doing so by the powerful grip of their peer culture, which intermediated between them and the greater society at large, incorporating into its own formulation those features of society that it desired and rejecting others for which it was not yet ready.

Chapter 10   Bringing It All Together

)

We have focused on a predominantly white, middle-class, preadolescent population and studied the nature of these children's lives. While the investigation could have centered on different aspects, we chose to approach their environment as much as possible through the children's own perspectives, to cast our emphasis on those things that they considered important. Working only loosely within the context of the major institutions of family, school, and after-school programs, we observed, interacted with, and asked children questions about the free time they constructed for themselves within these realms. It was within their social lives that they found the freedom to create and express themselves. This was where they forged the peer culture that set the standards against which they both evaluated the outside world and measured themselves. We have tried to portray children's experiences in the ways that they saw them, adding analytical elements that grew out of our own observations and interactions. We discussed issues related to their status stratification and dynamics, to their core nonacademic activities, to the sets of relationships that comprised their lives, influencing both their identity and social position. Taken together, these elements formed the foundation of their preadolescent peer lives and culture. Their peer culture fit in between the cracks structured by their mandated attendance in school and after-school activities, coloring their perceptions of and relation to those institutions and events. As they aged it also served increasingly as a cache surrounding their family base, providing the alternate, sometimes competing, sometimes aligning, set of norms, values, relationships, and lenses on their lives.

Characteristics of Preadolescence

GENDER

One of the primary variables through which children's lives have been analyzed has been gender. Throughout this analysis we have alternately considered and eschewed the influence of gender, at times typologizing boys' and girls' behavior together, while at other times separating and sharply differentiating between them. That boys and girls show different patterns of friendship and interaction has been well documented in the literature: boys have been found to play in large, competitive, athletically oriented groups, while girls lean toward small, intimate, and nurturant groups (Best 1983; Fine 1987; Goodwin 1980a, 1980b; Lever 1976, 1978; Thorne 1993; Thorne and Luria 1986). We saw these patterns replicated in the way boys and girls divided themselves into informal playground groups and interacted with their friends. Much male play (especially during school recess) occurred in large groups to foster athletic competition, whereas female play centered on small group intimacy and relationship work. During the middle elementary years this divergence of style and interest became so great that it fragmented boys and girls nearly entirely into gender-segregated friendship groups. Gendered groups generally occupied different locations on the playground, participated in distinct activities, and engaged in boundary maintenance work.

Variations by gender also emerged in the character of the preadolescent gendered peer cultures. Previous studies of elementary school children have pointed out that girls value social and nurturant roles (Best 1983; Borman and Frankel 1984) while they begin to focus on appearance and romantic issues (Eisenhart and Holland 1983). Boys have been found to gain status from competitive and aggressive achievement-oriented activities, with an emerging interest in the later grades in romance (Best 1983; Eisenhart and Holland 1983; Goodwin 1980a, 1980b; Lever 1976). Yet our research suggests that many of these peer focal concerns arise and become differentiated earlier than has been previously shown. Many of the factors hitherto considered primarily salient to adolescent gendered cultures have their roots in elementary school. Thus, girls we observed were already deriving status from their success at grooming, clothes, and other appearance-related variables; social sophistication and friendship ties; romantic success as measured through popularity and going with boys; affluence and its correlates of material possessions and leisure pursuits, and academic performance. Boys, even in the predominantly white, middle-class schools that we studied, were accorded popularity and respect for distancing themselves from the deference to authority and investment in academic effort, and for displaying traits such as toughness, troublemaking, domination, coolness, and interpersonal bragging and sparring skills.

At the same time, aspects of preadolescents' lives displayed a more mixed gender pattern. This was evident in the after-school realm, where boys and girls engaged in both overlapping and divergent types of activities. Boys and girls studied language and computers, developed their artistic skills, played musical instruments, and participated in sports and games. Girls leaned more heavily toward graceful and emotional activities such as drama and dance, while boys pursued more physically rough ventures, math and scientific enterprises, and outdoor activities. Boys were more involved in organized team sports than girls, although the differences between them in this area has clearly diminished. Many after-school activities were also segregated by gender, so that even if boys and girls did the same thing, they did it separately. Yet, at the same time, the overarching structure and value system guiding the after-school institution was common to boys and girls, giving them a fundamentally similar experience of moving through the extracurricular career and becoming socialized to the norms and values of adult culture.

Cross-gender interaction represents another area where gender influence was mixed. While boys and girls often socialized in segregated cultures, the internal characteristics of their attitudes and behavior toward each other showed considerable overlap. Both boys' and girls' groups contained a mix of members who had little interest in each other, who had interest but did not show it, and who were willing to make overtures toward the other. Boys and girls displayed these overtures in similar and different ways, teasing, talking, interrupting, calling, and approaching each other (cf. Voss, 1997). While some scholars have emphasized the great gender divide (cf. Best 1983; Eder 1995; Lever 1976, 1978; Schofield 1981, 1982; Thorne 1986, 1993), our research suggests that this analysis tells only part of the cross-gender story. First, the social segregation of preadolescent boys and girls appears less universal than previous research has claimed, with boys and girls voluntarily crossing over both individually and in groups, both briefly and for more extended periods, and both casually and more intensely. Preadolescence encompasses an era of gender separation, but it is not as complete as has been asserted. Second, this separation exists more strongly on the superficial, behavioral level than on the deeper level of children's attitudes and feelings. Many children indicated that they would have made more platonic and romantic crossovers had they not feared reprisal. This separation appears, then, to have been not as strongly desired as it was enforced. Cross-gender relationships, even throughout the gender-divide years, were subject to contradictory pulls. Many children's researchers studying gender, such as Thorne and Eder, have described the processual cross-gender rapprochement at the surface level of behavior, but they have underestimated most of the contacts/desire for contacts preadolescents experienced during the middle years and the role of peer stigma and censure in holding these back.

Finally, there are other ways in which the gender patterns of preadolescents were very similar, with boys' behavior closely approximating girls'. This becomes apparent the more we go beyond the social segregation and content of children's activities to the structure and dynamics of their friendship groupings. Here, research on children's gendered differences (Best 1983; Eder 1995; Fine 1987; Goodwin 1990; Lever 1976; Schofield 1981, 1982; Thorne 1993) is joined by the conventional folk wisdom on children's social behavior, which differentiates by gender, suggesting that girls lash out at each other verbally, wounding each other emotionally, whereas boys, who lack interpersonal skills, merely wound each other physically. While we were sensitive to these differentiations, our research found few significant variations by gender in either clique or middle friendship circle structure or dynamics; the stratification of children's peer societies into hierarchical groups and the interactional dynamics both within and among these groups appear to be fairly consistent for members of both genders. Boys and girls both displayed common patterns of inclusion and exclusion, followed similar cyclings through cliques, and generated similarly changing hierarchies. Boys appeared no less skilled at intricate emotional woundings and manipulations than girls. While boys and girls stratified themselves in popularity according to different factors, there was more similarity to the friendship structures and interactions across gender than up and down the status hierarchy. Boys and girls were both competitive and cooperative, hierarchical and leveling, and composed their peer societies into stratified groups that were fundamentally comparable in nature. We thus concur with those researchers who assert that there are some gender parallels, in contrast to the more conventional portrayal of gender differences.

AGE

Age is not commonly regarded as one of the prime demographic variables stratifying and characterizing people except at the older and younger ends of the life spectrum. Clusters of patterned distinctions do mark individuals, however, at both younger and older ages. Of these two, youth represents the most salient period for age demarcation because people are changing most rapidly in their younger years, and are stratified by outsiders and themselves into broad age groupings and specific subgroupings. Age thus represents one of the most prominent demographic variables for preadolescence, making childhood the only time when any other variable has the potential to overcome the importance

of race, class, and gender. On the one hand, preadolescents are physically removed from older children by being kept in elementary schools, while adolescents occupy the next educational strata (intermediate, junior high, or
middle schools). This protects them from contamination by adolescents, who
might infect them with the difficulties and precocity of their age. Preadolescents congregate more freely with younger children at school and are clumped
with them into childhood. They move through the later elementary school
years, conquering these domains, until they stand at the top of the age hierarchy, kings and queens of the school. They have size, maturity, status, and
power, until they move on to the next school and fall to the bottom of the hierarchy. On the other hand, they are institutionally substratified by school,
after-school, and other groups into strict age categories, with activities carefully delineated for people at different levels. Children, themselves, are looser
about intrapreadolescent clumping, mixing in their spontaneous play with
older and younger people, particularly in neighborhood and family groupings.
Yet they, too, even on their own, tend to reproduce age stratification, reserv-
ing certain kinds of friendships and levels of status for age contemporaries.

In our society, considerable attention has been focused in our society on
the age period of adolescence, for this is when people make the biggest leap from
childhood to adulthood. The period of preadolescence has received much less
notice. In fact, the construct of preadolescence is relatively recent, supple-
menting a host of increasingly divided age categories. Children now move from
infancy to toddlerhood, preschool age, elementary school, and adolescence.
Preadolescence demarks part of the elementary school phase only, the later
years. Yet preadolescence lies at the margin between childhood and adolescence, bridging the gap between these eras. A study of preadolescent peer culture must address the salience of this variable, articulating some generic
characteristics of preadolescence as an age grouping.

Preadolescents converge on several significant social dimensions. First,
they experience beginning thrusts toward independence and movement away
from their families. After their earliest years of school, they move toward becoming less physically, socially, and emotionally dependent on their families.
They are young, highly impressionable, and beginning to separate from their
parents and bond with their age peers for the first time (Elkin and Handel 1989).
They learn that this is their world, and that there is only so much their families (or other outsiders) can do to exert influence within it. At the same time,
their peer group is rising in influence. While adolescence marks the time when
their peer group will become the strongest locus of self, preadolescence marks
a significant stage in the journey along this path. Individuals juggle different
and often conflicting images of self between the childish self shown to their

families and the maturing self shown to their peers. Over time, this outside, peer self will become the truer reflection of their real level of maturity. Preadolescents start seeking their identity through accomplishment, through meaningful interaction with peers, and through attachment to social groups.

Second, preadolescents experience great intensity in their peer relations— for several reasons. Elementary school children are trapped within class and grade social systems that are limited in their size and mobility, thus restricting their avenues of escape from the clique social system. They stay in their homeroom location for most of the day and interact with the same people for most of the year. When separated from a best friend, they may well make a new best friend in their new class. At the same time, they may be tormented by bullies or clique members in their homerooms. These institutional arrangements become social enclaves that encapsulate them almost completely. With restricted social intercourse, the remaining social contacts take on an added power and influence.

Third, while adolescent social typologization and stratification divide middle and high school peer culture into a plethora of groups revolving around diverse substantive interests, elementary schools display a more limited, unidimensional group differentiation. This contrast may be due to such factors as the smaller size of elementary schools, the homeroom versus departmental educational structure, and the lesser maturity of elementary school–aged children. In any case, elementary, preadolescent peer society is organized into a single hierarchy of group status with only one popular group, the rest of the people falling into various strata of unpopularity. This forces people into social groups and identities tied to a single continuum and exposes the unpopular people to the whims of the more powerful, popular people.

Fourth, the behavior of preadolescents is more raw than adults', untempered by the social niceties and restraint that typically moderate adult social intercourse. Preadolescents enact the dynamics of power and dominance in a more explicit fashion, without the concern for mutual "face saving" that, according to Goffman (1967), characterizes adult interaction rituals. Although sharp features of clique behavior are discouraged, even banned (in their extreme), by supervising adults, they persist in their most elemental form in what Corsaro (1985) calls the "underlife" of the elementary school. Preadolescent experiences thus brand themselves searingly onto children's social consciousness, influencing their conceptions of group and societal dynamics and structures in the larger adult world.

Preadolescence represents a liminal state between childhood and adolescence, between the safety and security of childhood and the greater rewards and responsibilities of adolescence. Over the past several generations, we have witnessed the increasing "adolescentization" of society, as children have turned to adult pastimes and behavior at ever younger ages and young adults deferred their entry into full adulthood, staying in school and out of the labor force longer and refilling their parents' nests by moving back into the home. Adult influences are reaching down into adolescence, and adolescent influences into preadolescence. These trends are accompanied by identity shifting and role confusion, particularly among adolescents, but increasingly among preadolescents as well. Yet preadolescents are still trapped in the social cage of the family and the classroom, still defined by needing the care of baby-sitters. They find themselves buffeted by conflicting influences. Wolf (1991, 15) articulates this dilemma, noting that "the course of preadolescent childhood is played out in the continuing struggle between the mandate to grow up and the wish not to." They represent the last age of childhood, where we see the beginning emergence of peer identity, social preferences, and the roots of adolescent behavior patterns.

RACE AND CLASS

Along with gender, race and class form the triumvirate of demographic variables by which behavior and social status are currently most commonly assessed, distinguishing people, differentiating them into groups, and forming the basis for their identity. Because our population had limited diversity in these demographics, we gleaned less insight into the role of these variables for preadolescents than we might have desired. Yet even our small glimpse offers some sketchy patterns. Like gender, racial differences between children yielded significant variations in some types of situations but not others. Some of the neighborhoods and schools that we observed had larger populations of color than others. Where there were enough people of color in a given environment, these individuals often separated into discrete cliques and friendship circles, isolating themselves from whites. They sat and ate lunch together, formed their own social enclaves, and played together. They mixed in classroom settings and in other structured activities, but they came back together for spontaneous play. Still in the minority, these children in their separate groups ranked lower on the popularity scale than the white children and were not in the popular clique. The dynamics they reported in their cliques were similar to those experienced by the white children, and they formed the same types of friendships and cross-gender relations. Where there were not enough children of color to constitute separate friendship groups, however, they mixed in socially with the general population. When this happened, they acted and were treated like any other children. They were scattered among classes, after-school activities, and social groups. They fell into the popular clique and the middle friendship circles. They formed friendships and cross-gender romantic relationships with whites as readily as any others. While they did not have other people of color to significantly buffer them, they reported no feeling of prejudice or discrimination.

There was also a high degree of class homogeneity in our community. Some children came from trailer parks and apartment complexes, but there was limited low-income housing. The majority were middle- and upper-middle-class, living in single-family housing in a variety of price ranges. Like race and gender, class differences netted variable effects. This was a less visible factor than the other two, since most preadolescents dressed in the same general style of jeans, T-shirts, sweatshirts, and sneakers, and went to the public schools. Stories circulated about individuals who lived in big, fancy houses, or whose parents had unusually opulent material possessions (polo fields in the backyard, ranches in the mountains, airplanes), but being from a trailer park yielded no significant discussion. Preadolescents from poorer economic backgrounds fell into the full range of social strata, being included in the popular cliques, the middle friendship circles, and the pariahs. They played outside of school, formed friendships and cross-gender relations in the same ways as others. There were occasions where their participation in after-school activities was made somewhat difficult by economic limitations, and where organizations had to fund-raise to grant them scholarships. After-school participation extended into a wide range of class groups, however (Larreau 1991; Qvortrup 1990). While the parents of these individuals may have suffered occasional stigma in the parents' group, especially if they did not work to support their end of the fund-raising, most children were uninterested in such matters. These individuals passed the minimum economic threshold and were objects of neither curiosity nor scorn. At the same time, they were not eligible for the kind of popularity that some preadolescents derived from their more opulent material possessions and lifestyle. There were no discernible instances where they congregated into lower socioeconomic groups. The general flattening of class differences and relative invisibility of class distinctions resulted in children from less affluent backgrounds being generally integrated into the social group. There was some activity differentiation, but it was minor. People had a slight awareness of economic stratification, and a resulting identity differentiation, but it, too, was minimal.

It may well be that broader divergences in race and class would significantly affect the character of group typologization and stratification, injecting elements from the larger, adult society into the childhood model, or that the different ages of maturity characteristic of different population groups might affect the timing of the shift from the simpler to the more intricate model of development in ways that this research was unable to discern. Future research examining the stratification of children's social groups in populations with a broader or more comparative range of these demographic characteristics might help to answer some of these questions.

Play, Games, and Work

According to Stone (1965), recreation is an important bond that ties the individual to society. A symbolic process and collective representation, play reproduces the societal and historical forms in which it occurs. Stone and others have also asserted that the child's self becomes differentiated and integrated through play. Play enhances the development of role taking, emerges as a social construction and jointly sustained dramatic performance, invokes the complexity of patterned relations and their variance, and represents serious business for children (Corsaro 1985; Denzin 1977; Fine 1981; Goffman 1959; Mead 1934; Thorne 1993). As such, it is a major socializing influence.

In this research we have mostly focused on spontaneous play, with the exception of after-school activities. A relatively recent phenomenon, these activities have become increasingly salient to (especially) preadolescents' lives, serving as a new agent of socialization. Sociologists have been examining this phenomenon to gain a greater understanding of the socializing implications of the after-school period.

We see what Berlage (1982) calls the "homogenization of organizational America" through parents' widespread embrace of organizational leisure and its near monopolization over the after-school time period in children's days and lives. It reflects a society that has embraced the virtues and values of corporate-style organization. These adult-structured activities encourage professionalization and specialization, opposing children's unorganized tendencies toward recreation and generalism. They have also fundamentally changed the nature and dynamics of leisure and play. Play becomes transformed into games, and games into work. This contrasts with Mead's (1934) image of development as passing through the play, game, and generalized other stages. What is incrementally added on in this more contemporary model is the corporate character of the final stage. Previously, children were considered socialized upon being able to take the role of the generalized other and competently anticipate how an amorphous entity composed of "people" or "society" might respond to their self-presentations, thus enabling themselves to plan or modify their actions accordingly. This nebulous collective of evaluating others has been shaped more clearly for children by the adult-dominated world of today's leisure. Their developmental process now includes socialization to the after-school institution, one embodying an organizational framework that encompasses an implicit ascension up the ladder of adult, corporate-style norms, values, and structures. Complete socialization and self-development now require that children and adolescents become competent at "taking the role of the corporate other" and anticipating and understanding the organizational perspective. While they might have previously encountered and incorporated this view at a later age, our society has communicated its fundamental importance by bringing it more directly into the childhood socialization experience.

Yet children are not just passive recipients of adult society's exports; its features cannot be forced on them. Children's peer subcultures mediate between their incumbents and the norms and values of the adult world. Children have to like and accept the characteristics of adult offerings, or they will refuse to participate in them. As Corsaro (1986) suggests, children's withdrawals from adult rules and expectations are not directed toward the development of self-identity, as these are with adults, but toward the development of resistive youth peer cultures. The historical rise in the after-school movement shows that adults want to control children's activities and thereby inculcate them with adult values and directions. To do so, they have to structure leisure activities in ways that Goffman (1961) calls "engrossing," thereby enticing and holding kids to these endeavors without driving them away. Goffman suggests that encounters attain a euphoric quality, motivating participants to withhold their attention and concern from other interests and focusing them on the matter at hand (within the "interaction membrane"), in three ways: when they stimulate a certain level of tension (greater than everyday life, but lower than the breaking point), when they yield a process that permits the skilled display of participants' capacities, and when their timing is structured to attain a problematic outcome, so that the results will not be known until nearly the end.[1]

Adult-structured after-school activities encompass many of these qualities, bringing elements of intensity, dedication, seriousness, commitment, structured rules, and competition. Yet at the same time they also contain features that do not appeal to young people, such as selflessness and sacrifice (to the group), repetition (which creates boredom, especially in practices), deferred gratification, and the structured stratification of participants into hierarchies according to winning and talent.

In considering the benefits or harm generated by the infusion of adult control and the associated adult-oriented structures and values into the leisure of children and youth, we see elements of both. Our observations suggest that in progressing through the stages of after-school activities children learn several important norms and values about the nature of adult society. They discover the importance placed by adults on rules, regulations, and order. Creativity is encouraged, but acknowledged within the boundaries of certain well-defined parameters. Obedience, discipline, sacrifice, seriousness, and focused attention are valued; deviance, dabbling, and self-indulgence are not. Coordination with others, the organic model of working toward challenging and complex goals, stands as the ultimate model toward which young people are directed. Whether pursuing a collective activity in the sphere of music, athletics, academics, or nature, or working for individual achievement surrounded by a coterie of others who coach, support, transport, supply, and chronicle, young people learn that the highest, most rewarded levels of extracurricular participation embody the teamwork archetype. This anticipatory socialization to the organized, competitive world used to be the more exclusive domain of young boys, giving them what Borman and Frankel (1984) claim is a competitive advantage in the adult corporate world. But now that institutionalized competitive play has extended into the female realm, there may be greater gender equalization for this generation's future adults. In fact, girls' gender role images appear to be expanding to a much greater extent than are boys'. Girls, thus, are already beginning to change the world by moving into boys' realms.

At the same time, the earlier imposition of adult norms and values onto childhood, while contributing to children's successful socialization into the adult world, may rob them of developmentally valuable play, unchanneled and pursued for merely expressive rather than instrumental purposes. (Cf. Qvortrup 1993, who regards after-school activities as a form of social control.) By participating in increasing amounts of adult-organized activities, children forego some of the formative experiences embodied in spontaneous play, including forging collective decisions, learning how to negotiate and resolve problems through communication and cooperation, discovering the effects of stubbornness and withdrawal, and encountering the unfettered consequences of peer group dynamics. As a result, they are steered away from goal setting, improvisation, and self-reliance toward the acceptance of adult authority and adult goals. While these after-school activities may prepare children for the formally rational, hierarchical, and, in Foucault's (1977) words, disciplined adult world, children's spontaneous play may teach different but important social lessons. Adult-organized activities may prepare children for passively accepting the adult world as given; the activities that children organize themselves may prepare them for constructing alternative worlds.

Moreover, participating in these adult-organized activities draws children into junior versions of the existing social order. Adult society is reproduced in miniature there, both culturally and structurally. Hengst (1987) places this within a historical trend toward convergence and leveling between adults and children, closing the generation gap. Children are increasingly turned into miniature adults as they become consumers of clothing, entertainment, the media, and as their activities are transformed into work. Not only are the norms and values of adult culture embodied in organized after-school activities, but the structural inequalities of race, class, and, to a lesser extent, gender are somewhat inherent as well. It takes money to support a child going "up the ladder" of after-school activities, and while families from lower socioeconomic groups participate in these endeavors, they cannot afford them to the same extent as more affluent households (Erwin 1995; Qvortrup 1993). If these experiences prepare youngsters for the corporate work world—partly through their enhanced "cultural capital" (Bourdieu 1977a) of additional knowledge, skills, and disposition and partly through the "habitus" (Bourdieu 1977b), the attitude and experience of achievement they acquire—then after-school activities are yet another route to reproducing social inequities. The channeling of low-income racial group members into inexpensive, segregated activities may also become exacerbated as more extracurricular activities are moved from the realm of public education into the private domain. Finally, while girls' activities have made significant strides toward parity with boys' over the last decade, gender segregation and stereotyping still remain, with patriarchal structures and attitudes continuing to dominate significant portions of the field. The after-school arena may constitute a previously unaddressed venue of socialization contributing to social reproduction, augmenting existing studies of tracking (Bowles and Gintis 1976), the social relations of schooling (Bowles and Gintis 1976), class-based differences in linguistic codes (Bernstein 1977), and the relationship between aspiration and opportunity (Bourdieu and Passeron 1977). As such, it stands beside, rather than within, the educational institution.

The after-school phenomenon encompasses two processes: it serves as an extracurricular vehicle fostering the perpetuation of social inequality, and it is part of an institutionalized pathway encompassing funneled participation, specialization, professionalization, and conformity. For the latter, these activities represent the extension of a trend seen in high school, college, and the professional ranks, with participants entering the precocious world of semi-adult sophistication at ever earlier ages. These recreational activities offer a doorway into the youth subculture for adults. In exploiting this opening, adults have seized the opportunity to transform the character of children's play. What they have created, in so doing, is an ironic juxtaposition of work and play: play has become the vehicle for infusing adult work values into children's lives.

Peer Power: Culture, Socialization, and Identity

Preadolescence and its peer culture occupy a critical position in society. On the one hand, preadolescence as an age range stands as a developmental midpoint between the raw undevelopment of birth and the sophisticated functioning of adulthood. As Frønes (1994, 162) notes, "The structure and form of society influence socialization by shaping the social and cultural framework of childhood. Childhood thus functions as a conceptual bridge between societal and individual development." Preadolescence represents a time when people are learning about themselves and society, when they are changing dramatically. Individuals are sophisticated enough to understand what is going on around them, and to form beliefs and values. Yet they have not begun to seriously separate themselves from their families and determine their own lifestyles. They stand at a critical temporal midpoint.

At the same time, the culture of preadolescence is vital to mediating how individuals pass through this age period, how they develop and are shaped, and how they shape society, as they pass through preadolescence and later, as adults. Preadolescents do not perceive, interpret, form opinions about, or act on the world as unconnected individuals. Rather, they do all these things in concert with their peers, as they collectively experience the world, encounter problems, share their perceptions, and forge joint solutions to those problems. As Harris (1995, 467) notes in her theory of group socialization, neither parents nor society transmit their culture directly to children; culture is transmitted from the parents' peer group, and from society in general, to the children's peer group. From there, children's peer groups create their own culture by selecting and rejecting various aspects of the adult culture and by making cultural innovations of their own. Preadolescents adopt peer-guided interpretations to things around them, and they forge new interpretations as their environment changes and their experiences within it change. They impart these new interpretations to the collective peer culture. Preadolescent peer culture represents what Frønes (1994, 157) calls "the conceptual bridge between society and the individual, between personality and the cultural framework. . . . A counterculture of a subordinate age group, based on mechanical solidarity, a similarity of age, and position, in opposition to the adult world"; it incorporates elements of norms and values, of patterns and variations, of ideology and lifestyle. Kovarik (1994) likens it to a fortress, a place where it is safe to test resistance to adult authority. Understanding preadolescent peer culture is critical to understanding how children will develop into adults. It integrates their lives, concomitantly contributing to and being infused with elements of their experience. Any study of preadolescents would be remiss in not seriously addressing it.

Preadolescent peer culture is a dynamic entity, moderating and changing with its times, surroundings, and occupants. Symbolic interactionist theory has always viewed subcultures as recursive. No individual is born into a society devoid of occupants and their subcultures; these primary groups socialize and shape young people as they grow. At the same time, subcultures are ongoing and evolving, subject to change from within and without. Giddens's theory of structuration (1984, 25) echoes this theme, emphasizing the recursive duality of structure. Peer cultures, as structures, represent "organized sets of rules and resources, outside of time and space," but the social systems in which they are embedded "comprise the situated activities of human agents." As such, they exist apart from people but constrain and enable people, who adapt and change them as they use them. Corsaro and Eder (1990, 200), in a derivative of Giddens's work, propose that children's peer cultures are "interpretively reproductive." They suggest that "children become part of adult culture through their negotiations with adults and their creative production of a series of peer cultures with other children." Peer cultures are constituted in which children not only reproduce but also challenge and transform the world of adults so as to achieve self-control and a measure of autonomy (Corsaro 1986). Children get from and give back to adult culture. In short, preadolescent peer culture, while mediating between individuals and society, changes and evolves in an ongoing manner, in response to both individuals and society.

Preadolescent peer culture is a very powerful entity. The cement that bonds preadolescents, unifying their lives and their outlooks, it is something that they desperately try to align themselves within. Even as they vocally assert their rights to be individuals, they herd together like sheep. As children become preadolescents and then adolescents, they progressively locate their primary self-lodging away from their early primary groups and into their company of peers. Two of the most powerful functions associated with preadolescent peer culture are its socializing effects and its influence on the way individuals construct their identities. Through interacting with their peers, and by judging themselves against the standards and behavior of peer norms, people forge self-conceptions that lie at the core of their being. They learn the various aspects of peer culture and apply them to their sense of self in myriad ways. These derive, in part, from various aspects of their peer culture.

GENDERED PEER CULTURE

The differential popularity factors for boys and girls that we sketched in chapter 2 and throughout this work coalesce to constitute models of idealized gender roles that children and the generalized children's culture hold in high esteem. While boys and girls are surely born with differences in their character, aptitudes, and interests, our research suggests that they further accentuate these differences as a consequence of their interaction in gendered peer cultures. The pressure for conformity is very strong in preadolescence, and children aspire to fit themselves within the gender roles that they perceive as socially appropriate. This represents a form of anticipatory socialization, where children learn complexes of skills and values associated with accomplishing their gender roles satisfactorily.

The gender roles portrayed by girls and boys differ in regard to their active and passive, as well as their achieved and ascribed, natures. Both of these dichotomies can be seen, in overlapping and independent fashions. Boys' and girls' idealized gender images embody these differential polarities in several of the following cultural attributes. It is noteworthy, however, that these patterns are usually more apparent in the generalized roles themselves than in children's actual behavior.

Boys prosper in the youthful popularity system and carve out their gender identities through a successful internalization and expression of the male ethos. Their focal concerns evince an awareness of and aspiration toward the "cult of masculinity," through which they can demonstrate their growth, maturity, and distance from the femininity characterizing their early family-oriented lives. They try to adopt elements of the machismo posture through their toughness and defiance of adult authority, challenging prescribed rules and roles in class and distancing themselves from academics. To gain the admiration of, and popularity among their peers, they brag and boast about their exploits (despite norms of modesty) in the areas of sport, experiments with deviant behavior, success with girls, and dominance over other boys.

Boys' culture also embodies their "expression of physicality" in its central focus on active participation and prowess in sport. Boys spend most of their free time outdoors, carving out and conquering space, filling it up with their play and games, and overrunning the play of girls and younger boys (cf. Thorne 1986; Voss 1997). Their physicality is competitive and dominating, structured to involve contests where one individual or team bests the other and revels in the victory. Physical displays, both within and outside of the game structure, can also culminate in physical aggression and fights between boys, where masculinity is tested and dominance established.

The active nature of boys' lives is tied to their "orientation of autonomy." They know that part of growing up involves measuring up, or proving themselves as men. They prepare themselves for this eventuality by regularly measuring themselves against each other. They strive for independence from adult authority figures, for self-reliance and toughness. They cut themselves and each other off from the "cult of coddling" with sharp remarks and derogations against "babylike" behavior, toughening themselves in preparation for their adult role.

Finally, boys enter into the "culture of coolness," assuming suitably detached postures and attitudes both within and outside their groups. They act cool in distancing themselves from things they used to like but now define as feminine or nerdy. They act cool by repressing emotionality and dealing with others on a physical level. Most especially, they have to act cool to protect themselves in cross-gender relations, to avoid excessively weakening themselves due to their structural position of having to expose their interest in girls and face possible rejection.

Focal concerns of the girls' peer culture and gender role revolve around an entirely different set of skills and values. In contrast to the boys' defiance, girls become absorbed into the "culture of compliance and conformity." They occupy themselves with games and social interactions where they practice and perfect established social roles, rules, and relationships. Not only do they follow explicitly stated rules, but they extrapolate upon these, enforcing them onto others as well. Their superior performance in elementary school reflects not necessarily their greater innate intelligence but their more passive adherence to the normative order. Their instances of rebellion or misbehavior are more likely to be directed into social channels, toward other girls.

From an earlier age than boys, girls are attracted to the "culture of romance" (cf. Eisenhart and Holland 1983; Valli 1988). They fantasize about romantic involvements with boys and become interested, sooner, in crossing gender lines for relationships, both platonic and otherwise. They absorb idealized images of gendered ways of relating to boys based partly on traditional roles. This fosters passivity and dependence by encouraging them to wait for boys to select them. Girls who accomplish romance successfully, by attracting a boy who will actively pursue them, gain ascribed status among other girls.

Passivity is also inherent in the "ideology of domesticity" (cf. Valli 1988) that characterizes girls' play and interaction. Unlike the boys, who search for the physical limits of their bodies and the social limits of their school, group, and society through their efforts to challenge these limits, the girls carve out their inner space. They live indoor lives, draw indoor scenes, and concern themselves with nurturing, smoothing over problems or inequalities, and gathering others around them. They focus on the emotional dimension of expression and become more adept at intimate contact than at openly competing against others (cf. Deaux 1977; Gilligan 1982; Karweit and Hansell 1983b).

Hovering over all this is an "orientation of ascription" that is not found in as pronounced a manner among boys. From their parents and the mass media, they learn that the woman's role is to attract a man who will bestow upon her his status. While many of their mothers have careers, they see that these jobs are often accorded secondary stature within the family. Girls perceive, thus, that women partly get their status by its being attached to them. They therefore look to see what is attached to other girls. This comes out in their preoccupation with ascribed features of potential playmates such as material possessions, lifestyles, houses, and appearances. As part of this reflected role, girls also learn that women often get what they want through indirection and manipulation rather than direct action, and this becomes a part of their behavioral repertoire.

Yet although these ascribed/achieved and active/passive divergences are embodied in the popularity factors and the idealized gender images, it would be a mistake to assume that girls' and boys' activities reflect these dissimilarities. Our data show that girls are, in fact, no more passive in their everyday behavior than boys, that they work to get good grades, to play at sports, to be involved in extracurricular activities, and to stay embedded within their cliques. Boys, at the same time, display a passivity in leveling themselves academically to conform to peer group norms. Boys can be as manipulative and indirect as girls in their jockeying to maintain both boundaries around their friendship groups and their own positions within these.

What we see, then, is that boys and girls are active and passive within their own realms. They both employ agency within the structural framework provided by their gender roles, socially constructing their behavior so that it accords with the impressions they seek in order to achieve popularity among their peers. Under the guise of passivity and being attached, girls actively produce their peer status (although it may be done indirectly), while boys engineer images of themselves as forthright, active, and democratic, all the while working the back channels and scanning others for ascribed traits. Boys and girls actively create their roles of passivity and activity, achievement and ascription, in accord with their perceptions of the larger culture. These are patterns and roles that they learn in preadolescence and that they will continue to display as adults.

PEER GROUP DYNAMICS

Preadolescents also learn how to manage peer group dynamics through their subculture. Their experiences, particularly with the cliques that we discussed in chapter 3, not only teach them the dynamics of power and manipulation but impress upon them the importance of conformity. While social conformity has many prosocial functions, ensuring the survival of the group, it represents an opposing force to self-awareness (Diener 1980), and when carried to its extreme, can lead to what Janis (1972) calls "groupthink," the reduced capacity for critical reflection. Sociologists have long sought to discover the basis of social conformity, pondering citizens' adherence to totalitarian or repressive regimes, especially their passive acquiescence to the regimes of mass annihilation during the Second World War. Classical experiments, such as those by Asch

(1955) and Milgram (1963, 1965), shocked the academic world by documenting the lengths to which people will go, in response to mild social pressure, in
order to align themselves with others' instructions or behaviors. While subservience to peer groups is common in preadolescence, it becomes dangerous
under two conditions: when carried to an extreme, leading participants into
dangerous or immoral acts, or when children fail to grow out of it in adulthood
(Stone and Church 1984). The depth and severity of the pressures children experience toward group conformity through the clique dynamics of inclusion and
exclusion help to explain the strength of the early foundations of conforming
behavior, and the reward and punishment system through which it is socialized.

These clique dynamics also teach preadolescents to reproduce society's
strong feelings of differentiation between in-groups and out-groups. Individuals become highly sensitized to the opposition in which these groups are jux-
taposed and the sharply carved boundaries separating them. They form group
affiliation, the basis of in-group favoritism. At the same time they develop feelings of intolerance toward individuals not privileged to be accepted as members, adopting an ethnocentric perspective that accords their own attitudes,
values, and behaviors a higher degree of status, while devaluing those of others. Tajfel (1970) calls this the "generic norm of in-group/out-group bias," while
Harris (1995) considers these two sets of feelings for in-groups and out-groups
two of the "foundational" dynamics of peer group socialization. This fosters their
making what Pettigrew (1979) terms the "ultimate attribution error," leading
clique members to deny credit to out-group members while overrating the abilities of in-group members. Clique dynamics of inclusion and exclusion teach
young people the fundamental values of conflict and prejudice. As such, they
may form the basis for the societal reproduction of racism, anti-Semitism, sex-
ism, and other forms of bigotry and discrimination.

Finally, from these clique dynamics preadolescents learn the subtleties of
within-group jockeying for status, a third "foundational" predisposition of Harris's (1995) peer groups. They construct stratification systems based not on outside factors such as race or wealth, but on the internal factors of power,
popularity, and social status. This stratification is not fixed but, as in many locations in the adult world, fluid and changing. Internal group hierarchy is
something they will detect in every social group or organization they encounter.
From this, individuals learn *that* they should and *how* they should compete with
their friends. This includes both mechanisms for disadvantaging others as well
as advantaging themselves, through skillful combinations of leadership and
strategic followership. These dynamics constitute the politics of human group
life, from the microworld of everyday interaction, to the mesoworld of social
and work organizations, to the macroworld of governmental politics. Ironically,

while children exposed to more severe clique dynamics may suffer interpersonally, they master these characteristics of group functioning at an earlier age and henceforth adapt more successfully in peer interactions.

STRATIFICATION AND IDENTITY

The preadolescent peer culture further illuminates the relation of social position to identity. Scholars have long contemplated the precise nature of this relationship. Our research, particularly as discussed in chapter 4, suggests that the hierarchical ordering based on popularity and status is not strictly replicated in the identity arena. This varies from the direct stratification of status ranking and self-esteem found by sociologists studying the prestige hierarchy of occupations (Hodge, Siegel, and Rossi 1964) and the prestige hierarchy of ethnic and racial groups (Bogardus 1959). In addition, most social psychologists, as Rosenberg (1981, 603) notes, have "tended to take it for granted that those ranking lower in the various status hierarchies would have lower self-esteem than the more favored members of society."

The structural-relational hierarchy of identity inferred by our research is more complex than this, for it is grounded in two complementary elements: status and relationship. Status comprises four features: a pure *rank-orientation*, based on prestige, recognition, and visibility; an *attractiveness* component, tied to popularity and desirability; a *power and dominance* feature, embodying the ability to ridicule or pick on others while remaining safe from such degradation; and *leadership*, the ability to influence and have one's opinions accepted by others. Relationship is also defined by four component features: *camaraderie*, the freedom from loneliness that comes with having friends; *loyalty*, the degree of trust and allegiance in those friendships; *security*, or the stability and certainty of one's membership in the group; and *role in group*, involving one's core centrality versus marginality or peripherality in intragroup relations. Together, these two elements combine to stratify groups and their members along the identity hierarchy, as table 1 illustrates.

Table 1
A Hierarchy of Group Identity

	Status	*Relationship*
Popular	+	− +
Middle	−	+
Wannabe	− +	−
Isolate	—	—

The necessity of relational criteria in addition to those of pure status for understanding the identity hierarchy illustrates the need for integrating the perspectives of the processual and structural branches of symbolic interactionism. The processual approach focuses on the social situation as the context in which identities are interactionally negotiated, conceiving identity as situated, emergent, and reciprocal (Becker 1964; Blumer 1969; Glaser and Strauss 1965; Stone 1962; Strauss 1978). The structural interactionists emphasize identities as internalized roles, behavioral expectations associated with a position or status and thereby more directly tied to the social structure (Burke and Tully 1977; McCall and Simmons 1966; Stryker 1980). The importance of status elements to identity reifies the structuralists' concern with individuals' self-conceptions as based on social position and connected to social structure. The relational elements of identity are rooted in the emergence and negotiation of individuals' reciprocal friendship relations, thus evoking an interactional base in the social situation. Yet children's definitions and evaluations of self do not arise out of a combined patchwork of structural and processual influences, but are firmly grounded in a more integrated structural-relational foundation. This foundation is rooted in what Simmel (1950) considers the key element, or level of analysis, necessary to understanding society: "sociation"—those crystallized interactions binding groups of people and at the same time distinguishing them from each other. The crystallized interactions repeatedly characterizing children's interactions within and between groups are what mark the groups' character, distinguish them in relation to one another, and set the members' identities. This includes such patterned interactions as the repeated exclusion of wannabes by the popular clique members, the failures by the social isolates to find acceptance with any group, and the nonhierarchical, leaderless character of the middle friendship circles. This structural-relational identity shows us that processual and structural interactionists may have drifted too far from the critical center in their focus on negotiated interaction and social structure. These theoretical tensions may best be resolved by searching for the confluence of the two approaches at the Simmelian level of sociation rather than by focusing on their distinctiveness.

ROMANTIC IDENTITY

Finally, preadolescent peer culture encompasses a time period during which boys and girls go though a roller-coaster ride with regard to each other, varying between the extremes of high interest and intense disdain. It is also during this time that they begin to forge culturally sanctioned romantic pursuit of each other. As chapters 8 and 9 discuss, preadolescent cross-gender relations go through roughly three phases. During the first phase, gender integration, the youngest preadolescents generally regard each other with romantic neutrality. Although some individuals fantasize about romantic interest and liaisons, and others refer to their cross-gender friends (or are referred by others) as boyfriends or girlfriends, cross-gender friendships at this age are generally platonic. Boys' and girls' interests at this time overlap more closely, their differences in strength and size are fewer, and they play as relative equals. The period of gender integration is one where romantic awareness is low.

In the second stage, gender segregation is accompanied by a high level of romantic tension. The slightest indication of romantic interest brings pointed and painful teasing and stigma. People feel comfortable expressing interest in same-gender relations, but not in cross-gender ones. Although some would like to role-model the romantic relations of older friends and relatives, very few dare to express this openly. In general, during this period, cross-gender relations fall to their lowest ebb. Boys begin to get stronger, although not bigger, and their interests diverge widely from girls'. With some exceptions, when they do interact, it is for short time spans only, and it is fraught with tension.

The third stage, gender forays, is marked by a romantic awakening, during which preadolescents begin to acknowledge their burgeoning romantic feelings for members of the other gender and tentatively explore them. While boys and girls still hold many differences in their recreational interests, they are brought back together by their developing interest in each other. Some tread upon this path earlier and more courageously than others. This represents one of those critical transition points where individuals can make a lifestyle choice: they can advance forward toward social sophistication, or they can lag behind in security. It is for this reason that Frønes (1994) calls age a matter of individual choice and construction. Throughout these stages, individuals form self-images about themselves as romantic or nonromantic beings.

Critical to this pattern of stage progression is the role of preadolescent peer culture in first holding back, but then leading the way into, cross-gender romantic relations. While there is little talk or awareness of romance as a dimension in the early period, and strong norms and sanctions constrain it in the middle years, preadolescents diverge more in their romantic behavior during the later years, as some venture into this territory before others. The path of cross-gender romance is forged through a combination of the acts of these intrepid fore-runners and the legacy left behind by older people, including siblings and friends, who have made previous romantic forays. These stand as models for others to follow, and as social legitimations within the peer culture.

Those who make their romantic moves in the *early* phases of the period may engender a variety of identities. They may find success and status, being regarded as mavericks, looked up to and emulated by envious others. They may revel in the excitement they generate, both for themselves and others. They may enjoy the new opportunities they have opened for themselves by succeeding in forging a romantic liaison, acquiring peer status, and modeling the rewards and intimacy of the relationships they have observed among their parents and other adults. At the same time, they make this move with a certain amount of fear. Considerable attention is focused on those who lead the crowd, who try new things, who forge social change through deviance from social norms. They act in the fishbowl of the peer culture, and their greater visibility brings enhanced magnification of their success or failure. Those who attempt romantic forays risk shattering their sense of self-worth if their feelings are not reciprocated. This fills them with trepidation, paralyzing them into inaction. Overcoming their fear takes time and fortitude, and may be bolstered by the encouragement of friends. Failures have to manage their loss of status in the publicity of the peer culture. Ironically, people can meet with some success in this area and still suffer identity decline. While the popular, front-running crowd may encourage early romantic forays, others may look on these as disgusting, especially if they have any sexual overtones. People may be branded as shameful, dirty, and disgusting for acts that they commit, and even for reputations that exceed those acts. Because of the lingering double standard, girls are particularly prone to being labeled sluts if they engage in early romantic or sexual behavior.

Preadolescents who lean toward the *middle* path are safe. They can rest easily, nestled in the comfort and security of the cultural norms, neither challenging the bounds of new behavior nor being challenged by them. They have the benefit and detriment of generating the least peer attention, since they take no risks, generating neither admiration nor scorn. Nor do they receive the derision of unpopularity from romantic lagging; they carefully follow the trends set by others when the group social norms have moved the middle pathway to a given space. They are the ones who sit back and judge the front-runners and the laggards.

In the rear, those who are *late* on the romantic path encounter criticism and condemnation. This is not usually as severe as with those condemned for being out front, because social norms vary more widely in the rear, with people taking different amounts of time to catch up with the group. As we noted in chapter 4, people at the top of the status hierarchy generate more visibility than those at the middle and bottom, and this applies to those who are ahead of or behind developing trends as well. People who lag are less readily noticed or talked about than those in the lead. Such laggers may be labeled undesirable or uncool. If they lag excessively, people may begin to speculate that something is wrong with them. This lagging may take the form in the middle years of not giving up cross-gender platonic relationships, and in the later years of still thinking of members of the other gender as having "cooties." The most severely visible and stigmatized norm violators are those who violate the norms in the most radical ways: those who try repeatedly and unsuccessfully for romantic relations, especially in the middle years, or who inappropriately denounce what has come to be normatively accepted cross-gender romantic behavior. The identity consequences for people's relation to the culturally normative romantic path resemble Csikszentmihalyi's (1975) concept of the flow state, as something more engrossing than boredom, yet less engrossing than anxiety. People's identity in relation to the normative cultural path is represented in table 2.

Identity consequences of individuals' romantic progression in relation to the normative path may also be related to their sexual development and the onset of puberty. Physically, some people, especially girls, may be pushed into precocious sexuality before they are ready. Developing early secondary sex traits may result in their being treated by boys as sex objects. Girls who facilitate this treatment by responding positively to this attention may enhance their popularity. This teaches and reinforces their conceptions of self as physical commodities and sexual objects. Like girls who encounter early unwanted sexual attention within the family, they may develop lasting ways of relating to men through their sexuality. Yet girls do not similarly treat boys who enter puberty early. They may tease them for their cracking voices, or call them taunting names, such as "Ben Mustache." The precocious and popular girls may pay more attention to them, seek them out by chasing them at school and calling them on the phone at home. It appears, though, that the consequences to boys for precocious sexual development are not comparable to girls'. This difference is likely rooted in the broader society's cultural objectification of women as sexual commodities.

Although we noted in chapter 9 that some groups were more likely to see their members openly express romantic interest than others, this precocity may

Table 2
Identity and the Normative Path

	Gender Denouncing	Gender Isolated	Platonic	Romantic
Early	−	+	+	+
Middle	+	+	−	—
Later	−	+	+	+ / −

be tied more to normative acceptance of romantic expression, or to the power of group suggestion, than to the frequency of individuals in that group having romantic inclinations. Preadolescents' private development of romantic or sexual interest was not necessarily tied to their status group membership but tended to be more spread out across groups. These interests were culturally scripted by boys' and girls' gendered cultures, with boys more focused on sexuality earlier, and girls thinking about getting a crush or having a romance.

From these discussions, we see the power of peer culture, setting both the content and timing of preadolescent cultural norms and values. From their subculture, children learned the culturally acceptable behavioral guidelines and the consequences of violating them. They saw the positive and negative sanctions, social status and ridicule, applied to individuals based on their power, position, attitudes, and behavior. They learned and experienced the identity outcomes of their placement in relation to the peer culture. Their peer culture divided and unified them. It divided them by stratifying and setting them against each other. But it also forged them together in relation to older and younger groups in society. It took what was culturally appropriate (by preadolescent standards) out of the adult culture and translated it into preadolescent ways of thinking and communicating. It deconstructed and reconstructed elements of adult culture into preadolescent cultural forms. It supported age-related standards that stood in defiance of adult standards, that gave preadolescents their own beliefs and code. It fixed an age-related preadolescent collective identity that marked them apart from other age groups. It united and divided them, supported and destroyed them, gave them structure and process, and fit them as a distinctive subunit within the broader American culture.

Notes

Introduction

1. Sociological interest in the field of children's studies saw a renaissance during the last decade of the twentieth century. Sociologists reclaimed this field, which had been mostly ceded over to developmental psychologists and social workers, and produced an array of scholarly and institutional accomplishments: an annual research series devoted to children's studies (*Sociological Studies of Child Development*, see Adler and Adler 1986); an international effort, "The Childhood Project," coordinating research and publication on childhood across sixteen European countries (begun in 1987); several edited anthologies (see Handel 1988; Waksler 1991); a thematic working group on the "Sociology of Childhood" in the International Sociological Association (1990), a section on the "Sociology of Children" in the American Sociological Association (1992), and several scholarly monographs (see Corsaro 1997 for a complete review).

Chapter 1   The Parent-as-Researcher

1. For excellent overviews of methodological issues in studying children, see Corsaro (1996), Corsaro and Streeck (1986), Fine and Glassner (1979), and Fine and Sandstrom (1988). For more psychological approaches, see Damon (1977) and Rizzo, Corsaro, and Bates (1992).
2. Most ethnographers assume the position of either friendly observers (Best 1983; Corsaro 1985; Eder 1995; Glassner 1976; Goodwin 1990; Kless 1992; Opie 1993; Peshkin 1982; Rizzo 1989; Thorne 1993) or observing friends (Fine 1987; Mandell 1988). Waksler's (1986; 1996) retrospective method for studying children entails asking adults to recall their childhood experiences. Fine and Sandstrom (1988) articulate four roles available to adult ethnographers: the supervisor, the leader, the observer, and the friend.
3. Notable exceptions to this trend include Goodwin's (1990) work on the language of neighborhood street children, Willis's (1981) work on the culture of working-class youth, and Wulff's (1988) work on the ethnicity of South London girls.
4. See Ellis (1995), Karp (1996), Krieger (1991), and Ouellet (1994) for just a few recent book-length examples.
5. For discussions of the methodological approach of Erik Erikson, see Erikson (1973), Evans (1967), and Maier (1965); for that of Jean Piaget, see Evans (1973), Maier (1965), and Modgil (1976); and for that of Charles Cooley, see Jandy (1942) and Reiss (1968). It is interesting to note that the intellectual climate of their times was more receptive to the theories generated by their observational methods than to

the methods themselves, which were often viewed as excessively subjective and not sufficiently rigorous.

6. See Britsch (1995), Carere (1987), Daiker and Morenberg (1990), Goswami and Stillman (1987), Hustler, Cassidy, and Cuff (1986),and Pinnell and Matlin (1989).

7. See Cottle (1980) and Moustakas (1990).

8. We would like to thank Spencer Cahill for suggesting this concept to us. While the children never actually addressed us by the term "cool parents," they said such things as, "I could never talk to my parents like this," "You guys are so much easier to talk to," and "I could never tell my parents about this."

9. One of the most common dilemmas faced by adults who enter school settings as strangers and attempt to establish ethnographic research roles is pressure from institutional gatekeepers to enforce school disciplinary norms. Such authoritative behavior distances researchers from their subjects, yet noncompliance risks alienating them from their adult sponsors (cf. Eder 1995; Mandell 1988; Thorne 1993).

10. Ironically, however, when we were conducting interviews in the school the following year, a younger brother of this boy volunteered to be interviewed, and the parents spoke with us and gave us their consent.

11. While we primarily focused on preadolescents, we continued to monitor and stay in touch with many of our subjects even after they moved out of this age range. We occasionally used them at older ages for retroactive reflections and to follow up with trends and patterns begun in preadolescence and continued into later years (see chapter 9).

12. Gary Alan Fine, personal communication.

13. See Gusterson (1993), Hertz and Imber (1993), Rosaldo (1989). Numerous examples of studying down appear in the literature, ranging from anthropological (colonial) studies, research on criminal groups, studies of the disenfranchised and disadvantaged, and nearly all research involving children and other vulnerable populations.

14. Although we have found nothing specifically written about this subject, there is, however, discussion in some fields about negative effects of researchers' nonconsensual use of their children as subjects. In particular, the Child Language Data Exchange System, a compilation of parent-child transcripts donated by researchers (including some parent observers), is available to all language acquisition scholars. Stories of the subsequent resentment of children whose early language anecdotes have been written down, preserved indefinitely, and made accessible to hundreds of researchers have circulated informally in this field (James Morgan, personal communication).

15. This contrast is mirrored by the differential latitude afforded private investigators, who can enter locations and make inquiries relatively freely, whereas government officers, such as police, are bound by more restrictive investigative and evidentiary requirements.

16. One minor exception to this is the methodological reflection offered by Carere (1987) on the covert research she conducted while substitute-teaching elementary school children.

Chapter 2 *Popularity*

1. Many other scholars also note the importance of athletic ability to popularity; see Coleman (1961), Eder and Parker (1987), Eitzen (1975), Fine (1987), Schofield (1981).

2. Rituals of pollution refer to inter-gender activities where each gender accuses the other of having "germs" or "cooties." Thorne (1986, 174–175) notes that girls are

perceived as being more polluting than boys, and this anticipates and influences cross-cultural patterns of feminine subordination.

3. Children with older siblings were often more precocious than others, overcoming their reluctance to approach girls and initiating rites of flirtation and dating.

4. Dion and Berscheid (1974) note that friendship choices are often based on physical attractiveness. Dodge (1983) and Young and Cooper (1944) correlate low physical attractiveness with social rejection.

5. See Coleman (1961), Eder and Sanford (1986), Eder and Parker (1987), and Schofield (1981).

6. Simon, Eder, and Evans (1992) note that having a boyfriend enhances girls' popularity.

7. In the second grade, a group of popular girls, whose ringleader was extremely precocious, phoned boys on a regular basis. They asked them silly questions, giggled, and left long messages on their telephone answering machines. At one school outing, the dominant girl bribed a boy she liked with money and candy to kiss her, but when he balked at the task (after having eaten the candy and spent the money), she had to pretend to her friends that he had, so as to avoid losing face.

8. One girl even lied to her friends, pretending that she was going with a popular boy. When they found out that she had fabricated the story, they dropped her; so she lost both her status and her friends.

Chapter 3 *Clique Dynamics*

1. See Hallinan (1979), Hubbell (1965), Peay (1974), and Varenne (1982) for a discussion of cliques' sociometric characteristics.

2. They are primary groups, offering individuals the opportunity to select close friendships of their own choosing (Elkin and Handel 1989), to learn about society, to practice their behavior, and to evolve their selves and identities. Autonomous from the world of adults (Fine 1981), they are often forged in opposition to adult values (Elkin and Handel 1989), with a culture of resistance to adult standards (Corsaro 1985). They thus encompass a robust form of children's peer culture that is both unique in its own right yet at the same time a staging ground for future adult behavior.

3. Among these are studies focusing on the way children clump together into racial groups (Criswell 1937; Schofield 1981; Singleton and Asher 1977), into class-stratified groups (Coleman 1961; Gordon 1957; Hollingshead 1949), and into gender-segregated groups (Berentzen 1984; Best 1983; Goodwin 1990; Hallinan 1979; 1980; Lever 1976; Thorne 1993; Thorne and Luria 1986). Other studies look at the influence of structural characteristics of classrooms and schools such as size or organization (Dawe 1934; Gump and Friesen 1964; Hallinan 1979; Wicker 1969), the way shared student interests create bonds (Cusik 1973), and the influence of weak social skills (the social skill deficit hypothesis) (Asher and Renshaw 1981; Gottman, Gonso, and Rasmussen 1975; Kinney 1993; Oden and Asher 1977; Putallaz and Gottman 1981) on children's ability to form and be accepted into friendship groups. Another cluster of research within this genre employs sociometric measures to investigate the characteristics of friendship circles. Asking children to identify schoolmates they like or dislike, researchers generate models of reciprocal choice. These studies examine the number, size, exclusiveness, and stability of children's friendship groups (Glidewell et al. 1966; Hallinan 1979) as well as their sociometric exclusion, or social isolation, and its negative consequences (Asher, Oden, and Gottman 1977; Gronlund 1959; Hymel and Asher 1977; Roff, Sells, and Golden 1972). While the term "clique" is occasionally used in this literature, its definition differs from the way we are using it here. These previous scholars consider

cliques to be fundamentally equivalent to friendship groups, identifying anywhere from four to eight per grade level. This usage lacks the feature of exclusiveness, where only one clique dominates the upper status rung of a grade and is uniformly identified by members and nonmembers alike as the "popular clique." Where we start to see studies engaging the exclusivity feature is the research on popularity, which incorporates the element of status stratification, such that groups identified as popular are more likely to be true cliques. These studies focus primarily on identifying features designed to foster popularity in children (Asher, Oden, and Gottman 1977; Young and Cooper 1944).

4. Thick barriers exist between groups of popular and unpopular children, keeping them firmly socially separated (Kinney 1993). Research on relations between in-groups and out-groups discusses the conflict, hostility, and possible bias engendered by in-group toward out-group members (Hamilton and Gifford 1976; Sherif et al. 1961; Tajfel 1978; Tajfel et al. 1971). This is tied to the contact hypothesis, that lack of contact leads people to assume that out-group members are different and undesirable (Allen and Wilder 1979). Opposing this are two hypotheses: the similarity theory, that contact under favorable conditions will dissipate hostility between in-groups and out-groups and lead to friendship (Homans 1950); and the idea that some contact may make relations even worse than they were in the abstract (Perlman and Oskamp 1971; Schofield 1981; Triandis and Vassilou 1967). Looking internally at groups as social systems, studies have shown that contact with both competing out-groups and unpopular individual children can help in-groups to define their behavioral boundaries and make them more cohesive (Allen 1981; Best 1983; Sherif et al. 1961).

5. Corsaro (1981b, 1985) looks at the origins of cliques in a preschool, noting that the children he observes develop conflicts between others' attempts to be included in their play space and their resistance to these intrusions. Conjoint play thus forms the basis for friendship groups that include some and exclude others. Best (1983) traces the development of cliques in an elementary school, following a group of boys and their leaders through the early elementary grades and observing the progressive formation of the Tent Club, an exclusive group of popular boys that turns the others into outcasts.

   Other researchers articulate the presence of behavioral cycles engendered by cliques. Epperson (1963) looks at how excluded individuals react with behaviors that exacerbate their rejection, leading them to redouble their offensive efforts, only to cycle progressively farther into unpopularity. Eder (1985) describes the "cycle of popularity" characterizing popular middle school girls, who reach their peak popularity shortly after being accorded entry to the popular group, only to plummet downward thereafter as a result of their abandonment of old friends, their failure to respond to the friendly overtures of other out-group members, and their exclusive friendship with other popular girls. Others' earlier admiration and like for them are replaced by dislike and disrespect. Blau (1964) proposes a cyclic model of small group dynamics wherein individuals inflate the talents, abilities, and potential contributions they can offer a group in order to gain entry, only subsequently to diminish themselves modestly by flaunting their weaknesses, thereby reducing the competitive status striving within the group and promoting social integration. All of these cycles involve downward progressions, one by choice and two through the actions of others.

6. Davies (1982) notes that proximity, rather than liking, is often the most basic element in children's friendships.

7. Position maintenance involved the opposite of friendship realignment—friendship

stasis—and required a conscious effort to hold the primary loyalty and friendship of important clique members, so that they would not turn away from the leaders to potential rising stars. Since position maintenance falls outside of both inclusionary and exclusionary dynamics, we will not discuss it here. Membership challenge involved an attack on rising stars' popularity and power, accompanied by efforts to ostracize them from the group. Because this is an exclusionary technique, we will discuss it later in the chapter.

8. Oswald, Krappmann, Chowdhuri, and von Salisch (1987) note that one way children assert superiority over others and indebt them with loyalty is to offer them "help," either materially or socially.

9. Hogg and Abrams (1988) find that denigrating out-group members enhances a group's solidarity and improves the group status of people participating in such denigration. This tendency is particularly strong where two groups perceive themselves to be in conflict or competition.

10. Eder and Sanford (1986) and Merten (1994) note the same tendency among adolescent peer groups in middle school.

11. Eder (1991) also notes that when insiders pick on other members of their clique, this can have good-natured overtones, indicating that they like them.

12. Eder and Sanford (1986) and Eder and Parker (1987) discuss the importance of physical appearance, particularly hair, in adhering to group norms and maintaining popularity.

13. Merten (1994; 1996b) discusses the dilemma faced by children who are picked on, who would like to report the problem to a teacher but cannot do so out of fear that the teacher's intervention would incur the wrath of others. He notes the consequences for one boy whose mother complained to other parents about the way their children treated her son: when these others came to school the next day, they ridiculed the boy even more, taunting and deriding him for being a tattletale.

14. Bigelow, Tesson, and Lewko (1996) also note this "Lord of the Flies" phenomenon.

Chapter 4 *Clique Stratification*

1. On friendship groups as the most salient element of adolescents' school experience, see Coleman (1961), Cusik (1973), Everhart (1983), Gordon (1957), Hollingshead (1949), and Willis (1981). On friendship groups providing the basis for adolescents' forming and connecting to the peer culture, see Everhart (1983), Fine (1987), Willis (1981), and Wulff (1988).

2. For example, Coleman (1961) describes four groups in the stratification system of the adolescents he studies: the leading crowd, the exemplars, the local leaders, and a group he refers to as unpopular. Canaan (1987), Eckert (1989), and Eder (1995) discuss the formation of groups in junior highs or middle schools based on styles and interests, where people such as jocks, preppies, greasers, skaters, druggies, or eggheads can come together and find like-minded people. Researchers have also shown that adolescents stratify these clusters hierarchically in terms of popularity and prestige (Brown and Lohr 1987; Cohen 1979; Coleman 1961; Cusik 1973; Eckert 1989; Eder 1995; Hollingshead 1949; Ianni 1989; Kinney 1993; Larkin 1979; Lesko 1988; Lightfoot 1983; Merten 1996a; Schwartz 1987; Schwartz and Merten 1967; Schwendinger and Schwendinger 1985; Snyder 1972; Varenne 1982; Weis 1974).

3. See Canaan (1987) and Eder (1995) for a discussion of the diverse social groups in junior high and high school that do not exist in elementary school.

4. See Epstein (1973); Rosenberg (1979); Turner (1968; 1976). A central theme in the literature on the self-concept is that the content and organization of identities reflect the content and organization of society (Gecas 1982). Symbolic interactionists

have focused on the way identities are socially constructed in interaction, based on people's shared understandings of social roles, rules, symbols, and categories (Cooley 1902; Foote 1951; James 1890; Mead 1934; Stryker 1968; Thomas 1923). Identities are then expressed, maintained, negotiated, and modified in the enactment and presentation of these categories, through people's perceptions of the reactions and evaluations of others (Goffman 1959; McCall and Simmons 1966; Stone 1962; Weinstein 1969). Identities symbolize self-meanings and are acquired in particular situations based on people's comparison of their roles to others and others' counterroles (Lindesmith and Strauss 1956; Turner 1956). At the same time, identities form the core of our self-esteem, that emotional dimension of our selves. Identities thus specify the content and evaluation of our selves, and guide and regulate our subsequent thoughts, feelings, and behavior, operating cybernetically to reciprocally relate the individual and the social structure (Stryker 1980).

5. Kless (1992) notes only three clear groups: the leading crowd, the middlers, and the pariahs, failing to distinguish a wannabe cluster. This may be due to the larger size, greater diversity, and more variable classroom structure of the schools our subjects attended. For schools with a population of under eighty students per grade (such as Kless studied), that stratum tended to disappear, being replaced with only scattered individuals or not replaced at all.

6. Complicating and augmenting this typology of stratification were overlaps and movement between the ranks. Some people straddled ranks, occupying a gray zone between the popular, wannabe, or middle levels with friends in each, or drifting between isolation and a friend or two. Others aspired to and saw themselves in ranks where they were not fully accepted, commonly hanging out on the borders of the popular crowd, wanting to be accepted but achieving only sporadic success. Still others were in flux between ranks, having been kicked out of their group and searching to reestablish themselves, or temporarily drifting on their own, hoping to be taken back by their former friends.

7. Hallinan (1976) discusses the effect of classroom size and type on clique formation. She notes that traditional classrooms form strict hierarchies of popularities, while open classrooms create more room for age mates to gravitate toward people they like and form interest relations.

8. Merten (1996a) shows that when a high-status group of adolescent cheerleaders accepts a low-status girl as a member, they lose some of their popularity, prestige, and respect in the peer group.

9. Lippett and Gold (1959) find that children's sociometric status remains stable over the course of an academic year.

10. Hartup, Glazer, and Charlesworth (1967) observe that popular children know better than their unpopular counterparts how to pay the most attention to others when it is necessary, to praise them, to show them affection, and to willingly accede to their requests.

11. Eder (1995) specifically points out that this dynamic is common to both boys' and girls' subcultures.

12. As Rizzo (1989) notes, however, people were more likely to be closer friends with people in their class.

13. Eder (1995) also observes that nonathletes who try to imitate the dress of popular athletes are often viewed negatively.

14. Eder (1995) remarks on the prevalence of insecurity-based behavior in this age group, generally.

15. Youniss and Smollar (1985) note that friendship choices based on intimacy and openness, rather than popularity, do not become more widespread until adolescence.

16. According to Evans and Eder (1993), three main features serve to identify these people: unusual appearance, gender-inappropriate behavior, and deficient mental capacities. Coie (see Coie, Dodge, and Coppotelli 1982; Coie, Dodge, and Kupersmidt 1990; Dodge, Coie, and Brakke 1982) finds that rejected children exhibit fewer prosocial and more antisocial behaviors. As Eder (1995) also notes, people from lower socioeconomic strata and minority groups are disproportionately represented in this position.

17. This number is consistent with the relative number of isolates Hallinan (1979) observes in the elementary schools she studies.

18. Evans and Eder (1993) show that with a few exceptions, it is almost impossible for a low-status person to break the cycle of isolation.

19. Merten (1996b) notes that, ironically, being a social isolate increases adolescents' visibility, so that even people they don't know know them, and tease and pick on them.

20. Merten (1996b) notes that one "mel" gives up on trying to be accepted and hides behind a large winter coat, thinking to himself that this might lend him an aura of invisibility. In fact, it draws more attention to his unsuitability, leading his peers to tease and reject him more.

21. Corsaro (1979; 1985) observes that even preschool children rarely engage in solitary play. Children who find themselves alone usually attempt repeatedly to gain entry into ongoing peer interactions.

22. Merten (1996b) also sees the same increase in teasing under such circumstances. He notes that isolates sometimes hide their friendship with each other from the peer group to avoid this compound rejection, ignoring or even joining in when their friends are being ridiculed, and playing with them only when they are alone.

23. Merten (1996b) documents the way social isolates scrupulously analyze their social situations and behavior, trying to figure out what they are doing wrong.

Chapter 5   *After-School Activities*

1. See Berlage (1982), Eitzen and Sage (1989), and Frønes (1994), for a further discussion of the rise and extent of after-school participation.

2. The after-school phenomenon has its roots in the adult domination and control of children's play that began with the Playground and Muscular Christianity movements in the 1880s and 1890s. From within the public schools (the Public Schools Athletic League) and private associations such as the settlement houses, the YMCAs, and the Playground Association of America, adults moved to organize leagues of competitive athletics designed to lure ghetto immigrants from degenerative gang activities into team sports (Guttman 1988; Radar 1990; Riess 1989). In so doing, they hoped to instill youngsters with the values of physical and moral health such as daring, endurance, self-restraint, fairness, honor, courage, and cooperation (Cavallo 1981; Haley 1978). This movement saw its demise in the 1920s, as reformers despaired of achieving their desired goals and began to acknowledge that their programs were appealing more to middle-class youth than the original ghetto targets, and that competitive athletics might be detrimental to the character building of youngsters. In the 1930s more specialized organizations sprang up, offering adult-controlled play for youngsters like Pop Warner football, the Little League, and the Soap Box Derby, which drew middle-class youth into specialized athletic competition (Berryman 1978; Guttman 1988; Rader 1988; Riess 1989). These associations and others like them sustained a slow growth over several decades. In the 1970s and 1980s a broad expansion of adult-dominated children's leisure activities arose that was specialized in character yet not exclusively restricted

to sports. These activities took place primarily in the period of time following the conclusion of the school day, with some events taking place on weekends.

3. First, with the massive entry of women (especially middle-class women) into the labor force, a need arose for child care and/or child supervision following the school day. While we have seen the development of the "latchkey" kid (see Rodman 1990), we have more often seen activities where children could be taken care of, entertained, and enriched. After-school activities derived reinforcement from the prevalence of dual-career families and a social consciousness that demanded the cultural edification of children apart from traditional instruction offered in the classroom. Second, there were rising concerns about leaving children unsupervised in public, outdoor places (Cahill 1990). Parents became more sensitive to the potential dangers facing their "threatened children" (Best 1990), in response to a range of real and socially constructed societal transformations. After-school activities represented a safe place where children could spend recreational time.

4. Although some after-school activities for younger children may encompass day-care elements, and some of the sites we address offer day care (i.e., the YMCA), the focus of this book is not specifically directed toward examining child-care programs for working parents. Our focus, rather, is on extracurricular activities, some of which may involve child care.

5. Children from more educated and economically advantaged backgrounds receive more encouragement and support for regular participation in community organizations. They are twice as likely to be involved in after-school activities as children from lower social classes (Erwin 1995).

6. Extolling the benefits of adult-run leisure, some authors suggest that children exhibit a natural developmental progression to a point where they are amenable to and ready for adult direction (Leo 1994; Micheli and Jenkins 1994; Webb 1969). They think that children accept the inherent characteristics and values of adult-structured activities because these accord with children's increasing concern with success and their decreasing concern with fairness (Mantel and Vander Velden 1974). The world of youth, they assert, is equitable and can afford to be, but the world of adults is not so evenhanded. Competitive participation in exclusive after-school activities helps to prepare children for the adult world (Webb 1969). Others are less sanguine about the role of adults in the leisure play of children, claiming that this produces significant social and psychological harm (Devereaux 1976; Frey 1980; Frey and Eitzen 1991; Kohn 1994; McPherson 1978; Ogilvie 1979; Orlick and Botterill 1975; Underwood 1975; Wolff 1994; Yablonsky and Brower 1979). Too much attention is placed on success (Fallon 1975), with sportsmanship and morality falling by the wayside (Chissom 1978). Landers and Fine (1996) and Richer (1984) suggest that gender and status roles are reinforced even in the earliest stages of kindergardeners' participation in T-ball. Figler (1981) proposes that a conflict between children's and adults' needs in organized leisure may exist. Children desire to express themselves, to be spontaneous, to test their abilities, and can tolerate a greater degree of flexibility and chaos than adults. Adults prefer an orderly atmosphere with concentration on linear skill development. Adults may lose sight of their children's goals and become overly involved in satisfying their own needs for recognition (Lupo 1967; Waid 1979). Because adults are in control, however, the structure and nature of organized after-school activities favor their needs. As a result, children may develop feelings of failure and/or burnout (Coakley 1992). For an even-handed discussion of the pros and cons of organized youth sport, see Nixon and Frey (1996). The rise of institutionalized, adult-dominated after-school programs may thus constitute a social problem.

7. See Sutton-Smith (1971) and Finnan (1982) for a complete review and definition of children's spontaneous play.
8. Wallace (1970) suggests that such competitiveness may be a natural result of children role-modeling adults in society.
9. Carere (1987) posits that the phenomenon of adults subverting children to their rules and authority characterizes children's school worlds as well. She notes that teachers are involved in a continual battle of dominance in which they progressively restrict and narrow children's worlds, while children seek to attain fragments of freedom and autonomy.
10. See also Landers and Fine (1996) and Richer (1984).
11. Other instances of similar abuse have been reported where coaches gave pills to players to assist their gaining weight (Kaufman and Popper 1976) and injected the oranges players ate before games with amphetamines to "give them a little boost" (Underwood 1975, 95–96).
12. In discussing elite after-school activities, we will refer only to those kinds of elite pursuits readily available and engaged in by "ordinary" young people. Another whole range of "superelite" activities and ways to practice them are used by those individuals who aspire to be professionals or future Olympic stars, and who move out of their homes, for example, to live and train with coaches in different cities.
13. Webb (1969) suggests that this decision-making style accords developmentally with children's increasing emphasis on success and their diminishing concern with fairness.

Chapter 6 **Friendships: Close and Casual**

1. For research on the interactional capabilities of children, see Berndt (1989), Corsaro (1985), Corsaro and Eder (1990), Corsaro and Rizzo (1988), Davies (1982), and Deegan (1996). For a discussion of the age when children begin their education, see Damon (1983) and Davies (1982).
2. Ginsberg, Gottman, and Parker (1986) suggest that children's friendships provide the following functions: stimulation, physical support, ego support/enhancement, social companionship, and intimacy/affection. Goodwin (1985) and Mishler (1979) indicate the importance of communal sharing, trading, and bargaining in friendships. Adolescent close friendships have been found to provide the benefits of intimacy, to enhance individuals' interpersonal skills, sensitivity, and understanding (Youniss 1980), and to contribute considerably to cognitive and social development and psychological adjustment (Hartup 1993; Savin-Williams and Berndt 1990).
3. See Bossert (1979), DuBois and Hirsch (1990), Grant and Sleeter (1986), Hallinan and Smith (1985), Hallinan and Teixeira (1987a, 1987b), Hallinan and Williams (1987), Langworthy (1959), Schofield (1982), Schofield and Sagar (1977), and Troyna and Hatcher (1992).
4. See Foot, Chapman, and Smith (1980), Kurth (1970), and La Gaipa (1979).
5. Rubin (1980) notes the importance of psychological compatibility (shared outlooks and interests) in friendship selection patterns.
6. Dozens of studies have shown the tendency of friends to be approximately the same size, same age, same level of intelligence, and same degree of physical maturity (cf. Eder and Sanford 1986; Hallinan 1979; Hartup 1970; Lever 1978; Rizzo 1989; Schofield 1982).
7. Karweit and Hansell (1983b) show that age grading, curriculum tracking, and school size influence friendship selection.
8. Rizzo (1989) suggests that physical classroom proximity, even something as small as closeness of desk location, can have a strong influence on friendship selection.

See also Bigelow (1977), Bigelow and La Gaipa 1975; 1980), Damon (1977), and Selman (1981).

9. Rizzo (1989) indicates that as the school year progresses, children's choice of playmates becomes dominated by their classmates, with only a few holding on to neighbors as frequent playmates.

10. For another discussion of how children cultivate friends, see Rizzo (1989), chapter 7.

11. For a discussion of carpooling relationships and their socializing influence, see Adler and Adler (1984).

12. Oswald (1992) shows that for children's close friends, social norms may be suspended, territorial rules may not apply, tolerance of norm transgressions may be high, and there exists a trust that is very strong.

13. See Rubin (1980), chapter 8, on the composition of cross-age friendships.

14. Rubin (1980) shows how physical accessibility is related to friendship patterning. Epstein (1983) provides data on the likelihood of best friends living in geographical proximity. Selman (1981) discusses the particular importance of propinquity on friendship formation at younger ages.

15. See Epstein (1983) on the structure of schools and the probability of different types of friends.

16. At the same time, we note Blinde and Taub's (1992) research, marking the common existence of a lesbian stigma among female collegiate athletes.

17. See Rubin (1980) on the prevalence of cross-age neighborhood friendships and some of the problems associated with this.

18. Van Vliet (1986) finds that children who live in neighborhoods with relatively large numbers of peers have more extensive and satisfying friendship networks and share more activities with their friends.

19. In neighborhoods with many preadolescent boys, team sports and play in large groups are enhanced. There is also an increase in the spontaneity of social interaction (Medrich et al. 1982).

Chapter 7   Friendships: Compartmentalized

1. See Karweit (1983), who shows that friends are found in the same extracurricular activities.

2. For further discussion on the nature of obligatory transport relations, see Adler and Adler (1984), on car pool relations.

3. Increasingly, in the future, we expect to see these relationships augmented by electronic mail contact.

4. Rubin (1980) notes that people also form these relationships with former neighbors who had moved away.

Chapter 8   Cross-Gender Relations: The Early and Middle Years

1. Researchers taking this perspective include Damico (1974), Eder (1995), Eisenhart and Holland (1983), Lockheed and Harris (1984), Oswald et al. (1987), Pollard (1985), Rubin (1980), Sagar, Schofield, and Snyder (1983), Thorne (1986), and Voss (1997).

2. See Chafetz (1978) and Lewis (1972) for a discussion of the ways people treat infant boys and girls differently.

3. See Adler and Adler (1984) for a discussion of relationships formed for children by their parents based on carpooling convenience.

4. Oswald et al. (1987) report that most interactions between boys and girls at this age are of the "helping" variety.

5. See Finnan (1982), Oswald et al. (1987), and Thorne (1993) for further discussions of chasing and kissing games.

6. Interestingly, in 1996, several cases of kissing came to public attention. The one that generated the most interest was a case from North Carolina, where a first grader was suspended for kissing a girl and accused of sexual harassment. Public support for the youth was high, and he made several television talk show appearances. He discussed kissing as something he and his friends enjoyed doing to girls. (See Leland 1996.)

7. Rubin (1980) notes that gender separation is strengthened because boys and girls are often steered toward different types of activities: typically more active, physical play for boys and more sedate play for girls.

8. Rubinstein and Rubin (1984) report that girls prefer less turbulent interactions than boys.

9. In fact, research has shown that boys are more active in bothering others than girls, especially by invading their privacy, intruding into their territory, and quarreling with them (Maccoby and Jacklin 1980; Oswald 1992; Oswald et al. 1987; Voss 1997). Girls have been observed to react to such infractions by repeatedly rebuking boys for breaking school rules (Karweit and Hansell 1983b; Oswald 1992).

10. Oswald et al. (1987) note that by age twelve, girls tend to take a more active role in chasing games than they did previously, sometimes overcoming that of boys.

Chapter 9   *Cross-Gender Relations: The Later Years*

1. Rubin (1980) notes that boy-girl interaction at this age is typically strained, involving indirect or overheard indications of attraction, teasing, and "fooling around."

2. Oswald et al. (1987) find that at younger ages this type of helping behavior is where the genders are most likely to come in contact with one another.

3. Simon, Eder, and Evans (1992) discuss peer norms for such feelings, which guide people to appropriate levels by indicating that it is okay to feel this way, but not too much.

4. Shrum, Cheek, and Hunter (1988) find that the same-sex cliques of late childhood give way to cross-gender cliques and heterosexual coupling in middle to late adolescence, although this happens later for boys than for girls.

5. See Camarena, Sarigiani, and Petersen (1990) on differences in the way preadolescent boys and girls react toward and handle intimacy.

6. Rubin (1980) and Fine (1981) discuss how same-sex friends are often called upon to provide advice and support in the courtship process.

7. See Dion and Berscheid (1974) for further discussion of this point.

8. See Merten (1996d) and Fine (1987) for discussions of the emphasis on physical intimacy among boys.

9. See Merten (1996d) and Fine (1987) for further discussions of the use of the baseball metaphor for sex, and for elaboration of boys' sex talk.

10. See Holland and Eisenhart (1990) for a discussion of gender differences in approaching the opposite gender.

11. In fact, Merten (1996d) discusses the generally superficial and empty nature of "going with" relationships.

12. See Simon, Eder, and Evans (1992) and Merten (1996d) for discussions of the strong norm of exclusivity in dating.

Chapter 10   *Bringing It All Together*

1. Goffman's point about the increased level of tension in leisure activities accords with Csikszentmihalyi's (1975) discussion of the absorbing flow state that falls between boredom and anxiety.

References

Adler, Patricia A., and Peter Adler. 1994. "Social Reproduction and the Corporate Other: The Institutionalization of Afterschool Activities." *Sociological Quarterly* 35:309–328.

———. 1987. *Membership Roles in Field Research*. Newbury Park, Calif.: Sage.

———. 1986. "Introduction." In *Sociological Studies of Child Development*, vol. 1, edited by P. A. Adler and P. Adler. Greenwich, Conn.: JAI. Pp.3–10.

———. 1984. "The Carpool: A Socializing Adjunct to the Educational Experience." *Sociology of Education* 57:200–209.

Allen, Vernon L. 1981. "Self, Social Group, and Social Structure: Surmises about the Study of Children's Friendships." In *The Development of Children's Friendships*, edited by S. Asher and J. Gottman. New York: Cambridge University Press. Pp. 182–203.

Allen, Vernon L., and D. A. Wilder. 1979. "Group Categorization and Attribution of Belief Similarity." *Small Group Behavior* 10:73–80.

Asch, Solomon. 1955. "Opinions and Social Pressure." *Scientific American* 193 (November):31–35.

Asher, Steven, S. L. Oden, and J. M. Gottman. 1977. "Children's Friendships in School Settings." In *Current Topics in Early Childhood Education*, edited by L. G. Katz. Norwood, N.J.: Ablex. Pp. 203–221.

Asher, Steven R., and Peter D. Renshaw. 1981. "Children without Friends: Social Knowledge and Social Skill Training." In *The Development of Children's Friendships*, edited by S. R. Asher and J. M. Gottman. New York: Cambridge University Press. Pp. 273–296.

Bandura, Albert. 1969. "Social Learning and the Shaping of Children's Judgments." *Journal of Personality and Social Psychology* 11:275–83.

Bandura, Albert, and R. H. Walters. 1963. *Social Learning and Personality Development*. New York: Holt, Rinehart, and Winston.

Becker, Howard S. 1964. "Personal Change in Adult Life." *Sociometry* 27:40–53.

———. 1960. "Notes on the Concept of Commitment." *American Journal of Sociology* 66:32–42.

Berentzen, Sigurd. 1984. *Children's Constructing Their Social Worlds*. Bergen, Norway: University of Bergen.

Berlage, Gai. 1982. "Are Children's Competitive Team Sports Teaching Corporate Values?" *ARENA Review* 6:15–21.

Berndt, Thomas J. 1989. "Friendships in Childhood and Adolescence." In *Child Development—Today and Tomorrow*, edited by W. Damon. San Francisco: Jossey-Bass. Pp. 323–348.

Bernstein, Basil. 1977. "Social Class, Language, and Socialization." In *Power and Ideology in Education*, edited by J. Karabel and A. H. Halsey. New York: Oxford University Press. Pp. 478–486.

Berryman, Jack W. 1978. "The Rise of Organized Sports for Pre-adolescent Boys." In *Children in Sport: A Contemporary Anthology*, edited by R. A. Magill, M. J. Ash, and F. L. Smoll. Champaign: Human Kinetics Press. Pp. 3–18.

Berscheid, Ellen, Karen K. Dion, Elaine Walster, and George Walster. 1971. "Physical Attractiveness and Dating Choices: A Test of the Matching Hypothesis." *Journal of Experimental Social Psychology* 7:173-189.

Best, Joel. 1990. *Threatened Children*. Chicago: University of Chicago Press.

Best, Raphaela. 1983. *We've All Got Scars*. Bloomington: Indiana University Press.

Biernacki, Patrick, and Dan Waldorf. 1981. "Snowball Sampling." *Sociological Research and Methods* 10:141–163.

Bigelow, Brian J. 1977. "Children's Friendship Expectations: A Cognitive-Developmental Study." *Child Development* 48:246–253.

Bigelow, Brian J., and John La Gaipa. 1980. "The Development of Friendship Values and Choice." In *Friendship and Social Relations in Children*, edited by H. Foot, A. Chapman, and J. Smith. New York: Wiley. Pp. 15–44.

———. 1975. "Children's Written Description of Friendship: A Multidimensional Analysis." *Developmental Psychology* 11:857–858.

Bigelow, Brian J., Geoffrey Tesson, and John H. Lewko. 1996. *Learning the Rules*. New York: Guilford Press.

Blau, Peter M. 1964. *Exchange and Power in Social Life*. New York: Wiley.

Blinde, Elaine M., and Diane E. Taub. 1992. "Women Athletes as Falsely Accused Deviants: Managing the Lesbian Stigma." *Sociological Quarterly* 33:521–533.

Blumer, Herbert. 1969. *Symbolic Interactionism: Perspective and Method*. Englewood Cliffs, N.J.: Prentice-Hall.

Bogardus, Emory S. 1959. "Race Reactions by Sexes." *Sociology and Social Research* 43: 439–441.

Borman, Kathryn M., and J. Frankel. 1984. "Gender Inequalities in Childhood Social Life and Adult Work Life." In *Women in the Workplace*, edited by S. Gideonse. Norwood, N.J.: Ablex. Pp. 55–83.

Bossert, Steven T. 1979. *Tasks and Social Relationships in Classrooms*. New York: Cambridge University Press.

Bourdieu, Pierre. 1977a. "Cultural Reproduction and Social Reproduction." In *Power and Ideology in Education*, edited by J. Karabel and A. H. Halsey. New York: Oxford University Press. Pp. 487–511.

———. 1977b. *Outline of a Theory of Practice*. Cambridge: Cambridge University Press.

Bourdieu, Pierre, and Jean-Claude Passeron. 1977. *Reproduction in Education, Society, and Culture*. London: Sage.

Bowerman, C., and John Kinch. 1959. "Changes in Family and Peer Orientation of Children between the Fourth and Tenth Grades." *Social Forces* 37:206–11.

Bowles, Samuel, and Herbert Gintis. 1976. *Schooling in Capitalist America*. New York: Basic Books.

Brim, Orville G., Jr. 1960. "Personality Development as Role Learning." In *Personality Development in Children*, edited by I. Iscoe and H. W. Stevenson. Austin: University of Texas Press. Pp. 127–159.

Britsch, Susan J. 1995. "The Researcher as Teacher: Constructing One's Place in the Story of Events of Preschoolers." *Qualitative Studies in Education* 8:297–309.

Brown, B. Bradford, and Mary Jane Lohr. 1987. "Peer-Group Affiliation and Adolescent Self-Esteem: An Integration of Ego-Identity and Symbolic-Interaction Theories." *Journal of Personality and Social Psychology* 52:47–55.

Burke, Peter J., and Judith Tully. 1977. "The Measurement of Role-Identities." *Social Forces* 55:881–897.

Cahill, Spencer, 1994. "And a Child Shall Lead Us? Children, Gender, and Perspectives by Incongruity." In *Symbolic Interaction: An Introduction to Social Psychology*, edited by N. J. Herman and L. T. Reynolds. Dix Hills, N.Y.: General Hall. Pp. 459–469.

———. 1990. "Childhood and Public Life: Reaffirming Biographical Divisions." *Social Problems* 37:390–402.

Camarena, P. M., P. A. Sarigiani, and A. C. Petersen. 1990. "Gender-Specific Pathways to Intimacy in Early Adolescence." *Journal of Youth and Adolescence* 19:19–32.

Canaan, Joyce. 1987. "A Comparative Analysis of American Suburban Middle Class, Middle School, and High School Teenage Cliques." In *Interpretive Ethnography of Education*, edited by G. Spindler and L. Spindler. Hillsdale, N.J.: Lawrence Erlbaum.

Carere, Sharon. 1987. "Lifeworld of Restricted Behavior." In *Sociological Studies of Child Development*, vol. 2., edited by P. A. Adler and P. Adler. Greenwich, Conn.: JAI. Pp. 105–138.

Cavallo, Dominick. 1981. *Muscles and Morals: Organized Playgrounds and Urban Reform, 1880–1920*. Philadelphia: University of Pennsylvania Press.

Chafetz, Janet S. 1978. *Masculine, Feminine, or Human?* Itasca, Ill.: Peacock.

Chissom, B. S. 1978. "Moral Behavior of Children Participating in Competitive Athletics." In *Children in Sport: A Contemporary Anthology*, edited by R. A. Magill, M. J. Ash, and F. L. Smoll. Champaign: Human Kinetics Publishers. Pp. 193–199.

Coakley, Jay J. 1992. "Burnout among Adolescent Athletes: A Personal Failure or Social Problem?" *Sociology of Sport Journal* 9:271–285.

———. 1990. *Sport in Society*. 4th ed. St. Louis: Mosby.

Cohen, Jere. 1979. "High School Subcultures and the Adult World." *Adolescence* 14:491–502.

Coie, John D., Kenneth A. Dodge, and H. Coppotelli. 1982. "Dimensions and Types of Social Status: A Cross-Age Perspective." *Developmental Psychology* 18:557–571.

Coie, John D., Kenneth A. Dodge, and J. B. Kupersmidt. 1990. "Peer Group Behavior and Social Status." In *Peer Rejection in Childhood*, edited by S. R. Asher and J. D. Coie. New York: Cambridge University Press. Pp. 17–59.

Coleman, James. 1961. *The Adolescent Society*. Glencoe: Free Press.

Cooley, Charles H. 1902. *Human Nature and Social Order*. New York: Scribner's.

Corsaro, William A. 1997. *Sociology of Childhood*. Thousand Oaks, Calif.: Pine Forge.

———. 1996. "Transitions in Early Childhood: The Promise of Comparative, Longitudinal Ethnography. In *Ethnography and Human Development*, edited by R. Jessor, A. Colby, and R. A. Shweder. Chicago: University of Chicago Press. Pp. 419–458.

———. 1992. "Interpretive Reproduction in Children's Peer Culture." *Social Psychology Quarterly* 55:160–177.

———. 1986. "Discourse Processes within Peer Culture: From a Constructivist to an Interpretive Approach to Childhood Socialization." In *Sociological Studies of Child Development*, vol. 1, edited by P. A. Adler and P. Adler. Greenwich, Conn.: JAI. Pp. 81–101.

———. 1985. *Friendship and Peer Culture in the Early Years*. Norwood, N.J.: Ablex.

———. 1981a. "Entering the Child's World: Research Strategies for Field Entry and Data Collection in a Preschool Setting." In *Ethnography and Language in Educational Settings*, edited by J. Green and C. Wallat. Norwood, N.J.: Ablex. Pp. 117–146.

———. 1981b. "Friendship in the Nursery School: Social Organization in a Peer Environment." In *The Development of Children's Friendships*, edited by S. Asher and J. Gottman. New York: Cambridge University Press. Pp. 207–241.

———. 1979. "Young Children's Conceptions of Status and Role." *Sociology of Education* 52:46–59.

Corsaro, William A., and Donna Eder. 1990. "Children's Peer Culture." *Annual Review of Sociology* 16:197–220.

Corsaro, William A., and Thomas Rizzo. 1988. "Discussions and Friendship: Socialization Processes in the Peer Culture of Italian Nursery School Children." *American Sociological Review* 53:879–894.

Corsaro, William A., and Jürgen Streeck. 1986. "Studying Children's Worlds: Methodological Issues." In *Children's Worlds and Children's Language*, edited by J. Cook-Gumperz, W. Corsaro, and J. Streeck. Berlin: Mouton de Gruyter. Pp. 13–36.

Cottle, Thomas J. 1980. *Children's Secrets*. Garden City, N.Y.: Anchor Press/Doubleday.

Criswell, J. H. 1937. "Racial Cleavage in Negro-White Groups." *Sociometry* 1:81–89.

Csikszentmihalyi, Mihalyi. 1975. *Beyond Boredom and Anxiety*. San Francisco: Jossey-Bass.

Cusik, Phillip A. 1973. *Inside High School*. New York: Holt, Rinehart, and Winston.

Daiker, D. A., and M. Morenberg. 1990. *The Writing Teacher as Researcher*. Portsmouth, N.H.: Heinemann.

Damico, Sandra Bowman. 1974. "The Relation of Clique Membership to Achievement, Self-Concept, and School Attitude." *Dissertation Abstracts International* 35:717.

Damon, William. 1983. "The Nature of Social Cognitive Change in the Developing Child." In *The Relationship between Social and Cognitive Development*, edited by W. F. Overton. Hillsdale, N.J.: Lawrence Erlbaum.

———. 1977. *The Social World of the Child*. San Francisco: Jossey-Bass.

Davies, Bronwyn. 1982. *Life in the Classroom and Playground: The Accounts of Primary School Children*. London: Routledge and Kegan Paul.

Dawe, H. C. 1934. "Analysis of Two Hundred Quarrels of Preschool Children." *Child Development* 5:139–157.

Deaux, Kay. 1977. "Sex Differences." In *Personality Variables in Social Behavior*, edited by T. Blass. New York: Wiley. Pp. 357–377.

Deegan, James G. 1996. *Children's Friendships in Culturally Diverse Classrooms*. Bristol, Pa.: Falmer Press.

Denzin, Norman K. 1989. *The Research Act*. 3d. ed. Englewood Cliffs, N.J.: Prentice-Hall.

———. 1977. *Childhood Socialization*. San Francisco: Jossey-Bass.

Devereaux, Edward. 1976. "Backyard versus Little League Baseball: The Impoverishment of Children's Games." In *Social Problems in Athletics*, edited by D. M. Landers. Urbana: University of Illinois Press. Pp. 37–56.

Diener, Edward. 1980. "Deindividuation: The Absence of Self-Awareness and Self-Regulation in Group Members." In *The Psychology of Group Influence*, edited by P. B. Paulus. Hillside, N.J.: Lawrence Erlbaum. Pp. 142–163.

Dion, Karen K. and Ellen Berscheid. 1974. "Physical Attraction and Peer Perception among Children." *Sociometry* 37:1-12.

Dodge, Kenneth A. 1983. "Behavioral Antecedents of Peer Social Status." *Child Development* 53:1386–1399.

Dodge, Kenneth A., John D. Coie, and N. Brakke. 1982. "Behavior Patterns of Socially Rejected and Neglected Preadolescents: The Role of Social Approach and Aggression." *Journal of Abnormal Child Psychology* 10:389–409.

Dodge, Kenneth A., David C. Schlundt, Iris Schocken, and Judy D. Delugach. 1983. "Social Competence and Children's Sociometric Status: The Role of Peer Group Entry Strategies." *Merrill-Palmer Quarterly* 29:309–336.

DuBois, D. L., and B. J. Hirsch. 1990. "School and Neighborhood Friendship Patterns of Blacks and Whites in Early Adolescence." *Child Development* 61:524–536.

Dweck, Carol. 1981. "Social-Cognitive Processes in Children's Friendships." In *The Development of Children's Friendships*, edited by S. Asher and J. Gottman. New York: Cambridge University Press. Pp. 322–334.

Eckert, Penelope. 1989. *Jocks and Burnouts*. New York: Teachers College Press.

Eder, Donna (with Catherine C. Evans and Stephen Parker). 1995. *School Talk: Gender and Adolescent School Culture*. New Brunswick, N.J: Rutgers University Press.

———. 1991. "The Role of Teasing in Adolescent Peer Group Culture." In *Sociological Studies of Child Development*, vol. 4, edited by S. Cahill. Greenwich, Conn.: JAI. Pp. 181–197.

———. 1985. "The Cycle of Popularity: Interpersonal Relations among Female Adolescents." *Sociology of Education* 58:154–165.

Eder, Donna, and Maureen T. Hallinan. 1978. "Sex Differences in Children's Friendships." *American Sociological Review* 43:237–250.

Eder, Donna, and Stephen Parker. 1987. "The Cultural Production and Reproduction of Gender: The Effect of Extracurricular Activities on Peer-Group Culture." *Sociology of Education* 60:200–213.

Eder, Donna, and Stephanie Sanford. 1986. "The Development and Maintenance of Interactional Norms Among Early Adolescents." In *Sociological Studies of Child Development*, vol. 1, edited by P. A. Adler and P. Adler. Greenwich, Conn.: JAI. Pp. 283–300.

Eisenhart, Margaret A., and Dorothy C. Holland. 1983. "Learning Gender from Peers: The Role of Peer Groups in the Cultural Transmission of Gender." *Human Organization* 42:321–332.

Eitzen, D. Stanley. 1975. "Athletics in the Status System of Male Adolescents: A Replication of Coleman's *The Adolescent Society*." *Adolescence* 10:267–276.

Eitzen, D. Stanley, and George Sage. 1989. *Sociology of North American Sports*. 4th ed. Dubuque, Iowa: William C. Brown.

Elkin, Frederick, and Gerald Handel. 1989. *The Child and Society*. 5th ed. New York: Random House.

Ellis, Carolyn. 1995. *Final Negotiations*. Philadelphia: Temple University Press.

Epperson, David C. 1963. "Some Interpersonal and Performance Correlates of Classroom Alienation." *School Review* 71:360–375.

Epstein, Joyce Levy. 1983. "Friends among Students in Schools: Environmental and Developmental Factors." In *Friends in School*, edited by J. L. Epstein and N. Karweit. New York: Academic Press. Pp. 3–28.

Epstein, S. 1973. "The Self Concept Revisited or a Theory of a Theory." *American Psychologist* 28:404–416.

Erikson, Erik H. 1973. *In Search of Common Ground: Conversations with Erik H. Erikson and Huey P. Newton*. New York: Norton.

———. 1950. *Childhood and Society*. New York: Norton.

Erwin, Phillip. 1995. "Introduction to the Transaction Edition." In *Friendship and Social Relations in Children* (revised edition), edited by H. C. Foot, A. J. Chapman, and J. R. Smith. New Brunswick N.J.: Transaction. Pp.vii–xxxvi.

Evans, Cathy, and Donna Eder. 1993. "'No Exit': Processes of Social Isolation in the Middle School." *Journal of Contemporary Ethnography* 22:139–170.

Evans, Richard Isadore. 1973. *Jean Piaget: The Man and His Ideas*. New York: E. P. Dutton.1967.

———. 1967. *Dialogue with Erik Erikson*. New York: Harper and Row.

Everhart, Robert B. 1983. *Reading, Writing, and Resistance*. Boston: Routledge, Kegan and Paul.

Fallon, D. J. 1975. "Child's Play: A Run for the Trophy." *Quest* 24:59–62.

Figler, Stephen K. 1981. *Sport and Play in American Life*. Philadelphia: Saunders.

Fine, Gary Alan. 1987. *With the Boys*. Chicago: University of Chicago Press.

———. 1981. "Friends, Impression Management, and Preadolescent Behavior." In *The Development of Children's Friendships*, edited by S. Asher and J. Gottman. New York: Cambridge University Press. Pp. 29–52.

————. 1980. "The Natural History of Preadolescent Male Friendship Groups." In *Friendship and Childhood Relationships*, edited by H. Foot, T. Chapman, and J. Smith. New York: Wiley. Pp. 220–242.

Fine, Gary Alan, and Barry Glassner. 1979. "The Problems and Promise of Participant Observation with Children." *Urban Life* 8:153–174.

Fine, Gary Alan, and Kent L. Sandstrom. 1988. *Knowing Children*. Newbury Park, Calif: Sage.

Finnan, Christine Robinson. 1982. "The Ethnography of Children's Spontaneous Play." In *Doing the Ethnography of Schooling*, edited by G. Spindler. New York: Holt, Rinehart, and Winston. Pp. 356–381.

Foot, Hugh C., Anthony J. Chapman, and Jean R. Smith, eds. 1980. *Friendship and Social Relations in Children*. New York: Wiley.

Foote, Nelson N. 1951. "Identification as the Basis for a Theory of Motivation." *American Sociological Review* 26:14–21.

Foucault, Michel. 1977. *Discipline and Punishment*. New York: Pantheon.

Frey, James H. 1980. "Youth Sports: Who Really Benefits?" *Journal of the Nevada Association of Health, Physical Education, and Recreation* 1:1–9.

Frey, James H., and D. Stanley Eitzen. 1991. "Sport and Society." *Annual Review of Sociology* 17: 503–522.

Frønes, Ivar. 1995. *Among Peers*. Oslo: Scandinavian University Press.

————. 1994. "Dimensions of Childhood." In *Childhood Matters*, edited by J. Qvortrup, M. Bardy, G. Sgritta, and H. Wintersberger. Aldershot, England: Avebury. Pp. 145–164.

Garfinkel, Harold. 1967. *Studies in Ethnomethodology*. Englewood Cliffs, N.J.: Prentice-Hall.

Gecas, Victor. 1982. "The Self-Concept." *Annual Review of Sociology* 8:1–33.

Gelman, R., and R. Bailargon. 1983. "A Review of Some Piagetian Concepts." In *Handbook of Child Psychology*, 4th ed., edited by P. H. Mussen. New York: Wiley. Pp. 167–230.

Giddens, Anthony. 1984. *The Constitution of Society*. Berkeley: University of California Press.

Gilligan, Carol. 1982. *In a Different Voice*. Cambridge: Harvard University Press.

Ginsberg, Dorothy, John Gottman, and Jeffrey Parker. 1986. "The Importance of Friendships." In *Conversations of Friends: Speculations on Affective Development*, edited by J. M. Gottman and J. Parker. New York: Cambridge University Press. Pp. 3–50.

Glaser, Barney G., and Anselm L. Strauss. 1967. *The Discovery of Grounded Theory*. Chicago: Aldine.

————. 1965. *Awareness of Dying*. Chicago: Aldine.

Glassner, Barry. 1976. "Kid Society." *Urban Education* 11:5–22.

Glidewell, John, Mildred B. Kantor, Louis M. Smith, and Lorene S. Stringer. 1966. "Socialization and Social Structure in the Classrooms." In *Review of Child Development Research*, vol. 2, edited by L. W. Hoffman and M. L. Hoffman. New York: Russell Sage Foundation. Pp. 221–256.

Goffman, Erving. 1967. *Interaction Ritual*. New York: Anchor.

————. 1961. *Encounters*. Indianapolis: Bobbs-Merrill.

————. 1959. *The Presentation of Self in Everyday Life*. Garden City, N.Y.: Doubleday.

Good, Thomas L., and Jere E. Brophy. 1987. *Looking in Classrooms*. 4th ed. New York: Harper and Row.

Goodwin, Marjorie H. 1990. *He-Said-She-Said*. Bloomington, Ind.: Indiana University Press.

————. 1985. "The Serious Side of Jump Rope: Conversational Practices and Social Organization in the Frame of Play." *Journal of American Folklore* 98:315–330.

————. 1980a. "'He-Said-She-Said:' Formal Cultural Procedures for the Construction of a Gossip Dispute Activity." *American Ethnologist* 7:674–695.

————. 1980b. "Directive/Response Speech Sequences in Girls' and Boys' Task Activities." In *Women and Language in Literature and Society*, edited by S. McConnell-Ginet, R. Borker, and N. Furman. New York: Praeger. Pp. 157–173.

Gordon, C. Wayne. 1957. *Social System of the High School*. Glencoe, Ill.: Free Press.

Goswami, D., and P. R. Stillman, eds. 1987. *Reclaiming the Classroom: Teacher Researcher as an Agency for Change*. Portsmouth, N.H.: Boynton/Cook.

Gottman, John M. 1986. "The World of Coordinated Play: Same- and Cross-Sex Friendship in Young Children." In *Conversations of Friends*, edited by J. M. Gottman and J. G. Parker. New York: Cambridge University Press. Pp. 139–191.

Gottman, John M., J. Gonso, and B. Rasmussen. 1975. "Social Interaction, Social Competence, and Friendship in Children." *Child Development* 46:709–718.

Grant, Carl A., and Christine E. Sleeter. 1986. *After the School Bell Rings*. Philadelphia: Falmer Press.

Gronlund, N. E. 1959. *Sociometry in the Classroom*. New York: Harper and Brothers.

Gump, P. V., and W. V. Friesen. 1964. "Participation in Nonclass Settings." In *Big School, Small School: High School Size and Student Behavior*, edited by R. G. Barker and P. V. Gump. Stanford: Stanford University Press. Pp. 98–117.

Gunnarsson, L. 1978. *Children in Day Care and Family Care in Sweden*. Stockholm, Sweden: Department of Educational Research.

Gusterson, Hugh. 1993. "Exploding Anthropology's Canon in the World of the Bomb: Ethnographic Writing on Militarism." *Journal of Contemporary Ethnography* 22:59–79.

Guttman, Allen. 1988. *A Whole New Ball Game*. Chapel Hill: University of North Carolina Press.

Haley, Bruce. 1978. *The Healthy Body and Victorian Culture*. Cambridge: Harvard University Press.

Hallinan, Maureen. 1980. "Patterns of Cliquing among Youth." In *Friendship and Childhood Relationships*, edited by H. Foot, T. Chapman, and J. Smith. New York: Wiley. Pp. 321–342.

————. 1979. "Structural Effects on Children's Friendships and Cliques." *Social Psychology Quarterly* 42:43–54.

————. 1978. "The Process of Friendship Formation." *Social Networks* 1:193–210.

————. 1976. "Friendship Patterns in Open and Traditional Classrooms." *Sociology of Education* 49:254–265.

Hallinan, Maureen, and Stevens S. Smith. 1985. "The Effects of Classroom Racial Composition on Students' Interracial Friendliness." *Social Psychology Quarterly* 48:3–16.

Hallinan, Maureen, and Ruy A. Teixeira. 1987a. "Students' Interracial Friendships: Individual Characteristics, Structural Effects, and Racial Differences." *American Journal of Education* 95:563–583.

————. 1987b. "Opportunities and Constraints: Black-White Differences in the Formation of Interracial Friendships." *Child Development* 58:1358–1371.

Hallinan, Maureen, and Richard Williams. 1987. "The Stability of Students' Interracial Friendships." *American Sociological Review* 52:653–664.

Hamilton, D. L., and R. K. Gifford. 1976. "Illusory Correlation in Interpersonal Perception: A Cognitive Basis of Stereotype Judgments." *Journal of Experimental Social Psychology* 12:392–407.

Handel, Gerald, ed. 1988. *Childhood Socialization*. Hawthorne, N.Y.: Aldine de Gruyter.

Hansell, Stephen. 1984. "Cooperative Groups, Weak Ties, and the Integration of Peer Friendships." *Social Psychology Quarterly* 47:316–327.

Hardman, C. 1973. "Can There Be an Anthropology of Children?" *Journal of the Anthropological Society of Oxford* 4:85–99.

Harris, Judith Rich. 1995. "Where Is the Child's Environment? A Group Socialization Theory of Development." *Psychological Review* 102:358–389.

Hartup, Willard W. 1993. "Adolescents and their Friends." In *Close Friendships in Adolescence*, edited by B. Laursen. San Francisco: Jossey-Bass. Pp. 3–22.

———. 1970. "Peer Interaction and Social Organization." In *Carmichael's Manual of Child Psychology*, vol. 2, edited by P. Mussen. New York: Wiley. Pp. 361–456.

Hartup, Willard W., Jane A. Glazer, and Rosalind Charlesworth. 1967. "Peer Reinforcement and Sociometric Status." *Child Development* 38:1017–1024.

Hengst, Heinz. 1987. "The Liquidation of Childhood: An Objective Tendency." *International Journal of Sociology* 17:58–80.

Hertz, Rosanna, and Jonathan B. Imber. 1993. "Fieldwork in Elite Settings: Introduction." *Journal of Contemporary Ethnography* 22:3–6.

Hess, Robert D,. and Gerald Handel. 1959. *Family Worlds: A Psychosocial Approach in Family Life*. Chicago: University of Chicago Press.

Hodge, Robert W., Paul M. Siegel, and Peter H. Rossi. 1964. "Occupational Prestige in the U.S." *American Journal of Sociology* 70:286–302.

Hogg, Michael A., and Dominic Abrams. 1988. *Social Identifications*. New York: Routledge.

Holland, Dorothy, and Margaret Eisenhart. 1990. *Educated in Romance*. Chicago: University of Chicago Press.

Hollingshead, August B. 1949. *Elmstown's Youth*. New York: Wiley.

Holt, John. 1974. *Escape from Childhood*. Harmondsworth, England: Penguin.

Homans, George. 1950. *The Human Group*. New York: Harcourt, Brace.

Hubbell, Charles H. 1965. "An Input-Output Approach to Clique Identification." *Sociometry* 28:377–399.

Hughes, Everett. 1971. *The Sociological Eye*. Boston: Little, Brown.

Hustler, D., A. Cassidy, and E. C. Cuff, eds. 1986. *Action Research in Classrooms and Schools*. London: Allen and Unwin.

Hymel, S., and Steven R. Asher. 1977. "Assessment and Training of Isolated Children's Social Skills." Paper presented at the biennial meeting of the Society for Research in Child Development, New Orleans (ERIC Document Reproduction Service No. ED 136 930).

Ianni, Francis A. J. 1989. *The Search for Structure: A Report on American Youth Today*. New York: Free Press.

Inkeles, Alex. 1966. "Social Structure and the Socialization of Competence." *Harvard Educational Review* 36:265–283.

James, William. 1890. *Principles of Psychology*. 2 vols. New York: Henry Holt.

Jandy, Edward Clarence. 1942. *Charles Horton Cooley, His Life and His Social Theory*. New York: Dryden Press.

Janis, Irving. 1972. *Victims of Groupthink*. Boston: Houghton Mifflin.

Jensen, Ann-Magritt. 1994. "The Feminization of Childhood." In *Childhood Matters*, edited by J. Qvortrup, M. Bardy, G. Sgritta, and H. Wintersberger. Aldershot, England: Avebury. Pp. 59–76.

Joffe, Carol. 1971. "Sex Role Socialization and the Nursery School: As the Twig Is Bent." *Journal of Marriage and the Family* 33:467–475.

Karp, David. 1996. *Living with Depression*. New York: Oxford University Press.

Karweit, Nancy. 1983. "Extracurricular Activities and Friendship Selection." In *Friends in School*, edited by J. L. Epstein and N. Karweit. New York: Academic. Pp. 131–140.

Karweit, Nancy, and Stephen Hansell. 1983a. "Sex Differences in Adolescent Relationships: Friendship and Status." In *Friends in School*, edited by J. L. Epstein and N. Karweit. New York: Academic. Pp. 115–130.

———. 1983b. "School Organization and Friendship Selection." In *Friends in School*, edited by J. L. Epstein and N. Karweit. New York: Academic. Pp. 29–38.

Kaufman, Michael Jay, and Joseph Popper. 1976. "Pee Wee Pill Poppers." *Sport* 63:147–153.

Kinney, David A. 1993. "From Nerds to Normals: The Recovery of Identity among Adolescents from Middle School to High School." *Sociology of Education* 66:21–40.

Kless, Steven J. 1992. "The Attainment of Peer Status: Gender and Power Relationships in the Elementary School." In *Sociological Studies of Child Development*, vol. 5, edited by P. A. Adler and P. Adler. Greenwich, Conn.: JAI. Pp. 115–148.

Kohlberg, Lawrence. 1981. *The Psychology of Moral Development*. New York: Harper and Row.

Kohn, Alfie. 1994. "Sports Create Unhealthy Competition." In *Sports in America*, edited by W. Dudley. San Diego, Calif.: Greenhaven. pp. 17–20.

Kovařík, Jiří. 1994. "The Space and Time of Children at the Interface of Psychology and Sociology." In *Childhood Matters*, edited by J. Qvortrup, M. Bardy, G. Sgritta, and H. Wintersberger. Aldershot, England: Avebury. Pp. 101–122.

Krieger, Susan. 1991. *Social Science and the Self*. New Brunswick, N.J.: Rutgers University Press.

Kurth, Suzanne B. 1970. "Friendship and Friendly Relations." In *Social Relationships*, edited by G. McCall, M. McCall, N. Denzin, G. Suttles, and S. Kurth. Chicago: Aldine. Pp. 136–170.

La Gaipa, John. 1979. "A Developmental Study of the Meaning of Friendship in Adolescence." *Journal of Adolescence* 2:201-213.

Landers, Melissa A., and Gary Alan Fine. 1996. "Learning Life's Lessons in Tee Ball: The Reinforcement of Gender and Status in Kindergarten Sport." *Sociology of Sport Journal* 13:87–93.

Langworthy, Russell. 1959. "Community Status and Influence in a High School." *American Sociological Review* 24:537–539.

Larkin, Ralph W. 1979. *Suburban Youth in Cultural Crisis*. New York: Oxford University Press.

Larreau, Annette. 1991. "Structured Leisure: Social Class Differences in Children's Leisure Experiences." Paper presented at the annual meeting of the American Sociological Association, Cincinnati.

Leland, John. 1996. "A Kiss Isn't Just a Kiss." *Newsweek*. October 21, pp. 71–72.

Lemert, Edwin. 1972. *Human Deviance, Social Problems, and Social Control*. 2d ed., Englewood Cliffs, N.J.: Prentice Hall.

Leo, John. 1994. "Competitive Sports Are Beneficial." In *Sports in America*, edited by W. Dudley. San Diego, Calif.: Greenhaven. Pp. 21–24.

Lesko, Nancy. 1988. *Symbolizing Society: Stories, Rites, and Structure in a Catholic High School*. Philadelphia: Falmer Press.

Lever, Janet. 1978. "Sex Differences in the Complexity of Children's Play and Games." *American Sociological Review* 43: 471–483.

———. 1976. "Sex Differences in the Games Children Play." *Social Problems* 23:478–487.

Lewis, M. 1972. "Sex Differences in Play Behavior of the Very Young." *Journal of Physical Education and Recreation* 43:38–39.

Lightfoot, Sarah Lawrence. 1983. *The Good High School: Portraits of Character and Culture*. New York: Basic.

Lindesmith, Alfred R., and Anselm L. Strauss. 1956. *Social Psychology*. New York: Holt, Rinehart and Winston.

Lippett, R., and M. Gold. 1959. "Classroom Social Structure as a Mental Health Problem." *Journal of Social Issues* 15:40–58.

Lockheed, Marlaine, and Abigail M. Harris. 1984. "Cross-Sex Collaborative Learning in Elementary Classrooms." *American Education Research Journal* 21:275–294.

Lofland, John, and Lyn H. Lofland. 1995. *Analyzing Social Settings.* 3d ed. Belmont, Calif.: Wadsworth.

Lupo, J. 1967. "Case Study of a Father of an Athlete." In *Motivations in Play, Games, and Sports,* edited by R. Slovenko and J. A. Knight. Springfield, Ill.: C. C. Thomas. Pp. 325-328.

Lyman, Stanford, and Marvin Scott. 1989. *A Sociology of the Absurd.* 2d ed. Dix Hills, N.Y.: General Hall.

Maccoby, Eleanor. 1980. *Social Development.* New York: Harcourt Brace Jovanovich.

Maccoby, Eleanor, and Carol Jacklin. 1980. "Sex Differences in Aggression: A Rejoinder and Reprise." *Child Development* 51:964–980.

Maier, Henry William. 1965. *Three Theories of Child Development: The Contributions of Erik H. Erikson, Jean Piaget, and Robert R. Sears, and Their Applications.* New York: Harper and Row.

Maltz, Daniel N., and Ruth A. Borker. 1983. "A Cultural Approach to Male-Female Miscommunication." In *Language and Social Identity,* edited by J. J. Gumperz. New York: Cambridge University Press. Pp. 195–216.

Mandell, Nancy. 1988. "The Least-Adult Role in Studying Children." *Journal of Contemporary Ethnography* 16:433–467.

Mantel, Richard C., and Lee Vander Velden. 1974. "Relationship between the Professionalization of Attitudes toward Play of Pre-adolescent Boys and Participation in Organized Sports." In *Sport and American Society,* edited by G. Sage. Reading, Mass.: Addison-Wesley. Pp. 172-178.

McCall, George J., and Jerry L. Simmons. 1966. *Identities and Interactions.* New York: Free Press.

McPherson, Barry D. 1978. "The Child in Competitive Sports: Influence of the Social Milieu." In *Children in Sport,* edited by M. J. Ash and F. L. Smoll. Champaign, Ill.: Human Kinetics Press. Pp. 219–259.

Mead, George H. 1934. *Mind, Self, and Society.* Chicago: University of Chicago Press.

Medrich, Elliot, Judith Roizen, Victor Rubin, and Stuart Buckley. 1982. *The Serious Business of Growing Up: A Study of Children's Lives Out of School.* Berkeley: University of California Press.

Merten, Don E. 1996a. "Burnout as Cheerleader: The Cultural Basis for Prestige and Privilege in Junior High School." *Anthropology and Education Quarterly* 27:51–70.

———. 1996b. "Visibility and Vulnerability: Responses to Rejection by Nonaggressive Junior High School Boys." *Journal of Early Adolescence* 16:5–26.

———. 1996c. "Information versus Meaning: Toward a Further Understanding of Early Adolescent Rejection." *Journal of Early Adolescence* 16:37–45.

———. 1996d. "Going-With: The Role of a Social Form in Early Romance." *Journal of Contemporary Ethnography* 24:462–484.

———. 1994. "The Cultural Context of Aggression: The Transition to Junior High School." *Anthropology and Education Quarterly* 25:29–43.

Merton, Robert. 1957. "The Role Set." *British Journal of Sociology* 8:106–120.

Micheli, Lyle J., and Mark D. Jenkins. 1994. "Participating in Organized Sports Can Benefit Children." In *Sports in America,* edited by W. Dudley. San Diego, Calif.: Greenhaven. Pp. 25–32.

Milgram, Stanley. 1965. "Some Conditions of Obedience and Disobedience to Authority." *Human Relations* 18(February):57–76.

———. 1963. "Behavioral Study of Obedience." *Journal of Abnormal and Social Psychology* 67:371–378.

Miller, Walter. 1958. "Lower Class Culture and Gang Delinquency." *Journal of Social Issues* 14:5–19.

Mishler, Elliot. 1979. "'Won't You Trade Cookies with the Popcorn?': The Talk of Trades among Six-Year-Olds." In *Language, Children, and Society: The Effects of Social Factors on Children's Learning*, edited by O. Garnica and M. King. Elmsford, N.Y.: Pergamon. Pp. 221–236.

Modgil, Sohan. 1976. *Piagetian Research: Compilation and Commentary*. Windsor: NFER.

Morss, J. 1990. *The Biologising of Childhood*. Hillsdale, N.J.: Lawrence Erlbaum.

Moustakas, Clark. 1990. *Heuristic Research: Design, Methodology, and Applications*. Newbury Park, Calif.: Sage.

Musolf, Gil Richard. 1996. "Interactionism and the Child: Cahill, Corsaro, and Denzin on Childhood Socialization." *Symbolic Interaction* 19:303–322.

Nader, Laura. 1972. "Up the Anthropologist: Perspectives Gained from Studying Up." In *Reinventing Anthropology*, edited by D. Hymes. New York: Vintage. Pp. 284-311.

Nixon, Howard L. II, and James H. Frey. 1996. *A Sociology of Sport*. Belmont, Calif.: Wadsworth.

Oden, S., and Steven R. Asher. 1977. "Coaching Children in Social Skills for Friendship Making." *Child Development* 48:495–506.

Ogilvie, Bruce. 1979. "The Child Athlete: Psychological Implications of Participation in Sport." *Annals AAPSS* 445:47–58.

Opie, Iona. 1993. *The People in the Playground*. Oxford: Oxford University Press.

Opie, Peter, and Iona Opie. 1969. *Children's Games in Street and Playground*. New York: Oxford University Press.

———. 1959. *The Lore and Language of Schoolchildren*. New York: Oxford University Press.

Orlick, T., and C. Botterill. 1975. *Every Kid Can Win*. Chicago: Nelson-Hall.

Oswald, Hans. 1992. "Negotiations of Norms and Sanctions among Children." In *Sociological Studies of Child Development*, vol. 5, edited by P. A. Adler and P. Adler. Greenwich, Conn.: JAI. Pp. 99–114.

Oswald, Hans, Lothar Krappmann, Irene Chowdhuri, and Maria von Salisch. 1987. "Gaps and Bridges: Interactions between Girls and Boys in Elementary School." In *Sociological Studies of Child Development*, vol. 2, edited by P. A. Adler and P. Adler. Greenwich, Conn.: JAI. Pp. 205–223.

Ouellet, Lawrence. 1994. *Pedal to the Metal*. Philadelphia: Temple University Press.

Parker, Jeffrey G., and John M. Gottman. 1989. "Social and Emotional Development in a Relational Context." In *Peer Relationships in Child Development*, edited by T. J. Berndt and G. W. Ladd. New York: Wiley. Pp. 95–131.

Parsons, Talcott, and Robert Bales. 1955. *Family, Socialization, and Interaction Process*. Glencoe, Ill.: Free Press.

Passuth, Patricia. 1987. "Age Hierarchies within Children's Groups." In *Sociological Studies of Child Development*, vol. 2, edited by P. A. Adler and P. Adler. Greenwich, Conn.: JAI. Pp. 185–203.

Pavlov, I. P. 1927. *Conditioned Reflexes*. New York: Oxford University Press.

Peay, Edmund R. 1974. "Hierarchical Clique Structures." *Sociometry* 37:54–65.

Pence, A. 1988. *Intervention on 2nd General Meeting of Childhood as a Social Phenomenon*. Canada: Ganonoque.

Perlman, D., and S. Oskamp. 1971. "The Effects of Picture Content and Exposure Frequency on Evaluations of Negroes and Whites." *Journal of Experimental Social Psychology* 7:503–514.

Peshkin, Alan. 1982. "The Researcher and Subjectivity: Reflections on an Ethnography of School and Community." In *Doing the Ethnography of Schooling*, edited by G. Spindler. New York: Holt, Rinehart, and Winston. Pp. 48–67.

Pettigrew, Thomas. 1979. "The Ultimate Attribution Error: Extending Allport's Cognitive Analysis of Prejudice." *Personality and Social Psychology Bulletin* 5: 461–476.

Piaget, Jean. 1965. *The Moral Judgment of the Child.* New York: Free Press. (Originally published, 1932).

Pinnell, G. S., and M. L. Matlin, eds. 1989. *Teachers and Research: Language Learning in the Classroom.* Newark, Del.: IRA.

Pollard, Andrew. 1985. *The Social World of the Primary School.* New York: Holt, Rinehart, and Winston.

Polsky, Ned. 1967. *Hustlers, Beats, and Others.* Garden City, N.Y.: Doubleday.

Pooley, John. 1982. "The Contributions of Youth Sport Programs to the Quality of Life: Current Practices in Cross-National Perspective." *ARENA Review* 6:31–39.

Postman, Neil. 1994. *The Disappearance of Childhood.* New York: Vintage.

Punch, Maurice. 1994. "Politics and Ethics in Qualitative Research." In *Handbook of Qualitative Research*, edited by N. K. Denzin and Y. Lincoln. Thousand Oaks, Calif.: Sage. Pp. 83–98.

Putallaz, Martha, and John M. Gottman. 1981. "Social Skills and Group Acceptance." In *The Development of Children's Friendships*, edited by S. Asher and J. Gottman. New York: Cambridge University Press. Pp. 116–149.

Qvortrup, Jens. 1995. "Childhood in Europe: A New Field of Social Research." In *Growing Up in Europe*, edited by L. Chisolm, P. Büchner, H. Krüger, and M. du Bois-Reymond. Berlin: Walter de Gruyter. Pp. 7–20.

———. 1994. "Childhood Matters: An Introduction." In *Childhood Matters*, edited by J. Qvortrup, M. Bardy, G. Sgritta, and H. Wintersberger. Aldershot, England: Avebury. Pp. 1–24.

———. 1993. "Nine Theses about 'Childhood as a Social Phenomenon.'" Vienna: European Centre for Social Welfare Policy and Research.

———. 1990. *Childhood as a Social Phenomenon.* Vienna: European Centre for Social Welfare Policy and Research.

———. 1987. "Introduction." *International Journal of Sociology* 17(3):3–37.

Rader, Benjamin G. 1990. *American Sports.* 2d ed. Englewood Cliffs, N.J.: Prentice-Hall.

Reiss, Albert J., Jr., ed. 1968. *Cooley and Sociological Analysis.* Ann Arbor: University of Michigan Press.

Richer, S. 1984. "Sexual Inequality and Children's Play." *Canadian Review of Sociology and Anthropology* 21: 66–80.

Riemer, Jeffrey. 1977. "Varieties of Opportunistic Research." *Urban Life* 5:467–477.

Riess, Steven A. 1989. *City Games.* Urbana: University of Illinois Press.

Rizzo, Thomas A. 1989. *Friendship Development among Children in School.* Norwood, N.J.: Ablex.

Rizzo, Thomas A., William A. Corsaro, and J. E. Bates. 1992. "Ethnographic Methods and Interpretive Analysis: Expanding the Methodological Options of Psychologists." *Developmental Review* 12:101–123.

Robinson, Dawn T., and Lynn Smith-Lovin. 1992. "Selective Interaction as a Strategy for Identity Maintenance: An Affect Control Model." *Social Psychology Quarterly* 55:12–28.

Rochford, E. Burke. 1985. *Hare Krishna in America.* New Brunswick, N.J.: Rutgers University Press.

Rodman, Hyman. 1990. "The Social Construction of the Latchkey Children Problem." In *Sociological Studies of Child Development*, vol. 3, edited by N. Mandell. Greenwich, Conn.: JAI. Pp. 163–174.

Roff, M., S. B. Sells, and M. M. Golden. 1972. *Social Adjustment and Personality Development in Children.* Minneapolis: University of Minnesota Press.

Rosaldo, Renato. 1989. *Culture and Truth: The Remaking of Social Analysis*. Boston: Beacon.

Rosenberg, Morris. 1981. "The Self-Concept: Social Product and Social Force." In *Social Psychology*, edited by M. Rosenberg and R. H. Turner. New York: Basic. Pp. 591–624.

———. 1979. *Conceiving the Self*. New York: Basic.

Rubin, K. H., L. J. LaMare, and S. Lollis. 1990. "Social Withdrawal in Childhood: Developmental Pathways to Peer Rejection." In *Peer Rejection in Childhood*, edited by S. R. Asher and J. D. Coie. New York: Cambridge University Press. Pp. 217–249.

Rubin, Zick. 1980. *Children's Friendships*. Cambridge: Harvard University Press.

Rubinstein, J., and C. Rubin. 1984. "Children's Fantasies of Interactions with Same and Opposite Sex Peers." In *Friendship Formation in Normal and Handicapped Children*, edited by T. Field, M. Siegel, and J. Roopnarine. Norwood, N.J.: Ablex. Pp. 99–123.

Sagar, Andrew, Janet W. Schofield, and Howard N. Snyder. 1983. "Race and Gender Barriers: Preadolescent Peer Behavior in Academic Classrooms." *Child Development* 54:1032–1040.

Sanford, Stephanie, and Donna Eder. 1984. "Adolescent Humor During Peer Interaction." *Social Psychology Quarterly* 47:235–243.

Savin-Williams, Richard C., and Thomas J. Berndt. 1990. "Friendship and Peer Relations." In *At the Threshold: The Developing Adolescent*, edited by S. Feldman and G. R. Elliot. Cambridge: Harvard University Press.

Schofield, Janet W. 1982. *Black and White in School*. New York: Praeger.

———. 1981. "Complementary and Conflicting Identities: Images and Interaction in an Interracial School." In *The Development of Children's Friendships*, edited by S. Asher and J. Gottman. New York: Cambridge University Press. Pp. 53–90.

Schofield, Janet W., and Andrew Sagar. 1977. "Peer Interaction Patterns in an Integrated Middle School." *Sociometry* 40:130–138.

Schwartz, Gary. 1987. *Beyond Conformity or Rebellion: Youth and Authority in America*. Chicago: University of Chicago Press.

Schwartz, Gary, and Don Merten. 1967. "The Language of Adolescence: An Anthropological Approach to the Youth Culture." *American Journal of Sociology* 72:453–468.

Schwendinger, Herman, and Julia Schwendinger. 1985. *Adolescent Subcultures and Delinquency*. New York: Praeger.

Selman, Robert. 1981. "The Child as a Friendship Philosopher." In *The Development of Children's Friendships*, edited by S. Asher and J. Gottman. New York: Cambridge University Press. Pp. 242–272.

Sgritta, Giovanni. 1987. "Childhood: Normalization and Project." *International Journal of Sociology* 17:38–57.

Sherif, Musafir, O. J. Harvey, B. J. White, W. E. Hood, and C. W. Sherif. 1961. *Intergroup Conflict and Cooperation: The Robber's Cave Experiment*. Norman, Okla.: University of Oklahoma Book Exchange.

Shrum, Wesley, Neil H. Cheek, and Saundra M. Hunter. 1988. "Friendship in School: Gender and Racial Homophily." *Sociology of Education* 61:227–239.

Simmel, Georg. 1959. *Georg Simmel, 1858–1918: A Collection of Essays, with Translations and a Bibliography*, edited by Kurt H. Wolff and translated by David Kettler. Columbus: Ohio State University Press.

———. 1950. *The Sociology of Georg Simmel*, translated and edited by K. Wolff. New York: Free Press.

Simon, Robin, Donna Eder, and Cathy Evans. 1992. "The Development of Feeling Norms Underlying Romantic Love among Adolescent Females." *Social Psychology Quarterly* 55:29–46.

Singleton, L. C., and Steven R. Asher. 1977. "Peer Preferences and Social Interaction among Third-Grade Children in an Integrated School District." *Journal of Educational Psychology* 69:330–336.

Skinner, B. F. 1953. *Science and Human Behavior.* New York: Macmillan.

Sluckin, Andy. 1981. *Growing Up in the Playground.* London: Routledge and Kegan Paul.

Smith, Michael D. 1978. "Social Learning and Violence in Minor League Hockey." In *Psychological Perspectives in Youth Sports*, edited by F. Smoll and R. E. Smith. Washington, D.C.: Hemisphere Publishing.

Snow, David, and Leon Anderson. 1987. "Identity Work among the Homeless: The Verbal Construction and Avowal of Personal Identities." *American Journal of Sociology* 92:1336-1371.

Snyder, Eldon E. 1972. "High School Students' Perceptions of Prestige Criteria." *Adolescence* 6:129-136.

Speier, Matthew. 1970. "The Everyday World of the Child." In *Understanding Everyday Life*, edited by J. D. Douglas. Chicago: Aldine. Pp. 188–217.

Stone, Gregory. 1965. "The Play of Little Children." *Quest* 4:23–31.

———. 1962. "Appearance and the Self." In *Human Behavior and Social Processes*, edited by A. Rose. Boston: Houghton Mifflin. Pp. 86–118.

Stone, Joseph L., and Joseph Church. 1984. *Childhood and Adolescence.* 5th ed. New York: Random House.

Strauss, Anselm L. 1978. *Negotiations: Varieties, Contexts, Processes, and Social Order.* San Francisco: Jossey-Bass.

Stryker, Sheldon. 1980. *Symbolic Interaction: A Social Structural Version.* Menlo Park: Cummings.

———. 1968. "Identity Salience and Role Performance." *Journal of Marriage and the Family* 4: 558–564.

Sutton-Smith, Brian. 1982. "A Performance Theory of Peer Relations." In *The Social Life of Children in a Changing Society*, edited by K. Borman. Hillsdale, N.J.: Lawrence Erlbaum. Pp. 65–77.

———. 1971. "A Syntax for Play and Games." In *Child's Play*, edited by R. E. Herron and B. Sutton-Smith. New York: Wiley. Pp. 298–307.

Sutton-Smith, Brian, and B. G. Rosenberg. 1961. "Sixty Years of Historical Change in the Games Preferences of American Children." *Journal of American Folklore* 74:17–46.

Tajfel, Henry. 1970. "Experiments in Intergroup Discrimination." *Scientific American* 223:96–102.

———, ed. 1978. *Differentiation between Social Groups: Studies in the Social Psychology of Intergroup Relations.* London: Academic Press.

Tajfel, Henry, C. Flament, M. G. Billig, and R. F. Bundy. 1971. "Social Categorization and Intergroup Behavior." *European Journal of Social Psychology* 1:149–177.

Thomas, W. I. 1923. *The Unadjusted Girl.* Boston: Little, Brown.

Thorne, Barrie. 1993. *Gender Play.* New Brunswick, N.J.: Rutgers University Press.

———. 1987. "Re-Visioning Women and Social Change: Where are the Children?" *Gender & Society* 1:85–109.

———. 1986. "Girls and Boys Together, But Mostly Apart: Gender Arrangements in Elementary Schools." In *Relationships and Development*, edited W. Hartup and Z. Rubin. Hillsdale, N.J.: Lawrence Erlbaum. Pp. 167–184.

Thorne, Barrie, and Zella Luria. 1986. "Sexuality and Gender in Children's Daily Worlds." *Social Problems* 33:176–190.

Triandis, H. C., and V. Vassilou. 1967. "Frequency of Contact and Stereotyping." *Journal of Personality and Social Psychology* 7:316-328.

Troyner, Barry, and Richard Hatcher. 1992. *Racism in Children's Lives: A Study of Mainly-White Primary Schools*. London: Routledge.

Turner, Ralph H. 1976. "The Real Self: From Institution to Impulse." *American Journal of Sociology* 81:989–1016.

———. 1968. "The Self-Conception in Social Interaction." In *The Self in Social Action*, edited by C. Gordon and K. Gergen. New York: Wiley. Pp. 93–106.

———. 1956. "Role Taking, Role Standpoint, and Reference Group Behavior." *American Journal of Sociology* 61:316–328.

Underwood, John. 1979. *The Death of an American Game*. Boston: Little Brown.

———. 1975. "Taking the Fun Out of a Game." *Sports Illustrated* November 11: 87–98.

Valli, Linda. 1988. "Gender Identity and the Technology of Office Education." In *Class, Race, and Gender in American Education*, edited by L. Weis. Albany: SUNY Press. Pp. 87–105.

Van Vliet, William. 1986. "The Methodological and Conceptual Basis of Environmental Policies for Children." *Prevention in Human Services* 4:59–78.

Varenne, Hervé. 1982. "Jocks and Freaks: The Symbolic Structure of the Expression of Social Interaction among American Senior High School Students." In *Doing the Ethnography of Schooling*, edited by G. Spindler. New York: Holt, Rinehart, and Winston. Pp. 210–235.

Vaz, Edmund. 1982. *The Professionalization of Young Hockey Players*. Lincoln: University of Nebraska Press.

Vidich, Arthur J., and Joseph Bensman. 1964. *Small Town in Mass Society*. Princeton, N.J.: Princeton University Press.

Voss, Laurie Scarborough. 1997. "Teasing, Disputing, and Playing: Cross-Gender Interactions and Space Utilization among First and Third Graders." *Gender & Society* 11:238–256.

Vygotsky, L. S. 1978. *Mind in Society*. Cambridge: Harvard University Press.

Waid, R. 1979. "Child Abuse: Reader's Forum." *Runner's World*. September: 16.

Waksler, Frances Chaput. 1996. *The Little Trials of Childhood*. Bristol, Pa.: Falmer Press.

———. 1986. "Studying Children: Phenomenological Insights." *Human Studies* 9:71–82.

———, ed. 1991. *Studying the Social Worlds of Children*. Bristol, Pa.: Falmer Press.

Wallace, A. F. C. 1970. *Culture and Personality*. New York: Random House.

Watson, James B. 1970. *Behaviorism*. New York: Norton.

Webb, H. 1969. "Professionalization of Attitude toward Play among Adolescents." In *Aspects of Contemporary Sport Sociology*, edited by G. Kenyon. Chicago: Athletic Institute. Pp. 161–178.

Weber, Max. 1946. "Class, Status, and Party." In *From Max Weber*, edited by H. Gerth and C. W. Mills. New York: Oxford University Press.

Weinstein, Eugene. 1969. "The Development of Interpersonal Competence." In *Handbook of Socialization Theory and Research*, edited by D. Goslin. Chicago: Rand McNally. Pp. 753–775.

Weis, Joseph G. 1974. "Styles of Middle-Class Adolescent Drug Use." *Pacific Sociological Review* 17:251–286.

Weiss, Meira. 1994. "Nonperson and Nonhome: Territorial Seclusion of Appearance-Impaired Children." *Journal of Contemporary Ethnography* 22:463–487.

Wicker, A. 1969. "Cognitive Complexity, School Size, and Participation in School Behavior Settings: A Test of the Frequency of the Interaction Hypothesis." *Journal of Educational Psychology* 60:200–203.

Willis, Paul. 1981. *Learning to Labour*. New York: Columbia University Press.

Wolf, Anthony E. 1991. *Get Out of My Life, but First Could You Drive Me and Cheryl to the Mall*. New York: Noonday.

Wolff, Rick. 1994. "Participating in Organized Sports Can Harm Children." In *Sports in America*, edited by W. Dudley. San Diego, Calif.: Greenhaven. Pp. 33–41.

Wulff, Helena. 1988. *Twenty Girls: Growing Up, Ethnicity, and Excitement in a South London Microculture*. Stockholm Studies in Social Anthropology, No. 21. Stockholm, Sweden: University of Stockholm.

Yablonsky, Lewis, and Jonathan Brower. 1979. *The Little League Game: How Kids, Coaches, and Players Really Play It*. New York: Times Books.

Young, L. L., and D. H. Cooper. 1944. "Some Factors Associated with Popularity." *Journal of Educational Psychology* 35:513–535.

Youniss, James, and Jacqueline Smollar. 1985. *Adolescent Relations with Mothers, Fathers, and Friends*. Chicago: University of Chicago Press.

Index

About the Authors

Patricia A. Adler is professor of sociology at the University of Colorado in Boulder. Peter Adler is professor of sociology at the University of Denver. The Adlers' research has been centered on social psychology, sociology of children, sociology of sports and leisure, and microsociology. They have written and published widely in these areas, separately and together. Among their collaborative works are *Backboards and Blackboards*; *Construction of Deviance*; and *Membership Roles in Field Research*. They have also coedited *The Social Dynamics of Financial Markets* and the five-volume work *Sociological Studies of Child Development*.